Praise for *Portrait of a Burger as a Young Calf*

"Lovenheim's book is masterful! Never has a book so big, so poignant, so important been written about the people who produce our milk and meat for us and the 110 million cattle from which they earn their livelihoods. Peter Lovenheim confronts us with some unintended consequences of our eating habits."
—Franklin M. Loew, D.V.M., Ph.D.; member, Institute of Medicine, National Academy of Sciences; and former dean of the Cornell and the Tufts University Schools of Veterinary Medicine

"By focusing on the people involved at each step of this process, and by neither sentimentalizing nor anthropomorphizing the cattle, Lovenheim offers a graphic portrait of those whose labor and lives feed a nation and a world."
—*Booklist*

"A more generous view of the beef industry than Eric Schlosser's recent *Fast Food Nation* . . . an absorbing first-hand account."
—*Publishers Weekly*

"[Lovenheim] writes respectfully of farmers and expresses many of the same feelings I've had during a twenty-five-year career of handling farm animals. He also struggles with the ambivalence that both farmers and the public have about ending the life of an animal."
—Temple Grandin, author of *Thinking in Pictures,* and nationally recognized expert in farm animal handling and behavior

"This is wonderful writing about the process of farming and the people who farm. It's a serious book, lucid and endearing. Lovenheim is good company as he follows two calves from birth to griddle, but raises the hard questions we try not to think about—the same questions raised by E. B. White in *Charlotte's Web.*"
—Mark Kramer, director of the Narrative Journalism Program, Nieman Foundation for Journalism at Harvard University

"Peter Lovenheim hatched an intriguing plan. . . . *Portrait of a Burger as a Young Calf* is more than just the intriguing story of a man and his two calves. It is a behind-the-scenes look at where our food comes from."
—*Arizona Daily Star*

Portrait of a Burger as a Young Calf

THREE RIVERS PRESS
NEW YORK

Portrait of a Burger as a Young Calf

The Story of One Man, Two Cows,

and the Feeding of a Nation

Peter Lovenheim

Published by Three Rivers Press, New York, New York.
Member of the Crown Publishing Group, a division of Random House, Inc.
www.randomhouse.com

Three Rivers Press and the Tugboat design are registered trademarks of Random House, Inc.

Originally published in hardcover by Harmony Books, a division of Random House, Inc., in 2002.

Printed in the United States of America

Design by Leonard Henderson

Library of Congress Cataloging-in-Publication Data

Lovenheim, Peter.
    Portrait of a burger as a young calf : the story of one man, two cows, and the feeding of a nation / by Peter Lovenheim. — 1st ed.
    Includes bibliographical references
        1. Cattle—New York (State)   2. Cattle—Social aspects—New York (State)
    3. Animal industry—Moral and ethical aspects—New York (State)   4. Lovenheim, Peter.   I. Title.
SF196.U5 L68 2002
636.2'13'0974785—dc21   2001046509

ISBN 0-609-80544-4

10   9   8   7   6   5   4   3   2   1

First Paperback Edition

To Ken Schaeffer
In fond memory

Contents

Acknowledgments

I WANT FIRST TO THANK photographer Ariya Martin, who took most of the photographs that appear in this book. Ariya pulled on barn boots, climbed into cow barns, and hiked through pastures with me. She not only captured the people and animals of York but also helped me see more clearly the story I had written.

I thank author and playwright Diane Demeter for that walk at Chautauqua during which she told me something wise that freed me to begin thinking of undertaking a project of this scope. And to Jan Goldberg, my office-mate and friend, thank you for your steady counsel that helped me get started and stay the course. And to cattle dealer Jerry Miller for opening his farm to me and introducing me to so many people who later proved crucial to putting together this book.

Next, I thank Guy Kettelhack, author and talented "book doctor," who guided me through the first draft. I miss those long phone calls.

And thank you to my brother, film producer Robert Lovenheim, for pushing me to understand what the story was about.

Many people I met in the farming community who didn't make it into the book nevertheless provided useful information and encouragement. They include Alison and Dennis Fronczak; Beth Claypoole of Cornell Cooperative Extension; the Rev. Neil Frood Jr. of York Presbyterian Church; Bill and Phoebe Wilson, owners of "Dave the Ox"; Abbot John at the Abbey of the Genesee; cattle hauler Bobbi Johnson and her daughter, Kim Bennett; and everyone at Lawnel Farms, particularly Larry and Catherine Smith, office manager Chris Cromwell, and milker Alan Hatfield.

Several friends patiently helped me wrestle with a difficult choice. They include Rabbis Raphael Adler, Herbert Bronstein, and Marc Gruber; Mikel Finn, Dan Kolber, and Rafe Martin.

I thank Clayton "Bud" O'Dell, my finest teacher; the late Elizabeth Hart, an outstanding writing teacher, and Howard White, a former editor. Thanks, also, to the librarians at the Brighton, Penfield, and Rochester Public Libraries.

To the friends and family members who read early drafts of the manuscript, thank you for your interest, and good judgment. They are: Peter Guzzardi, Marie Lovenheim, Andrew and June Lovenheim, Irina Novozhenets, Joy Moss, Susan Kramarsky, Amy Mantell, Mary Anna Towler, Rabbi David Katz, and Herbert Siegel.

I appreciate, too, the work of my editor, Shaye Areheart, and agent, Loretta Barrett; their sensitivity to the lives of the people in this story have helped make it a better book.

To the Smiths and the Vonglises, I hardly know how to thank you enough. You opened your places of work, your families, and your lives to me. I tried each day to honor your trust, and I hope I've done so in the pages of this book.

To my children, Sarah, Val, and Ben, thank you for inspiring me, for listening at dinner to the stories of what I'd seen on the farm, and for tolerating the smell in my car.

And thank you to 7 and 8.

Introduction

In 1960, FOR SUMMER VACATION, my family drove from our suburban home in Rochester, New York, to California and back. I was seven years old. On the fourth day of our trip, somewhere in Iowa, I noticed from the back seat of my father's blue Buick Roadmaster a large herd of grazing cattle. I asked my older sister Jane, who sat next to me, why there were so many "cows," as I called them.

"That's where our hamburgers come from," she said.

My mother twisted around from the front seat. "Jane, shush!"

I asked my sister how cows become hamburgers.

"Oh, the farmers feed them," she said, vaguely.

"Then what do they do to them?"

"They take them for a train ride."

"Then what do they do?"

"Peter," said my mother, "let's play license-plate bingo."

In the forty years since that trip, I have eaten my share of steaks, roast beef, and hamburgers, but I have never quite gotten over either my curiosity about how we turn living things into food or my wonder and uneasiness at so many animals taking so many "train rides" to satisfy our appetites. At times, over the years, I ate less meat, taking what seemed the moral high ground. At other times I simply pushed the matter from my thoughts. Today my two older children's eating habits reflect my own ambivalence: one eats meat, the other doesn't.

In the spring of 1997, while standing in line at McDonald's with the daughter who eats meat, I was reminded of that long-ago road trip. McDonald's was giving away Teenie Beanie Babies with every purchase of a Happy Meal, and my daughter was hoping to get one. Despite having ordered 100 million of the stuffed toy animals, McDonald's couldn't keep up with the demand. The line in which we stood extended out the front door; at the drive-through, cars were backed up to the street.

As we waited, I glanced at a countertop display of Beanie Babies. Among them I was surprised to see a bright red bull named Snort and a black-and-white cow named Daisy. It struck me as odd that a company selling ground beef would offer toys in the shape of cattle. Were children really expected to hug and play with a toy cow while eating the grilled remains of a real one? It seemed to me the McDonald's–Beanie Baby promotion revealed a deep disconnect between what we eat and where it comes from.

This was not always the case. Until recent generations, every human culture knew intimately the source of its food. Today, however, fewer than 2 percent of Americans are engaged in farming. As a result, most of us know little about where our food comes from, and we are invested in keeping it that way because some aspects of animal agriculture make us uncomfortable. Collectively, we follow my Mom's advice: while the cattle graze around us, we play license-plate bingo.

But I began to wonder: What might happen if I could connect the dots and actually observe up close the process by which living animals become food? Could I meet the people who raise and care for these animals, watch them as they work, learn their thoughts as they labor to feed the rest of us? How would it affect me to understand deeply a process that has both fascinated and, frankly, scared me since childhood?

But how to begin? The numbers overwhelm: we eat more than 5 billion hamburgers annually, and to produce them we slaughter nearly 45 million cattle, almost 125,000 a day, 5,000 an hour, more than one each second.

I decided to simplify the task: to see if it was possible to move backward from "billions and billions served" to just one—one live animal, and to follow that one animal all the way from birth to burger, or—as an agriculture professor I later spoke with put it—"from conception to consumption."

My first thought was to catch a plane and head for Iowa, Kansas, or Texas to observe the vast cattle herds of the Midwest. This turned out to be unnecessary. As I soon learned, fast-food hamburger is a blend of fatty meat from cattle raised on pasture and feedlot in the South and Midwest, and lean meat from "cull" dairy cows—cows sent to slaughter when their milk production declines. Most fast-food hamburgers are at least one-half dairy cow, sometimes as much as 70 percent.

And then I learned something else I hadn't known: not only is the state I live in, New York, the third-largest dairy state in the nation (after Wisconsin and

California), but the westernmost counties that border my home in Rochester are the heart of the state's dairy industry. In other words, within a fifty-mile radius of my suburban home, I could observe firsthand the births, lives, and deaths of the cows whose meat comprises half or more of fast-food hamburgers. I could do all my research without taking another road trip through Iowa.

Who knows why particular images from childhood have the power to shape our lives? Or why, at midlife, we may feel compelled—if we are to remain vital—to confront those images and understand their power? For some, the confrontation may require a physical challenge, like climbing a mountain, hiking the desert, or sailing the ocean. For me, it required pulling on a pair of black rubber boots, climbing into a cow barn, and coming face to face with the reality of life and death.

To begin my journey, I bought a calf.

Portrait of a Burger as a Young Calf

1

A Calf Is Born

AT FOUR-THIRTY ON A MONDAY AFTERNOON in the herd office, Sue Smith peels off her navy blue farm coveralls and says good night. She's leaving to pick up her daughter, Kirsty, from swim practice at York Central High School, and probably won't be back to the farm today.

Just then, Andrew Smith, Sue's husband, herds a cow into the barn nearby. A Holstein with typical black-and-white coloring, this cow is one of the few on the farm with a name. She's called Darla. Andrew named her years ago for a reason he says he can no longer remember. Darla is not due to give birth for three more weeks, but Andrew checked her a few hours ago and felt two heads inside and got a feeling she's in trouble. He's called the vet, who should be here any minute.

Alerted to the problem, Sue pulls her coveralls back on. If she can't get to the high school, her daughter will know to get a ride home with one of her teammates.

Nearly forty, Sue Smith is of medium build, and slim. Her straight brown hair is cropped short, just above the ears, and streaked with blond. The large, rimless circular lenses of her eyeglasses dominate her thin face.

Sue grew up, one of seven children, on her family's dairy farm in a small town in central New York. Her father milked seventy-five cows. She studied physical therapy in college, then moved to western New York to work at an institution for the mentally retarded. There a co-worker fixed her up with Andrew Smith, one of three sons of Larry and Catherine Smith, owners of Lawnel Farms, a substantial family-run dairy in the small, western New York town of York. Their first date was a Smith family picnic.

As Andrew recalls it, after a year and a half of dating, Sue gave him an ultimatum: "Either tell me we're committed or I'm out of here." They married soon after.

Following the birth of their first child, Kirstin, Sue began working at the Smith family farm. She started in the farm office, then began helping with the cows. Later she took over as herd manager, responsible for all nine hundred cows.

Sue knows nearly all the cows not only by ear-tag number but also by sight. I once asked another herd manager how he could tell his cows apart. In reply, he asked how many students there had been in my high school graduating class. I said about three hundred. "Well, after being with them all that time, you could tell them apart, couldn't you?" he asked. "That's how it is for us with the cows."

Besides managing the herd, Sue also supervises most of Lawnel's sixteen non-family employees, all of which puts her among a small but growing number of women who manage dairy farms.

Each morning Sue rises between 4:00 and 4:30 A.M., several hours before Kirsty, now fifteen, and her son, Amos, fourteen. She arrives at the farm around 5:00 A.M., pulls on her navy blue coveralls (a patch over the left shirt pocket says, in bold capitals, LAWNEL FARMS; a patch over the right pocket says, in slender italics, "Sue"), and generally does not return home until twelve hours later. By 9:00 P.M. she's in bed again, often earlier in the winter.

In the barn, a red stanchion—a metal head lock used to restrain a cow—sits on a raised concrete platform. Andrew and Sue maneuver Darla toward the stanchion, then lock her head in at the front.

The vet arrives and injects an epidural of Lidocaine just above Darla's tail so she'll stop pushing. "We'll get her worked up and reach inside to see what's going on," explains the young vet, whose name is Craig. He pulls on a clear plastic vest with sleeves and gloves attached.

Sue pushes Darla's tail stump to the side, and holds it so it won't be in the vet's way. At Lawnel, all the cows' tails are cropped to about a third of their natural length. This keeps the cows from flicking manure onto employees and equipment during milking.

Craig pours hot, soapy water over Darla's vulva. Not yet thirty, Craig recently joined the veterinary practice that services Lawnel. Standing sideways to Darla, he reaches in with his gloved left arm up to the shoulder and scoops out blood and other fluids.

"Andrew, get the jack, please," Sue instructs her husband.

From an equipment room nearby, Andrew retrieves a heavy metal jack, about four feet long.

I step back and off to the side. I should get myself a pair of coveralls, but so far on my visits to the farm, I've just been wearing jeans and a light fall jacket.

At forty-five, Andrew Smith is a stocky, broad-chested man with a ruddy, round face, full mustache, and shaggy brown hair that curls out from under the back of his farm cap. His imposing shape is softened by his voice: he tends to speak slowly and softly, often with gentle irony.

"Oh, am I lucky I didn't try this myself," Andrew says, meaning pulling Darla's calves. "Craig's better at it than I am. Darla, give birth, please."

Andrew grew up on Lawnel Farms. As a boy, he was away only for the years his father, Larry, was studying for his masters and Ph.D. at Purdue, and even then he would come back to the farm for the summers and stay with his grandfather Nelson.

"I never thought of doing anything else but farming," he told me earlier. "I always liked it; it's not a job but a way of life. It's a cliché, I know, but it's true."

As did his father, Andrew attended Cornell and studied agricultural economics. But it didn't work out. After two years he flunked out and came back to the farm.

Later he was diagnosed with Graves' disease, a condition caused by a hyperactive thyroid. "That explained why at Cornell my weight dropped to one forty-five, my eyes were bugging out, and I had an attention span of about three minutes." Most of his thyroid was removed; he still takes pills daily for the condition.

With his health restored, Andrew tried college again. This time he enrolled at a state school and studied agricultural engineering. "I became a gearhead," he says, referring to someone skilled in working with machinery. "I started out in a class of thirty-six, which ended up with just eighteen, and graduated number eight."

That was about the time he met Sue on the blind date.

Neither of Andrew's two brothers chose a career on the farm. Marc, the oldest, lives in Syracuse and directs the state office of a government program that promotes land conservation and makes loans to farmers. Adrian, the youngest, is a landscape architect in Boston. "He designed Eddie Murphy's gardens in New York City," Andrew notes with pride.

While Sue manages the herd, Andrew does "crop and shop." He's responsible for planting and harvesting the crops, and buying and maintaining the machinery—combines, tractors, and trucks—often worth a quarter million dollars apiece.

Soon after I first met Andrew, I asked him to lunch, thinking at the time that farmers, like office workers, actually go out to lunch. Obligingly, he drove me to Cook's, a combination gas station and convenience store a couple of miles down the road. We picked up sub sandwiches, but, at his suggestion, ate them back at the farm. It was a good chance to get to know each other, but the last time we went out for lunch.

. . .

The jack used for pulling calves is a metal frame that fits behind a cow's rump. You attach it to one end of a chain, tie the other end around the calf's hooves, and crank the calf out. In an aside, Andrew says, "I prefer ropes because they're more humane on the calf's feet, but vets like to use chains because they're sterile."

A hoof appears from Darla's vagina, but quickly retracts. Craig reaches in to feel around.

"The calf is kind of . . . startin' to swell up in there," he reports. "I'm feeling two heads and a lot of feet."

Now Craig reaches in with both arms.

"I'm trying to make sure I have the right feet with the right head," he explains. He's sweating from the sideburns of his neatly cut, short brown hair.

Andrew, who is standing behind Craig, begins telling a story about how he just bought a small tractor from a farm dealer in the Midwest who specializes in repossessed equipment. "Lots of repossessions out there," he says.

I think Andrew's banter is meant to help calm the young vet.

It's 5:00 P.M. Andrew and Sue have been at work for nearly twelve hours.

Craig reaches inside Darla again and loops the metal chain over one hoof.

"Well, let's see what we got now," he says. "Let's just pull this foot a bit."

He and Andrew crank a single cloven hoof, white and pink, about six inches out of Darla.

Darla stretches her neck forward through the stanchion, trying to bellow, but she has little voice; the sound comes out high-pitched and weak.

"Two calves wanna come out at the same time," says Craig.

A few minutes later, Andrew asks, "C-section?" To me he says, "These are DOA, by the way. There's no movement in them legs."

I ask Andrew if he knew the calves were dead before the vet got here.

"Yeah," he says, "I suspected that was the case when I felt her up in the barn."

Craig says, "I didn't think this was going to be so difficult. This is turning into a project."

"You're sorry you took this call," says Sue, still standing by Darla's side, holding the cow's tail stump out of the way.

"They don't give me a choice what calls I take," says Craig, referring to the vet clinic where he works.

C-sections on dairy cows are sometimes done when a calf is too big to be born vaginally. The alternative, fetotomy, is generally considered much worse. That involves inserting into the vagina a long pole with a wire saw attached and cutting the calf up inside the uterus. A veterinarian once told me, "Sometimes I think it's better just to shoot the cow."

The one cloven hoof has somehow slipped back inside Darla, but now a black snout has emerged. "Okay," says Craig, "let's grab on this head and see what we can bring up."

"But the head's gonna come off," warns Andrew. "You know darn well it will."

"No," says Craig, "let's see."

I recall a dream I had two nights ago: a calf head with no body talked to me as it hopped around on its neck inside a cage. I feel sick to think that in a moment the image from my dream may come true.

An entire black calf head sticks out now from Darla's vulva. Then a hoof and a leg emerge alongside.

Craig quickly loops the metal chain around the head and leg.

Andrew cranks the jack.

The calf's neck begins stretching, the black hair parts, and the pink muscles under the hair begin to tear.

I don't want to see this.

Darla spits white foam.

Suddenly, Darla topples sideways off the concrete platform toward the barn aisle. In an instant, Sue and Craig throw their weight against her side and push her back up. Her neck is still locked in the stanchion. The danger is that she can choke to death.

Darla tries to bellow, but emits almost no sound.

The calf, red and stretched and raw, hangs limply outside Darla by the hips.

"Veal piccata," Andrew deadpans.

Craig pulls a few more times on the chain, and the calf slips entirely out of Darla and splatters onto the concrete floor. But it is only two-thirds of a calf. It has separated at the hips; the hind legs have not yet been born.

For a moment, Andrew, Sue, and the vet all turn their heads away from Darla, but I lean in for a closer look.

"Hey, Peter," asks Andrew, "you sure you're okay?"

"Yeah, I'm okay," I say.

"The smell doesn't bother you?" he asks.

I shake my head.

How bad all of this may smell is beyond me. I have nasal polyps; I can't smell anything. Surgery might help, but not having a sense of smell offers an obvious advantage on a dairy farm. It also has its drawbacks.

When I come home from the farm and enter the house, my wife and kids often have something to say about the smell of my clothes. And sometimes when friends ride in my car, I notice they'll sniff around; usually the problem is my barn boots in the trunk.

I'm sure earlier I had mentioned to Sue and Andrew that I have no sense of smell, and remind them of this. The vet is amused.

"You sure are in the right place!" he says.

Sue says to Andrew, "You want to hold her tail? I'm gonna leave to get Kirsty. She must not have been able to find a ride or she'd be here by now." Sue dips her hands in a bucket of soapy water, rinses just a second, and leaves.

Andrew loops the chain over the next set of hooves and, with the jack, cranks out the second dead calf. It's in one piece, legs reddened, tongue hanging out the side of its mouth, and falls. Andrew pushes it off the concrete platform and onto the barn floor.

"That *was* a heifer," he says. That the dead calf was female and could have become a productive dairy cow makes this a harder loss.

"Now we've gotta go in for the hips," he says.

Andrew cranks out two legs and a pair of hips. These, too, fall to the floor.

"No wonder this critter couldn't come out—these hips are huge," he says.

"They're all swollen," Craig agrees. "The calves were probably dead a couple of days ago."

A black Labrador that belongs to Lawnel's office manager enters the barn and sniffs at the carcasses.

Craig says Darla has massive infections made worse because the one calf split inside her. Nevertheless, he thinks that with antibiotics and fluids to rehydrate her, she has a better than even chance of surviving.

Andrew pets Darla on the head. "Hey, you know what, you did a good job for us," he tells her. "She wants a drink," he says to no one. "I'll get her a drink. She deserves a drink, doesn't she?"

Just then, Andrew and Sue's daughter, Kirsty, comes into the barn, wearing a purple high school jacket. On the back, in white letters, it says, YORK SWIMMING. Kirsty stops at the sight of the split calf on the floor.

"Oh, that is cool!" she exclaims. "Are they attached? Oh, they're all bloated!"

.   .   .

In her book *The Farm She Was,* the novelist Ann Mohin writes, "Preachers think they know all there is to know about birth and death, but it's the farmers and veterinarians who can tell you the truth."

It was Ken Schaeffer, an artificial inseminator, who first brought me to Lawnel Farms and encouraged me to meet Sue and Andrew Smith. I rode with Ken one day to watch him breed cows, and told him I was looking for a farm where I could follow one cow from birth to slaughter. "Lawnel's a well-run farm," he told me. "Big, but not too big, and the Smiths are real friendly. I think you'll like them."

I met with Sue and Andrew in the herd office. It's a small, plain room attached to the barn; you can walk right in without taking off your barn boots. On the right, as you enter, there's an old wooden desk with a computer. To the left is a small picnic table spread with copies of *Hoard's Dairyman* and other farm journals. On the facing wall is a time clock, and a corkboard with notices for the help and cartoons about farm life. Stacked on wall-mounted shelves are boxes of supplies: ear tags, rubber gloves, syringes.

Sue sat at her desk, Andrew pulled a chair into the middle of the room, and I sat at the picnic table. I asked about their farm: Was it typical in terms of the type of cows, the procedures followed? I wanted a typical farm—not a show farm, but nothing squalid, either.

They asked about my background: married, three kids, dog, and minivan; no farm experience. They asked about my education: nonpracticing lawyer with a background in journalism, early in my career I did legal work for nonprofit groups, including the Humane Society; I have run a mediation service for a half-dozen years but now devote most of my time to writing. And they asked about my project: a visit to McDonald's with my daughter got me curious about the disconnect between food and where it comes from, and the lives of the people who provide it for the rest of us.

I explained my plan to follow one animal from birth to slaughter, and that at another facility I'd already watched semen collected from a stud bull named Bonanza. Now I wanted to watch a cow, who had been inseminated with Bonanza's sperm, give birth. Without interfering, I'd then observe the calf through the normal, commercial production cycle—"conception to consumption."

Sue and Andrew seemed interested, but what closed the deal, I think, was when I told them I'd recently completed an eight-week "Herdsperson Training" course through Cornell Cooperative Extension. I took the course, which is designed for people in the dairy industry, to learn the basics of cattle husbandry. Topics included "Feed and Nutrition," "Animal Handling," "Calving and Calf Care," and "Milking Procedures and Equipment."

From the course, I not only learned a lot about raising dairy cows, I also learned the language. A "springing heifer" is a young female, pregnant for the first time and about to give birth; laminitis is soreness in the hooves; TMR stands for "total mix ration"—an all-in-one feeding program.

Within twenty minutes, Sue and Andrew had agreed that for as long as I needed—a year or maybe two—I could go anywhere on the farm, see anything, talk to anyone, day or night. Sue ran a computer printout showing that 106 Lawnel cows had been bred with semen from Bonanza. Four of those cows were due to freshen—give birth—within the next three weeks.

. . .

"C'mon, girls, c'mon, sweeties." Sue Smith's soprano singsong urges four pregnant and wary cows toward a metal stock trailer attached to her pickup. "C'mon 'n' get in. C'mon, 4923, don't be a problem. Get on the trailer."

"Yip, yip, yip," she calls, slapping the reluctant cow on its side.

"This is a big trip for them," says Sue, explaining their hesitancy. "They know they're going somewhere, and they don't like the change."

We are in a barn at Lawnel Farms among a herd of about fifty "dry" cows—cows that are not being milked because they'll soon bear calves. Letting the cows dry off allows them to conserve nutrients they'll need to give birth and resume giving milk. Sue's moving the four to a maternity barn, where she expects they'll each freshen within a ten-day period at the end of this month.

These four cows—all artificially inseminated with sperm from the stud bull Bonanza—are the ones I've come to see. If I can manage to watch even one of them give birth and then follow the life of that calf, I'll be able to achieve my mission of watching one cow from birth to slaughter.

Sue gives the cows two needle stabs in the rump; thin lines of blood run down their sides. These are vaccines, one for salmonella, the other to prevent "scours"— what farmers call diarrhea in cows. The one for diarrhea, says Sue, is "for the baby; it goes into the baby's bloodstream."

After fifteen minutes in the barn, Sue has rounded up and put in the trailer three of the four cows on our list: 1523, 4923, and 1458. One, 4854, is reluctant.

Sue calls her again. "Here, 4854," she says, as we walk through the barn, scanning ear tags to find the cow.

At Lawnel, as on most large dairy farms, cows are identified by numbers assigned in sequence at birth. Each cow gets a three- or four-digit number. The number is printed in black numerals on both sides of a pair of yellow, two-inch square rubber tags inserted just after birth, one into each ear.

"She heard me call her; I know she did," Sue insists.

Does she really think a cow recognizes the sound of its number?

"Oh, sure," she says. "I can go into a barn and call any cow by her number and, chances are, she'll come—maybe not all the cows, but some will. This one's just running away because she knows something's up. She knows I'm going to move her."

As we walk through the barn, cow 4854 sprints the other way, slips on wet concrete, bunches up in a corner with other cows as if to hide, then breaks away and runs into the yard, then back again, and away from us down the center aisle.

"Some cows are interested in communicating with people and some are not," Sue told me later. "Most all of them communicate with each other, though, by the way they stand near each other, lick each other, that sort of thing. But I definitely think most of them know their numbers."

After some minutes we give up on trying to catch 4854. With three cows in the stock trailer, we ride in Sue's pickup a half mile or so down the road and unload the cows into the maternity barns. Sue will return for 4854 in a few days.

.   .   .

York, New York, straddles Route 36, a two-lane country road that runs north-south through the Genesee River valley of western New York State. The regular speed limit on Route 36 is fifty-five. As you drive through York, you have to slow down to thirty-five, but you don't have to stop because the main intersection has neither a traffic light nor a stop sign.

At the main intersection, on one side of Route 36, is a restaurant called York Landing, a tiny post office, and a hair and tanning salon. Across the street is a hardware store and a historical marker noting that Chester Arthur, who became president upon the assassination of James A. Garfield, attended elementary school in York. His father served for several years as minister of the local Baptist church. That congregation worships today in a lovely wood-frame building down the street from the post office; just up the road the other way is a handsome brick structure that houses the Presbyterian church.

But, to my mind, the most impressive building in York is the Town Hall. Built originally as a church, this white, two-story structure is in the style of a Colonial home with a cupola (holding a bell that chimes every hour) beneath a large clock that in turn supports a weathervane topped by a bronze sculpture of a goose in flight.

Behind the Town Hall, about two hundred thin marble tombstones stand in a graveyard. Many lean to the right or left; some are cracked and lie on their sides. The worn names, often barely legible, reflect the Scottish origins of this community's earliest settlers: MacDonald, McIntyre, Duncan, Burns. Most died before the Civil War. Originally they called their town Inverness, after the Scottish town on the North Sea, but later, perhaps when English residents came to outnumber Scots, the name was changed to York.

The founders set their town on the Genesee River, near a U-shaped bend that they called York Landing. They built a flour mill, a warehouse, and wooden docks to service barges moving wheat and corn up and down the river, and later along a canal. Though commercial river traffic peaked more than a century ago and the canal has long since been abandoned, York nevertheless endures, owing largely to its location in the heart of the Genesee River valley, an area of temperate climate and rich pastureland that supports one of the densest concentrations of dairy farms in the state.

On the front lawn of the York Town Hall stands a flagpole and an illuminated lawn sign. Messages on the sign change weekly, promoting events such as public meetings, pancake breakfasts, and spaghetti suppers. Today the sign announces a square dance next Saturday at 8:00 P.M., open to the public, featuring "The Old-Time Fiddlers."

If I can succeed in watching a certain calf born between now and then, I just may go to the square dance to celebrate.

. . .

Though Sue Smith has pledged her cooperation, my plan to watch the Bonanza-bred cows give birth presents some challenges. Lawnel Farms is only thirty-five minutes from my home in suburban Rochester, but cows can give birth at any hour of the day or night. Moreover, each of these four cows has already had three or four calves, and when cows have already had multiple births, their subsequent labors are likely to be brief.

I've given Sue my office and home phone numbers with instructions to call any-time, day or night, if it appears that one of the four cows might be starting labor. As an afterthought, I've rented a pager and given her that number, too. I've laid out warm clothes on a chair in the corner of the bedroom so I'll be able to leap from bed at a moment's notice and dress for the near-freezing weather common in late November in western New York. I've packed the back seat of my car with note-book, pens, camera, flashlight (for observing a birth at night), trail mix, blanket, and pillow (in case I need to sleep in the car)—my own bovine Lamaze bag.

My teenaged daughters, I've noticed, have stopped asking me to give their friends rides. I know they're embarrassed that their dad's got all this stuff in the back of his car, not to mention the farm aroma so unfamiliar to suburban kids.

. . .

Lawnel Farms is located on Craig Road, the first cross street as you head south out of York on Route 36. There are several private homes on the street, a shoot-ing club that doubles as the VFW post, and a small, seventy-head dairy; but much of the land on either side of this stretch of Craig Road belongs to the Smith fam-ily and is part of Lawnel Farms.

The "Nel" of Lawnel is Nelson Smith. He bought the original tract of land in 1923 and ran it as a vegetable farm. Now ninety-one, Nelson is spry, with a shock of white hair, and he wears a hearing aid in one ear. He resides in an assisted-living center in nearby Batavia.

The "Law" of Lawnel is Lawrence Smith, Nelson's oldest son. After teaching agricultural economics at a nearby college for four years, Larry joined his father on the farm. (There is still a bit of the professor in Larry. The day after I met him and told him of my plans to write a book about farming, he faxed me a reading list of eleven recommended titles.) It was Larry who bought the first dairy cow and expanded the enterprise by buying, over many years, five other farms on or near Craig Road. Today, Larry Smith, sixty-five, is semiretired.

With more than two thousand acres and nine hundred cows, Lawnel is not the largest dairy farm in the area—there are farms with 1,100 and even 1,500 cows within a half hour's drive of here—but by any measure Lawnel is substantial. It also represents a trend, both in New York State and nationally, toward fewer but larger dairy farms.

The original Lawnel property—what the Smiths call "the main farm"— includes barns to house all of Lawnel's cows while they are milking. There is not enough barn space, however, to keep all the cows, calves, and heifers there all the time. Depending on its age and stage of life, an animal may be housed at another of the five farms now integrated into the Lawnel operation, and periodically moved from one farm to another. For example, heifers—young females—ready to be artificially inseminated for the first time are kept at the farm called Curry; cows ready to freshen are kept at the Hanna Farm. One of the drawbacks to this arrangement, Sue Smith admits, is that it requires Sue and her staff to spend a good deal of time driving around to the various farms, checking on animals and moving them from place to place. It was at Valley View Farm, for example—which sits right next to Sue and Andrew Smith's home—that I had watched as Sue rounded up the Bonanza-bred cows to move them to the Hanna Farm to give birth.

. . .

It was not long after I began visiting Lawnel Farms that I realized my original plan to follow a dairy cow from birth to slaughter would be impractical. Dairy cows, I learned, typically live five years: two years before they're first bred, and then three years giving milk. After that, most cows' milk production declines, and they're sent to slaughter. I was willing to invest a couple of years following a cow, but not five.

Fortunately, there was an alternative: instead of following a cow, I could follow a bull.

Bulls born on dairy farms generally have no economic value. They're not going to grow up to give milk, and they're not efficient beef producers. This is because milking breeds, like the Holstein, have been manipulated over the years to be tall and bony, to carry a heavy udder; beef breeds tend to be stockier and more compact. Bull calves born on a dairy farm typically are shipped to auction within a few days of birth and sold for next to nothing—fifty dollars or less. Most are slaughtered immediately—their meat often goes for pet food—and some are raised for four months for veal.

Nevertheless, I learned, some Holstein bull calves are raised for beef. Farmers select the heartiest ones at auction and raise them for about sixteen months, up to a slaughter weight of about 1,200 pounds. The meat, called "dairy beef," generally ends up as inexpensive steaks and chops in midpriced restaurants, and some is also ground and mixed with other meats to produce fast-food hamburger.

By following a bull calf raised for dairy beef, I could observe one animal from birth to slaughter, and the entire process would take less than two years.

•   •   •

Lawnel's "bull pen"—where newborn bull calves are kept—is located on the main farm in an old barn that connects to the herd office. The pen consists of a concrete slab covered with a thin layer of straw. It is a very thin layer; in many spots the concrete shows through.

This morning there are nine bull calves in the pen. One appears dead and another seems unable to rise; several are shivering. A tattered blue blanket, large enough to cover maybe half of one calf, lies unused on top of the straw.

Nearby, behind a locked gate leading to the fresh cow area, a cow bellows loudly. The gate is open at the bottom about a foot. The cow sticks her nose beneath the gate and exhales sharply. The vapor of her breath on this 35 degree November morning slides in two streams, one from each black nostril, under the gate and toward the bull calves.

Behind the gate, Sue Smith calls a cow that's recently given birth: "C'mon, sweetie, c'mon, girl, c'mon, sweetheart, oo-you—you!"

Two little bull calves stick their heads through the wooden fence of the bull pen. They lick and nuzzle the leg of my jeans.

A woman in her early twenties enters the barn. Shiny auburn hair—her most striking feature—hangs in a long braid down the middle of her back. This is Jessica Treuthart, Lawnel's calf manager. She's in charge of all calves born on the farm, which may be as many as twenty or thirty in a week.

Jessica is looking for a heifer calf she had temporarily placed among the bull calves. She goes to each calf lying on the concrete, lifts its leg until she finds the heifer, and gently pushes it out of the pen. She'll move it to the heated greenhouse where newborn heifer calves are raised.

Jessica has been working at Lawnel for only three months. Before that, she was a hairdresser for seven years after high school. "I did everything," she says. "Perms, color, cutting, makeup. I like this better, though," she says of working as calf manager. "I like being outside."

Jessica spots the dead calf and drags it from the pen by one hind leg into the center aisle of the barn. Why might the calf have died?

"Oh, I don't know," says Jessica. "Sometimes they just die."

Twice a day, Jessica feeds the bull calves milk replacer—dry milk mixed with water and minerals and vitamins. But unlike the heifers in the greenhouse, bull calves do not receive colostrum, the thick, creamy milk rich in nutrients and antibodies that cows, like women, secrete in the first few days after giving birth. Heifer calves get colostrum, but colostrum requires significant labor to collect, freeze, thaw, and prepare, so bull calves generally don't get any. Neither do they receive medications against diarrhea or other diseases.

In the herd office, a photocopy of an article from a farm magazine is posted on the corkboard. The headline reads, A CALF WITHOUT COLOSTRUM DOESN'T HAVE A CHANCE.

Jessica returns from another room in the barn with a red plastic snow sled, the kind children ride in the winter. She lifts the dead bull calf onto the sled and pulls it down the aisle and out of the barn. The calf's rear legs hang off the end and drag on the ground.

From behind the gate to the maternity barn, a cow bellows.

• • •

In midmorning I stop in the maternity barn to check on the four Bonanza-bred cows. They are mixed in among a dozen or so other cows. As I enter, I see that one cow is starting to freshen. It's not one of the Bonanza-bred cows, but when a 1,500-pound animal begins to give birth, it's hard not to watch.

This cow, 1602, lies on her side on a thick layer of straw. Earlier I had asked Sue Smith if it was safe to walk around in a maternity barn. "Yeah," she said, "just watch your back. One or two of the cows might become a little too protective." I decide to watch 1602 from behind a low fence at the front of the barn.

About 90 percent of the time, dairy cows are able to give birth unassisted. When calves must be pulled—as Darla's were—or cut out by C-section, it's usually because the calf's head is too big or the calf is turned around in an abnormal position, such as breech (backward). In a normal presentation, a calf's front feet come first, followed by the head, shoulders, middle, hips, and then the hind legs and feet.

The cow laboring in front of me is black around the head and tail, and mostly white in the middle. She bellows once and looks back, wide-eyed, over her shoulder. I'm not sure if she can see what I see: protruding about four inches from her vagina is a single cloven hoof. It is yellowish white, the color of stained teeth, delicate and slender; it looks as if you could fit it with a high-heel shoe. The yellowing effect, sometimes called "golden slippers," results from viewing the hooves through the sheen of the fetal membrane that still envelopes the calf.

Cattle belong to the mammalian order Artiodactyla, hooved animals with an even number of toes. A cow's natural habitat is open grassland or savanna, and it was in order to lengthen the legs and thus increase the speed with which cows could outrun predators that they and other hooved animals—deer, sheep, and goats among them—evolved what is called *digitigrade locomotion*—that is, they walk on their toes. The split, or cloven hoof, is simply the thickened nail on the enlarged third and fourth toes. The remaining toes have either disappeared or been reduced to vestiges known as dewclaws, little points of flesh higher up on the leg.

But cloven hooves have somehow acquired a sinister reputation. Satan, for example, is usually portrayed with them. Indeed, the name of the official bulletin of the Church of Satan, according to that organization's website, is *The Cloven Hoof.*

I watch 1602, a single split hoof sticking out from her backside as she rests between contractions, and wonder how those little golden toenails became the symbol of such evil.

As I watch, the head of 1602's calf emerges, then the shoulders, then the rest slides easily out and onto the dry straw. In a swath of sunlight cast through the open east side of the barn, the calf lies motionless. It's mostly white with a pink nose, and it has a patch of black on the left side of its face. Its mother rises to her feet and immediately begins licking her calf. Two other cows, including 1523—one of the Bonanza-bred cows—walk over and stand nearby.

Through an open window in the back of the barn, I can see the silver silo of another small dairy down the road. A similar scene—a cow licking a newborn calf—is likely occurring there as it is on every dairy farm in America this morning, as indeed it is even on this farm in the next barn over, where another cow is licking another calf born just minutes before I arrived. The nation's 9 million dairy cows produce about 7 million calves a year, about twenty thousand a day, one every four seconds.

A truck pulls up in front of the barn. It's Jessica, the calf manager. The temperature is in the thirties, but she wears no coat, only a plaid flannel shirt. She enters the barn and lifts the calf's leg. "It's a boy," she says. Jessica gently lifts the calf with both arms extended under its belly, puts it in the front seat of her truck, and drives off.

I had been so focused on watching 1602 lick her calf that it seemed Jessica arrived to take it away only minutes after it had been born. I check my watch, though, and actually the calf had been with its mother for nearly forty minutes.

1602 sniffs the straw where her calf had lain, then walks to the fence and bellows. Four other cows follow. She goes to the feed bunk and grabs a mouthful, to the water trough and drinks quickly, then to the fence and bellows. She walks from one barn to the other, then back again, then to the place in the straw where her calf had lain, and bellows. Every cow in the barn stands still except 1602; she paces. She walks to the fence again and sniffs the ground. She moos, softly.

In the natural state, the cow-calf bond is strong. Calves will nurse from their mothers for the better part of a year. In one study of domesticated cows, contact between cow and calf for as little as five minutes after birth was shown to produce a strong maternal bond; in another, cows did not break the bond with a calf even when another calf was born a year later.

.   .   .

Toward the end of the afternoon, I check back at the bull pen to see how 1602's calf is doing. ("1602's calf" is the only way to refer to this animal because bull calves at Lawnel, owing to their short stay on the farm, are not even given numbers.) The calf lies shivering, along with three other bull calves born today.

From another part of the barn, where cows who have recently given birth are kept, a cow sticks her nose under the wooden gate and bellows continuously. Curious what cow is making so much noise, I look over the gate to read her ear tag. It's 1602. She seems to know her newborn calf lies nearby.

•   •   •

It's not easy to watch a newborn calf taken from its mother, or to see a little bull calf shivering on a concrete floor. I try to keep my emotions in check, however. Everything about this farm is still new to me: I hardly know one building from another or which piece of equipment does what; I haven't even met half of the farmhands. Before I let myself react emotionally, I want to understand the whole picture—particularly from the farmers' point of view.

•   •   •

Two days later, on a Friday morning, I arrive at Lawnel at nine, only to be told by Sue Smith that the first of the Bonanza-bred cows freshened at three o'clock this morning on pasture at the Hanna Farm. No one called me because no one saw it. The mother, 1523, has already been moved to the main farm and is in the barn for fresh cows. The calf, a heifer, is also at the main farm, in the greenhouse.

The greenhouse, a domed, wood-frame structure about forty yards long and ten wide, is covered on all sides with plastic sheeting and is heated on this cold morning to a comfortable fifty degrees. Inside are two long rows of pens made from four-foot-high wire fencing. Each pen holds one heifer calf. It's easy to find the calf born to 1523 this morning, because the calves are all arranged in birth order: the oldest, born last month, is on the left as you enter, followed by younger and younger ones as you move down the row. I have to look all the way down the left side and then start back up the right side until I find the last occupied pen.

Inside stands a black-faced calf with just the tiniest spot of white hair precisely in the middle of her forehead, a black body with just a thin band of white over her back, and four white legs. In this, she resembles her mother, 1523, who, except for a thin horizontal band of white on the forehead and another on the rump, is black in body and face, and white on all four legs. The calf is about the size of a large dog and meets, on this first day of her life, all the criteria for cuteness: large head, big eyes, warm to the touch, wobbly, gentle, and totally helpless.

Jessica stands in the pen gently holding her to her feet and feeding her a bottle.

"I'm giving colostrum," she says. "Also, just before you got here I gave her what we call a 'first defense' pill—it helps protect them from diseases. Since she was born at night on pasture, we're not sure if she might have gone a few hours before getting colostrum." A calf's ability to absorb antibodies from colostrum declines rapidly within about six hours of birth.

The calf sucks eagerly from the bottle. If it were not inclined to do so, Jessica explains, "I'd have to tube her." That means force-feeding the colostrum through a tube placed down the calf's esophagus.

Jessica also disinfects the calf's navel, which hangs red and twisted about five inches below its belly, by dipping it in iodine. (Later, when I asked Jessica if there were any similarities between hairdressing, which she did for seven years, and caring for calves, she said, "Yeah, I still come home with my hands stained, only now it's not from hair dye but from the iodine dip.") She also gives the calf two injections in the upper part of the left hind leg: one of iron and one of selenium and vitamins.

Finally, putting one leg over the calf's back to steady it, Jessica punches a yellow tag with printed black numerals into the calf's ear. From now on, this newest Lawnel calf will be known as 6717.

· · ·

By late morning it has started raining. In the bull pen, 1602's calf—born two days ago—has stopped shivering. I don't know if this is because the weather has warmed just a bit or because he has become stronger.

As I'm watching, Andrew herds several cows into this part of the barn. One of them is ready to freshen, but has a problem. "Everything's in line, but her cervix is tight," he says. He's going to pull her calf.

He leaves the other cows unattended in the aisle and puts the one about to freshen in the red metal stanchion across from the bull pen. This is the same stanchion where the vet pulled Darla's stillborn twins. Already I can see two hooves emerging from the cow, one on top of the other; both glisten in the fluorescent light hanging from the barn's low ceiling.

Andrew ties a nylon rope around the top hoof and reaches into the cow's uterus with his right arm, covered to the shoulder with an orange glove. Then he gets the calf-puller and begins cranking. As the head emerges, I see that the calf is listless; its tongue hangs from the side of its mouth. The calf hits the concrete floor and Andrew pulls it into the center aisle. He kneels over it. He pushes on one of its eyes and pokes a length of straw up one nostril, looking for a response. He begins rhythmically pushing on the wet calf's chest.

"C'mon, girl," he urges.

After a minute, he drags the lifeless heifer calf out of the barn by the nylon rope around its hoof.

"Excuse me, ladies," he says, as he passes two other cows standing nearby.

• • •

As has become my habit, I stop at York Landing restaurant to review my notes before heading home. "The Landing," as it's called, sits at York's main intersection. Built around 1850, the two-story redbrick structure is thought originally to have housed a bakery, then a hardware store, and then maybe a general store. For about the past ten years it has been a restaurant. Its current owners are a warm and energetic couple in their thirties, Larry and Joan Alexander.

I find the Landing an ideal place to rest and warm myself, particularly after a cold day of tromping through cow barns. As the restaurant's front door opens, a cowbell clangs gently. The first thing you see is the bakery case, usually filled with homemade brownies, cookies, and lemon bars. The interior space is inviting: sturdy brick walls, the ceiling and floor covered in dark hardwood planking.

I find the building itself to be comforting, and once paced out the dimensions of its rectangular shape. Not surprisingly, they very nearly comport with what classic Greek architecture called "the Golden Rectangle," a particular ratio of length to width that was thought to create the most aesthetically pleasing of spaces.

Behind the bakery case is a large service counter—with a cash register on one side and coffee on the other. The coffee is self-service: just help yourself and pay later. Over the counter hangs a wooden fan, and behind that, suspended from the ceiling and stretching toward the back, are hand-lettered signs from the building's past: CREAMERY, ICE CREAMERY, BAKERY.

On the wall to the left, a chalkboard lists the daily specials. There's usually a burger, a main dish like chicken and biscuits or beef stew, a cold sandwich, and homemade soup. Last week, Joan Alexander made fried salmon patties from her grandmother's recipe. I remember my own mother making salmon patties. Joan's are delicious.

The Landing's interior walls are hung with large black-and-white photos of early life in York. One, of York Landing itself, shows a flour mill and a warehouse that once stood at a turning point along the canal that ran parallel to the Genesee River. The photo that most intrigues me, though, is of a 1912 road rally. It shows classic cars—many fitted with American flags—lined up in the street on a snowy day. There's a brass band with a big bass drum. Watching the cars are a group of men in long cloth coats and driver's caps, and two boys in knickers. They all stand in front of the same building in which I now stand looking at their picture.

Toward the back of the restaurant is a cabinet with Native American blankets and other crafts offered for sale. I've already bought a ceramic candle holder, which I keep on a night table beside my bed, and a wood-framed mirror that hangs in my office. Now I've got my eye on a wooden birdhouse in the shape of the Landing itself.

Along one wall, customers are free to post notices: a men's prostate support group is forming, York Emergency Medical Services needs volunteers, Kiwanis is holding a chicken barbecue, a new mother is looking for a baby-sitter, someone has hay to sell.

There's plenty of seating at the Landing. There are square wooden tables and round, marble-topped tables such as you might see in an ice cream parlor, but I always sit at the booth in the front, just to the right as you walk in. It's made of knotty pine, and built right into the space in front of the window. Seven or eight people could fit at it. Sitting here, I can see cars and trucks go by on the street and watch people as they enter the restaurant. I can also hear most conversations at the bakery counter and register. Larry Alexander later told me that this table— which I've come to think of as "my" table—is, in fact, everyone's favorite table, and for the same reasons. He and his wife, Joan, he says, refer to it as "the Table of Knowledge."

"It's gossip central," explained Larry. "If you sit there long enough, sooner or later you're gonna find out everything happening in this town." The former town supervisor, he recalled, used to meet at the table with his road crew.

Larry offered this rundown of who sits at the Table of Knowledge on a typical morning:

5:30. Highway crews: snow plowers in the winter, road crews in the summer; also farmhands coming in to work and night milkers coming off their shift.
6:30. Commuters on their way to work in Rochester.
7:30. Farmers done with morning chores, coming in for a snack.
8:00. Walkers, also known as the "hoofers and woofers," a group of eight to ten women who walk their dogs together. On Fridays they stay at the table for a game of dice, for which Larry keeps extra quarters on hand.

As I sit at the Table of Knowledge, reviewing notes of my day at the farm, I over-hear someone mention Lawnel. Two people in the kitchen, probably students who work here part-time after high school, are speculating about whether Larry Smith, now in his sixties, still owns the farm, or whether Sue and Andrew Smith have taken over. One says Larry has retired, but the other insists he's still working. And just at that moment, the cowbell on the front door clangs, and Larry Smith himself, wear-ing a Lawnel Farms cap, walks in. I invite him to join me for coffee, but he says he's just picking up an early dinner and needs to go. One of the young people from the kitchen comes out, greets Larry warmly, and hands him his take-out order.

. . .

The following Monday I return to Lawnel. "Did you hear that calf you were watching died yesterday?" Jessica asks me, her long red braid swinging across her back.

She's referring to 1602's calf in the bull pen. She doesn't know why it died, but two other bull calves died, too. Jessica says Sue's checking to make sure there's nothing wrong with the milk replacer they've been feeding the calves. To disin-fect the bull pen of any bug that may be lurking there, Jessica has removed the straw and covered the concrete with lime. She's temporarily put the calves out in front of the pen, in the barn's concrete aisle.

Jessica excuses herself to check something in the herd office. While she's gone, Joe Hopper, the cattle hauler, arrives with his stock trailer to pick up calves for the livestock auction. Joe, about fifty years old, wears brown coveralls. He has a kindly face, with a soft brown mustache and a warm smile.

Joe enters the bull pen. "C'mon here, girl, boy, whatever," he calls softly. "Some are lazy," he says to me. "Get up, you," he coaxes, prodding the calves to their feet. "Okay, there you go."

In the natural state, calves this young don't walk much, nor do they need to. The mother hides them and they sleep a great deal while she grazes on nearby pasture, coming back frequently to check them and give them milk.

Even without the three calves that died, there are still eleven ready to go today. None of them looks too healthy, though. One lies literally on top of another. Joe picks the top one up by the ears. He gently kicks the one on the bottom, but it hardly moves.

"This one ain't goin' nowhere today," he says.

He begins gently coaxing the others with a nudge here and there. None move.

"C'mon, kids," he urges. "C'mon, c'mon, c'mon. My back is hurting me today. Be nice to me, kids."

Jessica returns to the barn.

"Hey," says Joe, brightening, "I'm all set now. I got my hairdresser with me."

Working as a team, they start moving the calves one by one out of the barn and up the ramp to Joe's trailer.

"C'mon, you," Joe says to a calf as he walks it slowly toward the truck. "Of all days I left my juicer home."

I ask him what a juicer is.

"I got this little prod," he explains. "I give 'em a touch on the back and it wakes 'em right up—gives 'em some energy. It's kinder than hittin' 'em—I don't believe in hittin' 'em."

Joe turns one listless calf over and lays it facedown. He raises it to its back legs, then its front legs, then pushes it gently toward the ramp.

"I've had thirty-two calves this morning," says Joe.

Finally there is just one calf left, lying on its side on the concrete floor, its legs shaking. It is obviously ill and unable to stand.

"I ain't takin' that one," says Joe, but then reconsiders. I think he means he's not supposed to bring sick animals to the auction. "I shouldn't carry you, but . . ." he says to the calf, and then bends down and lifts it under its belly and carries it out of the barn and into the trailer.

•   •   •

I'm curious what has become of 1602's calf. Jessica says its body has already been put in the compost.

It takes just a couple of minutes to walk to the Lawnel compost pile. It's out past the cow barns, beyond the manure lagoon and the retaining pond, under some shade trees. Actually, there are two piles, each about four feet high. At first glance, all I see are mounds of rich soil, lots of straw, sticks and leaves. But as my eyes adjust, I begin to notice, sticking out of the piles here and there, little bones, clumps of hair, a hoof. Somewhere in here is 1602's calf.

•   •   •

The following day, the phone in my bedroom rings at one-thirty in the morning. Both of my teenaged daughters are home in their beds, so my first thought is that one of my parents, both of whom are in their eighties, may be ill. When I answer I'm relieved to hear Sue Smith's voice. She says one of the night milkers just called her at home to say that 4923, one of the Bonanza-bred cows I'm watching, is ready to freshen. Sue says she thought the cow was looking close—ready to give birth—yesterday, so she moved her from the Hanna Farm to the maternity barn at the main farm.

I quickly dress and drive the forty minutes to Lawnel. I've driven Route 36 many times, but never in the middle of the night. In the beam from my headlights the number 36 catches my attention for the first time. In Jewish tradition, numbers have special meanings. The number 18, for example, stands for "life," as in the Hebrew toast *"L'chaim,"* which means "to life." By extension, the number 36 would stand for "double life." It's a good omen: maybe this cow will have twins.

At Lawnel, one look at the cow tells me she's not anywhere near freshening. I've been reading about how to tell when cows are ready to give birth, and she has none of the signs: there's no mucus discharge from her vagina, she doesn't hold her tail up, and she's still eating.

I decide to stay at the farm until 5:00 A.M. when Sue arrives for work, so she can take a look at the cow, just to be sure.

So it won't be a total loss, I stand outside and study the sky. It's a clear and cold night. I can't remember the last time I've seen so many stars. Orienting along the Big Dipper, I locate the North Star just over the three Lawnel silos, facing back toward York.

I decide to use the pillow and blanket I've been carrying around in my car for the last two weeks, but the car's back seat proves an uncomfortable place to sleep. When Sue arrives for work, I'm still awake, and exhausted. She checks on 4923 and quickly agrees the cow is not in labor.

Before I leave, I change my deal with Sue: if any of the three remaining Bonanza-bred cows goes into labor, call me, but only *after* 5:00 A.M.

·   ·   ·

The next day the telephone rings again and I stumble from bed. I mumble a dry hello.

"Good morning, Peter, this is Sue Smith." She has a cheery, wide-awake voice. "4923's water broke just a few minutes ago. I think we're going to have a calf for you this morning."

I tell Sue I'll be there in forty minutes.

"By the way, what time is it?" I ask.

"It's five-fifteen," she says. "See you soon."

. . .

As I slow my car to forty-five miles an hour to drive through York, I pick up an early-morning talk show on a Rochester station. The co-hosts, Beth and Chet, are discussing their Thanksgiving plans. Beth says she follows a "near-vegetarian" diet and talks up nonmeat substitutes for Thanksgiving turkey. "We're going to convert you all," she kids her co-host. Then he teases her: "What are we supposed to do, Beth, gather around our Thanksgiving tables tomorrow and say grace for 'this soybean loaf'?"

. . .

At 6:00 A.M. at Lawnel, I walk quickly past the old bull pen to the maternity barn where 4923 stands in profile, quiet and alone. Her tail stands up at a thirty-degree angle to her back. She hunches up and expels a gush of water; a tell-tale strand of mucus hangs from her.

She is a mostly black cow. I can easily recognize her by the large white mark on her forehead that looks like a backward question mark.

Sue is in the milking parlor, helping milk a group of sick cows.

Andrew is where he usually is, in the equipment barn; he's changing the oil on Sue's Chevy Suburban, which they'll drive to New Jersey tomorrow to spend Thanksgiving with Andrew's brother. They are hoping to get into Manhattan first to see the Macy's Thanksgiving Day Parade.

"Hey, take a look at that," says Andrew, gesturing toward a green tractor in the barn. He says it's a repossessed tractor he bought from a dealer in Indiana. He'll use it as a manure scraper. "It only has 215 hours on it," he says. "That's nothing. That's like five thousand miles on a passenger car." This must be the tractor he was talking about last week while trying to calm the young vet pulling calves out of Darla. Andrew says that to get the tractor he drove round-trip to Indiana in two days with just two hours' sleep. The slight bravado I've been feeling about having made back-to-back forty-minute night drives from Rochester to York starts to fade.

. . .

As the sun rises, the three Lawnel silos appear as silhouettes against the reddening sky. A light frost covers the ground. I am standing in a postcard-perfect picture.

In the greenhouse, Jessica is pouring warm milk replacer into buckets for the heifer calves that have finished with colostrum. She also gives injections of Gastro-Cote, which she describes as "like Pepto-Bismol." Cow 6717, born earlier this week, rests quietly in her pen.

. . .

At a quarter to seven, in the maternity barn, 4923 lies on her left side on a thin bed of straw. A single bright halogen light illuminates most of this old barn from above. Outside, a front-loader with headlights on dumps feed into the back of a Mack truck. I wonder if the artificial lights and loud engine noises affect the cows' ability to relax and give birth.

The sky has lightened now. 4923 still lies on her side; she's extended her rear leg and is pushing. Her vagina has opened. I can see the sac inside.

Ten minutes later she stands, reaches under a fence, and rubs noses with a cow on the other side. She walks to the end of the barn, and then back.

Outside the milking parlor, a fourteen-wheel stainless-steel milk truck arrives. Dave Slocum, the driver, comes to Lawnel every morning to haul the farm's milk to a processing plant about forty miles south of here. Dave's truck can hold 63,000 pounds of milk—nearly 30,000 quarts.

It's been more than two hours since 4923's water broke. Her vagina is swollen and red, and I can see the sac again. But she's still walking around, and she's not pushing. I wonder if maybe I'm making her nervous by standing too close.

A half hour later, Andrew enters the barn and announces, "I'm going to pull her. It's been too long since her water broke."

Jessica also appears in the barn. Andrew tells her to get some dry straw.

"C'mon, you know where to go," says Andrew, leading 4923 to the red metal stanchion across from the old bull pen, now covered in lime.

The cow enters the stanchion without resistance and Jessica drops straw on the cement floor under her tail. Andrew pulls an orange, shoulder-length glove onto his right hand and arm, stands sideways to the back of the cow, and reaches in.

"Twins," he says. "Looks like the water broke on one but not the other. That's why she hasn't freshened."

As Andrew pulls and pushes a bit inside her, one white, cloven hoof emerges. He cups his hands and pours soapy water over the vulva and the vagina contracts.

Two hooves now emerge. Andrew ties one end of a nylon rope around them and the other end to the calf puller, and cranks. 4923 bellows as one wet calf slips quickly from her and falls with a thud to the straw-covered floor, a distance of almost five feet. Andrew drags the calf into the aisle, glancing at its underside as he does.

"It's a heifer," he says.

The value to the Smith family of this female calf will depend on the sex of her twin. If the other calf is also a heifer, 4923's pregnancy will be a double bonus: two valuable milk cows from one pregnancy. But if the other calf is a male, the pregnancy will be a near-total loss. This is because in about 85 percent of cases in which a female calf is born twin to a male, the male hormones circulate into the unborn female and render her sterile. The female twin, called a freemartin, (perhaps from the Anglo-Saxon *faer,* meaning "empty," and the Gaelic *mart,* meaning "a spayed female") is assumed to be infertile and, rather than being raised as a milk cow, is sold at auction like a bull calf.

Another hoof emerges; Andrew ties the rope around it and pulls. Now the head comes out: mostly black, with eyes wide open. Andrew keeps cranking; 4923 bellows loudly.

With a gush, the second calf slips out. It hits rear first against a white bucket of soapy water on the floor and then bounces the rest of the way to the concrete floor. Andrew drags it into the aisle.

"Bull calf," he announces, betraying no emotion.

.   .   .

The bull-heifer twins are a wipeout for Lawnel, but not for me. This little bull calf lying at my feet is the one I've been waiting for. Son of Bonanza, daughter of 4923; if this calf survives, it can be the one I watch grow through the sixteen-month production cycle for dairy beef.

Andrew releases 4923 from the stanchion and begins to lead her back to the maternity barn, but then agrees, at my request, to leave her here with her twins, at least for a little while, so I can watch them together. He cleans the stanchion and leaves the barn.

Both calves, mostly black, lie sprawled on the concrete floor. The bull is bigger than the heifer, and has a white triangle on its forehead that extends down to its nose. The heifer also has a white triangle on her forehead, but hers does not extend down to the nose. This is the simplest way to tell them apart. Both calves, but especially the bull, seem to have enormous ears for the size of their heads.

I think of them as "donkey ears," like those on the boy Lampwick when he turns into a donkey in *Pinocchio*.

4923 stands over the bull calf. The calf is wet all over and bawls; he tries to stand, but can't. She bends to him and begins licking his neck, his ears, and across his face.

4923 moves to the heifer calf and licks her head, shoulders, and back. Three minutes later she comes back to the bull with big, long licks across the rump, the back, the neck, the face, and then back to the rump. I time her at about ninety licks per minute. I wonder if the birth fluids taste good to her and that is why she licks, or if it's just instinctual. Experts say the licking establishes a bond between cow and calf, dries the birth fluids so the calf doesn't get chilled, and stimulates the calf to stand and begin looking for a teat from which to nurse.

These little calves are all ears and heads and faces.

The bull calf tries to stand, but slips on the floor, which is wet with amniotic and vaginal fluids.

4923 licks her bull calf's face, across its eyes, forehead, ears, shoulder, stomach, and back.

The twins briefly rub heads together.

Their mother licks silently; the only sound in this barn is that of a rough tongue moving against short, wet hair.

I never understood the term *cowlick* before; now I see that it's hair that stands up as if licked by the coarse tongue of a cow.

The heifer calf rises; 4923 licks her rump and tail. She staggers toward her mother's enormous udder and puts her face to the back of it, not quite reaching a teat. Then she falls again. From 4923's right front teat, milk drips.

The bull calf tries again to stand, but still can't get enough traction on the slippery floor.

Ten more minutes and the heifer calf is once more on her feet. 4923 continues licking the bull calf, who hasn't yet stood. He begins to shiver, lying in the unbedded concrete aisle amid now-cold birth fluids and blood.

Minutes later, Jessica enters the barn with encouraging news: starting today, bull calves will be kept in a new outdoor "superhutch" near the greenhouse. A farmhand is building a base for it now. Also, she'll be giving bull calves colostrum—not the best colostrum, which comes from mature cows, but younger cows' colostrum, which until now they've been throwing away. Colostrum from younger cows doesn't have as many antibodies as colostrum from older cows, because the younger cows haven't been exposed to as many diseases—but it's still helpful and will be an improvement over milk replacer.

As Jessica leaves, the heifer twin, still standing, pokes at the underbelly of her mother, but still hasn't found a teat. The bull calf remains unable to stand; its back legs keep doing splits on the slippery floor. If 4923 would just push him forward about three feet, where the floor is drier, I bet he could stand.

· · ·

A loud electronic horn outside plays a few bars from "Old MacDonald Had a Farm." It's the Snack Shack, the coffee and food truck from York Landing restaurant that stops at Lawnel every morning around this time. I decide to take a break.

Joan Alexander, who, with her husband, Larry, owns York Landing, says the restaurant is doing well in getting local people to come in, but there just are not enough people around. That's why six months ago Joan created the Snack Shack. Each morning, starting at seven-thirty, she drives to about a dozen of the larger farms—a loop around the county of about one hundred miles—offering breakfast sandwiches (egg, cheese, bacon, ham, or sausage on bagel, muffin, or croissant), doughnuts, and Danishes. The Snack Shack itself is a Toyota pickup with beverage, sandwich, and bakery sections built of pressure-treated wood in the back. When Joan and Larry bought the vehicle, it already had 200,000 miles on it. Today it has about 25,000 more. I buy a peach Danish.

· · ·

When I return to the barn fifteen minutes later, both calves are lying in the aisle, but 4923, their mother, is gone. Her nose and mouth stick under the gate from the maternity barn. I don't know who moved her. The heifer calf walks jerkily down the long concrete aisle toward the gate and her mother.

Just then, Jessica returns. She's wearing a raincoat, a yellow slicker. The new calf hutch is ready, she announces. She picks up the heifer calf, both arms under its belly, and carries it outside to her pickup to drive the hundred yards or so over to the new hutch.

When she returns, she tries to pick up the bull calf, but he's too heavy. Jessica gets the red plastic sled—the one she uses to pull dead calves out of the barn— and puts the bull calf on it. But he is so big that when she begins dragging it, he falls off the back.

I have to make a decision: I want to help Jessica, but I've planned to be an observer of what happens on this farm, not a participant. Yet something in me wants to touch and hold this bull calf, this newborn I'm going to follow until its death.

"Do you have another raincoat?" I ask. Jessica gets one from the calf office. I strip off my winter jacket and put the yellow slicker on over my sweatshirt. Jessica lifts the back end of the bull calf, and I, with my arms under his wet belly, lift the front, holding his chest against my own. Together we carry him to the truck and put him in the front, on the floor next to his sister.

In the awkward position in which he's wedged backward on the floor, the bull calf's red umbilical cord is exposed. I remove my glove to touch it. It feels like the thin, slippery skin of a roasted red pepper.

At the superhutch, we take the two calves from the truck. The covered hutch, enclosed on three sides, is made of white fiberglass and thickly bedded with straw. Probably a dozen calves could fit in it.

Unaided, the heifer calf walks over to the hutch. Jessica and I manage to get the bull calf to his feet next to the truck, but he's unsteady and won't move. Another farmhand—the pocket patch on his coverall reads "Bennett"—comes over and asks if we are done with the truck, because he needs it. He climbs in and starts to back up, but we signal him to wait until we move the bull calf out of the way. Bennett quickly gets out of the truck and, without a word, drags the bull calf by its ears over to the hutch.

After Bennett leaves, I ask Jessica what she thinks of Bennett handling the calf that way.

"I wouldn't do it," she says, "but the calves don't seem to mind. I don't think it hurts them."

The twins lie in the hutch. One at a time, Jessica coaxes them to their feet and, straddling them, bottle-feeds them colostrum. They both drink eagerly.

I comment to Jessica how gentle and nurturing she is with the calves. She says, "It's funny, 'cause I never took care of anything before I worked here." She has no younger siblings, nieces, or nephews, and never baby-sat. She says that until she quit hairdressing and started working at Lawnel, she also knew nothing about cows. "I used to drive by farms and not even notice," she says. Now she's beginning to think "some of the cows are pretty smart," and she finds herself "getting attached to some of them."

Jessica says that if this is the bull calf I want to follow, I should mark it, because more bull calves will likely be born today and be put into the hutch. Since they don't get numbers, it will become difficult to tell them apart. Also, if I mark the calf, on Monday, Joe Hopper, the cattle hauler, will know not to take it to auction.

In the calf office, I find an orange livestock marker, a kind of thick fluorescent crayon. By the time I return to the calf hutch, another bull calf, born at Hanna this morning, already has joined the twins.

I climb into the white fiberglass hutch, bend to the bull calf lying in the thick straw, and firmly rub the marker up and down over the white triangle on his forehead. Later I'll pay the Smiths for this calf, but for now the orange mark brands him as mine; literally, I've put my mark on him. Immediately, I feel an unanticipated sense of responsibility for this animal's well-being. My first thought is to see if I can get Jessica to slip him a little extra colostrum. I'll need to work at maintaining a professional distance; my intention, I remind myself, is to observe farm procedures, not interfere with them.

I mark the heifer calf, too, with the thought that it will be nice to keep the twins together. I can't keep either of them here at Lawnel, of course; there's no room on a dairy farm for bull calves or freemartins. I'll have to find another farm where they can be raised for beef.

· · ·

As I leave, the bull calf is shivering, but I'm not too concerned: he's lying in thick straw next to two other calves, the open side of the hutch faces south, and even though it's still quite cold, the sun is shining.

I return the yellow raincoat to the office and head for my car. Wearing the slicker hasn't really done much good; the zipper was broken. Nearly twelve hours after I began this day, I drive home, my clothes spotted with blood and amniotic fluid.

· · ·

The inside of York Town Hall is alive this Saturday night with fiddle music. Dark wooden floors and wainscoting warm the hall, despite its high ceiling. On the stage, the Old-Time Fiddlers, a seven-piece band, warms up: fiddles, guitar, accordion, and keyboard. Admission is five dollars paid to a woman seated at a folding table as you come in; a man next to her stamps your hand.

Folding metal chairs line three sides of the place. The crowd is ample; there must be about seventy or eighty people, many of them about that old, too, although a few are younger, say in their sixties. I think farmers would have to be retired to come to a dance at night; otherwise how could they get up early enough the next morning to begin work? Some of the men wear string ties; many of the women are dressed in boots and colorful skirts.

On a word of welcome from the caller, everyone is up on the floor and quickly formed into groups of four couples. If a group lacks a couple or two, someone raises a hand with the number of fingers indicating how many couples they need. My wife and I join three couples in need of a fourth. My brother, who is visiting for Thanksgiving, and his girlfriend join another group.

I don't know how to square dance; the last time I tried, I think, was in fourth-grade gym class, and there we mostly made fun of it and tried to avoid touching the girls. But when the music begins, and the caller starts talking us through the do-si-dos and allemandes, the other couples in our group eagerly help us follow the calls and move about the circle more or less in time. By the third dance, I am working up a sweat and truly enjoying it.

There is something both comforting and exhilarating in moving to music so swiftly around a circle, reaching out your hand and finding someone else's hand at just the right place and moment, and grasping it. And then reaching again, and again, and each time a hand is there just where and when it's supposed to be, even though these are people whom you've never seen before and may never see again.

After three square dances the band plays a few swing numbers, then takes a break. Snacks are available in a little kitchen off the main hall. People have made cookies and left them on paper plates on a countertop. A sign says COOKIES, 25 CENTS, TAKE 2 OR 3.

After another set of square dances, I'm tired. The dance will continue until midnight, but I'm ready to go home. As we leave York Town Hall around 10:00 P.M., I look up at a clear sky, filled with so many stars that I cannot see from my own home. I think about the calves, one in a greenhouse and two others in a hutch, with orange marks on their foreheads that I put there. I wonder how they are doing on this cold night, but oddly I'm not concerned enough to drive the two or three minutes to Lawnel to check. In a hectic week, I had reached for the fundamental experience of watching the calves born, and with all the uncertainty and near misses and with the help of the Smiths and the people who work for them, I had been fortunate enough to do exactly what I'd set out to do, and for the moment that is enough.

2

Collecting Bonanza: A Flashback

BEFORE I'D EVER HEARD OF LAWNEL FARMS—and before my twin calves were born there—I'd spent two days learning how calves are conceived. The first day was at Genex, watching the stud bull Bonanza "collected"—Bonanza would later become the father of my calves. The second day I rode with an artificial inseminator to watch him breed cows. I back up in my story here to recount those two days.

· · ·

As a Holstein bull was led into the Genex ring by a nose lead, I lowered my pen and notebook and stared, openmouthed. I was stunned. I had never seen a bull so large. The man handling the bull stood five feet eight inches—about my own height—but this bull was so huge, the top of the man's head didn't even reach its shoulder.

"He probably weighs twenty-five hundred pounds," said a Genex technician.

That's nearly twice the weight of a mature dairy cow.

I was inside Production Center No. 2, a one-story redbrick building set on a high plateau overlooking Cayuga Lake, just outside Ithaca, New York. Owned by Genex Cooperative, an artificial-insemination company, the facility housed some fifty stud bulls. I stood at an observation window facing an indoor arena called the "collection ring."

Just then the bull let out the loudest, longest bellow I had ever heard, something like a foghorn.

"What's that all about?" I asked.

"I don't know," said the technician, not showing much interest. "I don't have the slightest idea what he might be saying."

The man leaned in closer to the window, shielding his eyes from the fluorescent light above.

"Can you read what it says on that ear tag?" he asked.

He was referring to a green plastic tag hanging from the lower half of the bull's right ear.

I couldn't make it out; the writing was too small.

"I think that might be Bonanza," he said excitedly.

Then I saw it. That enormous animal was, in fact, Bonanza—one of Genex's most up-and-coming young studs.

"Well, you're in luck," he said. "Bonanza's just about to be collected."

.   .   .

Artificial insemination of dairy cows was commercially developed in this country in the late 1930s. The technique quickly became popular because it offered farmers clear advantages over natural matings: it promised greater profits by genetically manipulating a herd over time to produce more milk; it also eliminated injury to cows during mating, and danger to farmers from keeping aggressive bulls.

Universal adoption of artificial insemination (AI for short) was delayed, however, by the problem of storage and transportation of semen: at room temperature, bull semen remains viable for only one to two hours. Early efforts to freeze semen had mixed results. In order to service cows on farms far removed from bulls, semen sellers had to be resourceful. Reminiscing in the pages of *Hoard's Dairyman* in 1996, former Massachusetts county agent Miles R. McCarry recalled:

[We] once tried to get around liquid semen's limited shelf life by hiring a barnstormer to fly it to technicians in Indiana in a [World War II] surplus plane. They dropped semen packages from the plane, which floated to earth on little parachutes to be collected by technicians who would rush them to the cows. Technicians spread sheets in their yards as targets. . . . One day, a big storm blew in, causing the floating semen packages to miss their drop sites. I bet to this day there are many gray-headed Ohio and Pennsylvania women still wondering what got all over the wash they hung out to dry that breezy day in 1950.

The discovery, in 1960, that semen could be frozen in liquid nitrogen greatly boosted the AI industry. Now semen from any bull could be available anywhere in the world. The first calf conceived from frozen semen was named Frosty.

Today, AI is used in 90 percent of U.S. dairy herds, and, partly as a result, yearly milk production in the United States has grown from 7,000 pounds per cow—about 814 gallons—in 1960, to about 22,000 pounds today—more than 2,500 gallons.

As the AI industry has grown, local farmer cooperatives have merged into regional or national firms; for-profit companies have also entered the field. Genex, with more than three hundred technicians, enjoys more than $68 million in semen sales annually and claims to inseminate each year more than 1.2 million of the nation's 9 million dairy cows. If you have eaten hamburger recently, there is about a one-in-eight chance that the biological father of the dairy cow from which part of the meat came was a Genex bull.

Of the popularity of AI, a breeding technician I spoke with cited control as the main attraction: "Dairy farmers like AI because it's one thing on the farm they can control—they can't control the weather or prices, but they can control their cow's genes."

Competing AI companies make it easy for farmers to buy semen from them. In the comfort of their homes, dairy farmers can study color catalogs picturing each company's stud bulls, and select the one to whom they want their cows bred.

Each catalog entry resembles a kid's baseball card: there's a color photo of the bull—usually standing in profile against a pastoral scene, often with front feet slightly elevated on a mound of grass. A box next to the picture lists the bull's statistics: gallons of milk his daughters produce per year; percentage of fat and protein in the milk; his daughters' body traits, such as rump angle, foot angle, size of udder, and length of teats. Under the stats are pictures of two or three of the bull's daughters. They also stand in profile, but with rumps slightly angled toward the camera to offer a better view of their udders.

According to the Genex catalog, Bonanza's mother was a cow named Ned Blaze, who gave 39,960 pounds of milk in one year, nearly double the national average. Her milk, and the milk of Bonanza's daughters, scores higher in protein content than in fat. This is an important selling point. Years ago, dairy farmers were paid more for milk high in fat, but as consumers have come to prefer less fat, milk rich in protein commands the higher price.

That stud bulls—like Bonanza—have names is significant. Most dairy farmers today don't name their cows, let alone bulls. If cows have names, it's because someone took a special interest in them (like Darla at Lawnel) or they are celebrities, such as Elsie, the Jersey on the Borden Milk can (whose real name before she was used in advertisements was "You'll do, Lobelia"). As a rule, though, cows and bulls today are not named. To be a Holstein bull and to have a name reflects one's economic worth.

●   ●   ●

I had no trouble getting into Genex. The man who had taught the "Reproduction" class in my Herdsperson's Training course is a Genex breeding technician. When I called and asked if he would host my visit, he kindly agreed.

In the collection ring, I saw that Bonanza's coloring was the typical black and white of the Holstein breed, but he was significantly more black than white. His head, neck, back, and rump were black. A band of white lay across his shoulders like a narrow scarf; his underbelly, legs, and feet were also white. His genitals were striking. The pink sac that hung between his legs was about a foot long and nearly as wide. There was just no way that one could not notice it. AI companies are not shy about discussing this feature of stud bulls, one even lists the predicted circumference of a sire's son's scrotum in its catalog.

Several techniques have been developed by which bull semen can be collected for artificial insemination, the most popular of which is that used at Genex: the artificial vagina. In this method, the stud bull mounts either a dummy or live "jump stock," and at the moment of ejaculation a technician covers the tip of the penis with a special tube to catch the semen.

Another method is electric stimulation, also called electro-ejaculation. This technique involves placing a probe fitted with electrodes up a bull's rectum and delivering a microcurrent of from five to thirty volts to stimulate the sacral and pelvic nerves. This method is especially useful with bulls that will not or cannot mount properly, or that lack libido. The method sounds bizarre, but I have read of its use with men who cannot ejaculate normally, such as those with neurological problems. Genex does not use electro-ejaculation regularly in part because it is difficult to do it properly. There appears to be some scientific support for this position. Researchers at Colorado State University studying sixty-nine Angus bulls collected by electric stimulation found, by measuring vocalizations and release of hormones, that the higher the voltage and the less skilled the person handling the equipment, the more disinclined the bulls were to tolerate the procedure.

I noticed that about a quarter of the way around the perimeter of the collection ring, another Holstein animal, about two-thirds the size of Bonanza, was standing quietly, its head tied at about a forty-five-degree angle by a nose lead to a metal hook on the floor, called a "hold-down anchor." In this posture, the animal's rump stuck out toward the center of the ring.

At first I assumed the animal with its head down, who evidently was going to be the jump stock for Bonanza, was a cow or maybe a castrated bull, but then I noticed its scrotal sac. Like Bonanza, it was an intact bull.

A slender young man in gray coveralls, with a blond brushcut, took Bonanza by a nose lead and positioned him behind the smaller bull. The man smoked a cigarette with one hand while with the other he slowly waved Bonanza's huge black head left and right over the smaller bull's rump. The man slouched, looking bored, as if helping stud bulls ejaculate was the beginning of just another workday.

Suddenly, Bonanza reared up on his hind legs and leaped onto the other bull's back.

And then just as quickly it was over; Bonanza dismounted and was again standing on the crushed limestone surface of the collection ring.

"That was just a false mount," a nearby technician told me. Bulls, he explained, seldom ejaculate on the first mount. In fact, handlers don't want them to; arousing a bull gradually through several mountings over fifteen to twenty minutes produces a better quality and quantity of sperm.

Cows are not used as jump stock because they would not be strong enough to withstand the repeated mountings of the heavy stud bulls. Instead, other bulls are used as the mounts. At Genex, mounts are usually failed studs, young bulls that had been accepted into the sire program but then discontinued. "A mount might be a bull we had intentions of drawing semen from, but, due to poor sperm production or poor conception rate or no market for the sperm, we dropped it," a technician explained.

One of the bull handlers later put it more succinctly: "The mount's daughters didn't produce enough milk, simple as that."

When a bull is dropped from the sire program to become a mount, he loses his name, and instead receives a number assigned in sequence. Bonanza's mount that morning wore a green ear tag with the number 339.

In most cases, sires willingly mount other intact bulls. They don't copulate rectally, but they do become aroused and go through precopulatory motions. A Genex officer explained, "These bulls haven't seen a cow since they were six months old on their farms, so they never had natural service," meaning they never had sexual relations with a cow.

Sires are brought into the collection ring two mornings a week, are expected to ejaculate twice, and each time are given a choice of two or three mounts.

"What a bull works on Tuesday he may not even look at on Friday," a handler explained. "Or he may work on the same mount three weeks straight and then get tired of it and not want it again. And then some bulls will work on anything, anytime, anywhere."

At the time of my visit, twenty-one mounts were serving fifty sires.

Mounts are kept in the ring for three hours at a stretch, during which time four or five bulls may mount them. With each bull mounting up to four times before ejaculation, a mount may be mounted twenty times in a morning. To help cushion the impact of repeated mountings, each mount stands with front hooves on quarter-inch-thick rubber floor mat over the crushed limestone surface of the collection ring.

Only one mount seemed reluctant to take his position, a brown bull that resisted when led into the ring. A handler shouted, "You fucking cocksucker!" and kicked the mount in its side.

For a bull, being a mount must be the lowest job in the world: to have begun life with the promise of being a stud, only to end up, in effect, a "prison bitch." I wondered if a mount, at some point, realizes that no one is calling him by his name.

. . .

Bonanza leaped again onto 339's back. His penis—bright pink and perhaps two feet long—came out momentarily, but quickly retracted as he backed down off the mount.

A bull's penis is normally held within the body, folded in an S shape, by the retractor penis muscle. During sexual excitement, erection is achieved by the rapid relaxation of this muscle, allowing the penis to straighten.

While dismounting, there is some danger that a bull might land on a bull handler's foot. For protection, handlers' shoes are fitted with metatarsal shields.

*   *   *

Most Genex sires are active for just a year or two: rarely, a few continue producing sperm until twelve to thirteen years of age. "When they're done, they're hamburger," said a technician. "We don't sell them to anyone else to use."

Genex vice president Herb Rycroft explained, "Sires in active service stay for a couple of years—I'm talking about the middle-of-the-road bulls. They sell some semen and then leave after a while. Those at the top of the list—like Bonanza— may stay much longer.

"Bonanza could continue for five or six years. What does change is the quantity of semen, because the cells in the testicles that produce sperm begin to die off.

"Also, the market changes. Like in any business, the customer is interested in the newest product. When a bull is popular, customers are interested for a while, then they're on to the newer ones. Our oldest bull, Beltone, just died last month after fifteen years and produced eight hundred thousand straws. [A straw is a thin cylindrical piece of plastic, much like a drinking straw, but closed at each end.] If you figure a fifty percent conception rate on inseminations, you can figure he had four hundred thousand offspring."

That's impressive, but far from the world record. That honor goes to a bull named Sunny Boy, who died recently at twelve and a half years of age. According to *Hoard's Dairyman,* this Holstein sire from the Netherlands produced more than 2 million straws of semen, including 250,000 in his peak year of 1991. It is said that during Sunny Boy's prime, a son or daughter of his was born every two minutes somewhere in the world.

*   *   *

On Bonanza's third mounting, his penis became erect and aimed near 339's rump, but soon retracted. Bonanza jumped down and resumed licking the mount's anus.

*   *   *

Another young man in gray coveralls entered the ring and approached Bonanza. He held a long tube about the size of a rolled-up wall poster. This was the artificial vagina. It had been kept warm in an oven at 120 degrees. Artificial vaginas are made of a plastic outer tube, about three feet long, and a shorter inner tube that holds warm water in a thin rubber sheath. One end of the tube is open to allow the bull's penis to enter, and the other end is attached to a clear plastic bottle to receive the semen.

Suddenly, Bonanza reared up on his hind legs and leaped onto the mount, the white underside of his massive chest resting on the mount's black back. Bonanza, that huge beast, was so high in the air his head came within a foot of the fluorescent light hanging from the ceiling over the collection ring.

The semen collector took a position on Bonanza's right side, holding the artificial vagina in his outstretched hand.

Then Bonanza, his white front legs squeezed against the mount's black sides, hopped up on both back hooves—for one remarkable moment he was airborne.

In a movement so swift I had trouble following it, the semen collector reached under Bonanza and touched the open end of the artificial vagina to the tip of Bonanza's extended penis; the feel of the warm water at the end of the tube, it is believed, triggers the bull's ejaculation.

I anticipated a great orgasmic bellow, but heard nothing.

• • •

Bonanza dismounted, and several things then happened quickly.

The semen collector left the collection ring, unscrewed the jar at the end of the artificial vagina, and placed it in a wall box that passed through to an adjacent laboratory.

The handler took Bonanza by the nose lead and moved him out of the collection ring.

The mount, still tied by the nose lead to the hold-down anchor, defecated. A technician ran into the ring and shoveled it away. Then another man approached with a bucket and a long-handled brush, and washed the mount's rump with disinfectant. A handler explained, "After each successful mounting, we wash anywhere there might be body fluids from the bull—saliva, seminal fluid on the rump—anywhere disease could be spread."

The mount would remain in the ring a couple more hours that morning to service other sires.

• • •

In the laboratory, Melissa Clark rolled her desk chair over to the pass-through window to retrieve the bottle of Bonanza's semen. Her lightly curled brown

hair hung to the middle of her back. Bonanza's ejaculation that morning produced 9 cc of white, milky liquid, higher than the average for bulls, which is 7
cc. Nine cc is a small amount of liquid: if you were to hollow out your thumb,
9 cc wouldn't quite fill it. A human male ejaculates, by comparison, on average
about 5 cc.

Melissa grew up in farm country near Ithaca, and came to Genex in 1986, her
first full-time job after graduating from high school the previous year. By the time
of my visit, she had been analyzing bull sperm for Genex for nearly twelve years.
Wearing blue jeans and sneakers, she rolled her chair over to a table on which sat
a 200-power phase-contrast microscope.

She prepared a slide of Bonanza's semen and placed it under the lens. "I try to
keep in mind when I'm looking under the microscope at the sperm," she said,
"that some poor farmer is paying good money for this. You know, we're serving
farmers, and the quality of the sperm is really going to have an effect on someone's business."

Melissa evaluated the morphology, or structure, of Bonanza's sperm, looking
for signs of abnormality. As a reference, she consulted a paper on which was drawn
a normal sperm cell with a healthy, paddle-shaped head and straight tail, and then
examples of abnormal variations: a head that was tapered or pear-shaped or too
small; appearance of bubbles or craters on the head; a broken, bent stump, or a
coiled tail; a tail with sharp angles, or a sperm with no tail at all (called a "free
head").

Melissa also checked for motility. "I want to see them moving in a straight line
or nearly a straight line," she said. "I don't want to see them with their tails bent
or going in circles."

How is it for her as a woman, I wondered, to work with bull semen all day?

"It did feel strange at first," she said, "but now I don't think about it. I mean,
the sex quickly became a non-issue, like it's very easy to disassociate yourself from
using terms like 'penis.' Still, it is interesting at parties when people ask me what
happened at work today."

Melissa gestured toward the microscope. "Take a look," she offered.

I bent over the eyepiece. In the circular field of view, I saw what appeared
to be thousands of frantic sperm swimming about. I tried to follow just one. It
swam in a circle. I tried another, and managed to hold it in my view for a second or two. This was it, the real beginning of my journey: cattle sperm on a
microscope slide.

Bull semen is so heavily concentrated—1.5 billion sperm in an average ejaculate—that it can be diluted by a factor of fifty and still be potent enough to impregnate a cow. By contrast, the average human ejaculate contains just 100 million sperm.

To "extend" Bonanza's semen, Melissa mixed it with whole milk—just as you'd buy in the supermarket—and then added in antibiotics to inhibit bacterial growth. The original thumbful of semen grew to about a quart.

Bull semen is sold encased in narrow plastic tubes called straws, about the size of the little straws attached to juice boxes. During insemination, a straw is opened at one end, placed into the cow's vagina up to the cervix, and the sperm released. One straw is used in each insemination.

Genex aims for 20 million sperm per straw, and at that density would be able to produce about one thousand straws from Bonanza's two ejaculations that morning. Given twice-weekly collections, that would add up to about 100,000 straws in a year. With each of Bonanza's straws selling for about twenty dollars—straws range in price from about five dollars to about forty dollars—that means Bonanza's ejaculate earns nearly $2 million a year.

Melissa pulled on a parka and took Bonanza's extended semen into a walk-in cooler. Its temperature began dropping from 35 C. to 5 C., slowing the metabolism of the sperm. She then inserted the cooled semen into individual plastic straws. Straws come in different colors: Bonanza's that day were bright green; others are yellow. Later she would pack the straws in canisters and lower them into a smoky, stainless-steel tank of liquid nitrogen where, in seven minutes, the semen would chill to −140 C. Once frozen, bull sperm can be banked for up to twenty years. In this way a cow could be bred with the sperm of a bull long dead.

The last step was to imprint each straw for permanent identification with a series of words and numbers.

I noticed a bunch of yellow and green straws discarded in an open trashcan. They were rejected probably because of a flaw in the plastic or the imprinting. I asked Melissa if I could take one as a sample, and reached in and picked at random a green straw. It was one of Bonanza's.

As I left Production Center No. 2, a Genex employee exited through the same door carrying a container of liquid nitrogen. I stepped aside so as not to bump him.

"Hey, thanks," he said, as the door swung shut behind him. "I got eighty thousand dollars' worth of semen in here."

Outside, on a patch of grass just off the parking lot, stood two jagged, rectangular stones about four feet tall that resembled tombstones. Each was inset with a metal plaque. One said, in letters about six inches high, "LUCIFER 1938–1956," and the other, "IVANHOE 1952–1963."

These markers, I learned, were moved from the headquarters of an old AI company in Pennsylvania with which Genex merged in 1996. Ivanhoe and Lucifer were among the most active sires in that company's program. "These two had major impact on the Holstein breed over many years," a Genex officer explained. "They were so good they were the sires of sons. That means their sons also became sires, which is the highest compliment to a bull."

In the parking lot, an eighteen-wheel tractor-trailer idled noisily. It was filled with frozen semen for delivery throughout the Northeast. On the truck's side was painted the Genex logo: the word GENEX with the G cleverly composed of a sperm and egg uniting, and, underneath, the Genex slogan: "A Tradition of Genetic Excellence."

I walked to my car, a green plastic straw of bull semen warming in the pocket of my shirt.

· · ·

"The dairy cow is an exploited mother," writes British veterinarian John Webster in his book *Understanding the Dairy Cow.* "To exploit her we have to ensure that she grows up, becomes pregnant, gives birth and lactates."

The "becoming pregnant" part—at least for many dairy cows in western New York—is up to Ken Schaeffer, an artificial inseminator for Genex. He agreed to let me ride with him for a day to watch him inseminate cows.

I'm not sure what I expected an artificial inseminator to look like, but it wasn't Ken Schaeffer. At forty-seven, he was slender and fit, of medium build, with neatly trimmed brown hair and beard. He had intense gray-blue eyes. A pair of aviator-style glasses hung over his chest on a cloth cord. He wore a blue baseball-style cap rather than a high-brimmed farm cap. If not for his one-piece, gray Genex coverall, I might have taken Ken for a college professor who also coaches the tennis team.

His territory includes most of Livingston County, an area of about six hundred square miles, most of it within the Genesee River valley. In his moss-green pickup, Ken visits the larger farms daily, or sometimes twice a day. For smaller farms, he is available on call.

Ken grew up in Copiague, New York, on Long Island. His father was a police officer in Astoria, Queens. At fourteen, Ken's life changed when his parents sent him for the summer to visit his father's aunt who lived on a farm in Winderset, Iowa.

"That's the area where *The Bridges of Madison County* was filmed," he said. "From that summer, I think I always wanted to live in the country and work with animals."

Ken returned to his aunt and uncle's farm the next summer and for many summers after that, and decided to become a large-animal veterinarian. After finishing high school, he enrolled at Kansas State University, then transferred to Cornell to study animal science with a pre-vet curriculum. During his senior year he lived and worked on a college-owned dairy farm.

But he didn't get into vet school.

Not sure what to do next, Ken worked on a friend's father's dairy farm. "An AI—artificial insemination—technician would visit to service the cows," he recalled, "and that's when I got the idea that the next-closest thing to being a large-animal vet would be to become an AI technician myself."

He did, and has been doing it for twenty-five years, all of those years with Genex.

Most days, Ken makes his rounds of up to a dozen farms accompanied by his four-year-old, mixed-breed German shepherd, Buster.

"He usually sits where you are," said Ken, motioning to the front passenger seat of his pickup. "I left him home today, and he didn't think much of that."

•   •   •

The reproductive cycle of the cow is similar to that of the human female: a period of fertility occurs every twenty-one days; gestation lasts just over nine months. After giving birth, a cow lactates nine months to a year, with the volume of milk gradually diminishing after about six months.

Heat, or estrus, describes the period of eight to sixteen hours before an egg is released from a cow's ovary. During heat, levels of the hormone estrogen increase and cause changes in the cow's appearance and behavior. A good part of successful dairying involves detecting when cows enter heat, so that they can be inseminated at the right time for conception to occur. If a heat is overlooked, or if a cow is inseminated a day or even half a day too early or late, the cow will not become pregnant. Every day a cow that is ready to become pregnant remains unbred—or "open," as it is called—costs the farmer three to five dollars in lower milk production. By this calculation, in a herd of three hundred cows, one estrus cycle missed per cow over the course of a year will cost the farmer nearly $30,000.

For this reason, farmers spend a lot of time watching for cows in heat. A goal on many farms is to detect 80 percent of heats, although on most farms half or more of heats are missed and as many as 20 percent of cows inseminated actually are not in heat at all. Some farms pay employees a bonus for detecting heats accurately.

In the wild, bulls efficiently detect cows in heat through odors and probably other chemical markers. Similarly, when farms kept bulls for breeding, the bulls did the heat detection. But since artificial insemination has been so widely adopted, it is mostly up to farm employees to detect heat.

The most reliable sign of heat is when a cow will stand still to let another cow mount her. Mounting a cow can also be a sign of heat, but of the two behaviors, standing to be mounted is considered the more reliable sign. Studies of isolated herds of cattle living in the wild report that cows in a natural state do not mount each other. Instead, a cow in heat is quickly detected by a bull who then guards the cow from the rest of the herd.

Other signs of heat include general restlessness, nervousness, and excitability; sniffing another cow's genitals, frequent bellowing, lack of appetite, swelling of the vulva with or without discharge of clear mucus, and dilated pupils.

Vigilant as farmers may want to be, no farm can afford enough help to watch cows twenty-four hours a day to detect heats. Many techniques and commercial products, therefore, have been developed to assist farmers in this task.

The most common technique is simply to place a bright chalk or crayon mark on a cow's rump. This is called "chalking the tail head." The idea is that when a cow comes into heat and stands to be mounted, the chest of the cow on top will rub against the rump of the cow on the bottom and smudge the chalk mark, thus leaving evidence that the cow on the bottom is in heat and ready to be bred.

Dairy magazines are filled with advertisements for innovative devices to help detect heat. There's a cow pedometer, for example, that measures the number of steps a cow takes in a day; if the number is far above a predetermined norm, a light will flash on the pedometer, indicating the cow is in heat. Some farmers bring dogs into the barns and let them try to sniff out cows in heat.

·   ·   ·

Ken married in his twenties, but divorced when his two boys were five and three years old. Both of his sons, now in their early twenties, live in Rochester.

Ken dates some, but has not remarried. "I've been gun-shy ever since the divorce," he said. "I pretty much spend time by myself, but that's mostly because of my long work hours."

Typically, he works fourteen hours a day. "I get up at five-thirty, go for a jog, check my calls to see if I have to go out right away for any emergencies, do my chores—I've got two horses, a rooster, and ten hens, plus two dogs. Then I shave and clean up. By seven-thirty it's time to leave.

"I'm on the road the whole day. Sometimes I'll stop for lunch, but if I haven't got the time, I'll just eat while I'm driving. I'm usually on the road till 8:00 P.M.—more often nine or ten o'clock; once in a great while I may go till 1:00 A.M. On an average day I'll breed thirty to thirty-five cows."

Ken gets five days off a month, but sometimes works two weeks or more without a break.

It was to provide himself with some companionship that he got dogs. He took one that was going to be euthanized by its previous owner, and the other—Buster—he adopted from the pound.

I heard no trace of New York City in Ken's speech. After half a lifetime upstate, he spoke with the pleasantly slow, deliberate cadence of people raised on farms in this area.

When he does get a few days off, Ken likes to go camping in Canada. Sometimes he goes with friends, but more often just with his dog Buster. "We just hike and canoe around in the parks up there. It's so beautiful and quiet. At night the stars are so bright it looks unreal."

He also runs marathons. Recently he flew to San Diego to run in a Leukemia Society marathon. Many of his customers sponsored him, and he raised $3,600.

. . .

After brief stops at two smaller farms, we pulled into Lawnel's dirt driveway. I didn't know it at the time, of course, but this would be the first of a hundred or more visits I'd eventually make to Lawnel.

The herd office was empty, so I didn't meet Sue Smith that day, but I remembered Ken mentioning how rare it is in the dairy industry for a woman to manage a large herd.

He also noted that many of his customers were busy elsewhere on their farms when he shows up to breed cows. "I could go most of the day without talking to anyone," he said.

Sue had left a note for Ken indicating that nine Lawnel cows had been seen in heat. Ken entered the number of the first cow on Sue's computer and interpreted the data on the screen for me: "She's three and a half years old, has had one calf. At an average of eighty-one pounds daily, her milk production is good."

Eighty-one pounds of milk—more than nine gallons—would fill about half a bathtub.

"She looks like a pretty good animal," said Ken, "so I'll use a good bull." He checked to see who the cow's father was, to avoid inbreeding. You can easily get undesirable traits by breeding a cow with her own father, brother, or other close relative. The risk has increased with widespread use of artificial insemination: for the 9 million or so cows in the United States today, at any given time there are probably fewer than a thousand stud bulls providing semen.

"Maybe I'll use Jeff on her." At twenty-four dollars a straw, Jeff is a high-quality Genex bull.

He entered the next cow's number: "This one's nearly five years old. Her milk production is only fifty-seven pounds a day, and she's going into her fourth lactation."

Farmers speak of cows in terms of the number of times they have lactated rather than the number of times they've given birth. On most farms today, cows average just three lactations before their milk production falls and they are removed, or "culled," from the herd.

"I'm going to use a young sire on her, just four dollars a straw. She's got such low production, she's probably not going to hang around long."

After checking computer entries for the other cows, Ken returned to the truck.

In the back were two three-foot-tall metal tanks containing liquid nitrogen and semen from thirty-eight different Genex sires. Ken carefully opened a canister and, using extra-long metal tweezers, pulled out a straw of semen.

"You want to be careful around this stuff," he said, admitting he has spilled a few drops of liquid nitrogen on his fingers over the years. "It definitely burns."

Gently, Ken wrapped the frozen straw inside a brown paper towel and tucked it upright inside the left breast pocket of his coverall. His body heat would help the semen thaw evenly.

Many farms, Lawnel included, leave it up to the breeder to find in their herds the cows who need to be bred. "Cow catching," as Ken called it, consists of walking into a barn about half the size of a football field with a hundred or more cows milling about, and picking out by ear tag number the ones you want to breed. Ken's got at most fifteen minutes to find them before the semen thaws too much.

Ken and I entered the barn. This was a free-stall barn, which meant cows were free to roam the three long aisles running the length of the barn or to lie and rest in any of the hundred or so stalls—each bedded with finely chopped wood shavings. Ken started down one aisle, looking for the low milk producer. As he did, another cow, not on our list, followed him closely, trying to lick his shirtsleeve.

"They can smell fluids on my clothes and smell other cows I've serviced that are in heat," he said. "They almost consider me the bull."

At that time, to be in a free stall barn with one hundred or more cows roaming about intimidated me. It's hard to convey just how large a mature Holstein cow is. Imagine an upright piano walking around on long legs. The keyboard is about shoulder high to you. Any one of those cows, if it wanted to, could crush a person.

Still, despite the presence of so many large animals, the barn was remarkably quiet. All I could hear was the occasional clank of metal bars as a few cows pushed at stanchions—headlocks—to lick up feed, the splash of urine hitting the concrete floor and manure falling with a splatter; on the roof of the next barn over, a huge flock of black birds sat in a row—a few of them cawing. Sometimes a cow coughed or gently mooed, but this was a peaceful place.

The barn floor was concrete, with shallow grooves pressed into it for better footing. Still, the floor was covered nearly everywhere with urine and wet manure, as well as some other fluids. Sometimes a cow would slip on the slick surface after taking a turn too fast. I saw one cow slip and fall completely on its side, then right itself.

I was glad I'd gotten myself a pair of barn boots. I hadn't bought them right away when I started visiting farms; they seemed so much a part of a real farmer's work clothes, somehow I didn't feel I'd earned the right to wear them. But after I'd completed the Herdsperson Training course, I put twenty dollars on the counter at a farm supply store and got a pair.

Barn boots are made of soft, lightweight rubber that fits over your shoes and goes up to about the tops of your calves. There's tread on the sole, which helps you keep from slipping.

Ken stopped to show affection to one of the cows, something I hadn't seen him do before.

"She's my pet," he said. "I named her."

The cow is called Rosebud. She was born about eight years ago. "I bred her when she was just a virgin heifer. I can't remember how I chose the name

Rosebud. But she still comes up to me every time I come out here and I say, 'Hey, Rosebud,' and rub her ears."

Ken continued down the aisle, reading tags, and then called to me: he'd found the cow.

She was standing quietly in a stall, the smudged remains of a streak of pink chalk visible on her rump.

Ken pulled an orange plastic glove onto his left hand and unrolled the plastic sleeve up to his shoulder. From the inside of his right, unbuckled barn boot, he pulled out a bottle of mineral oil and squirted a bit onto the glove.

"I try to stand back and a little to the side," he said, taking this position behind the cow. "That way if she kicks, she'll get me in the hip, not the knee." A kick in the knee once laid him up for six weeks.

He then pushed to one side the foot-long stump of the cow's tail. "Thing about these cropped tails," he commented, "if they hit you in the head it's like getting hit with a club."

Finally, like a runner flexing before a race, Ken leaned into the cow, inserting his gloved arm into her rectum up to his elbow. He felt around for a moment, then retracted his hand.

"I like to clean out the anus," he explained. "It gives me more room to feel the uterus."

The rectum and uterus of a cow are in roughly the same positions relative to each other as they would be in a human female on all fours. By pushing down while inside the rectum, Ken can locate the exact spot where he'll want to deposit the semen: just beyond the cervix, in front of several rings of cartilage that separate the vagina from the uterus.

"Once you feel the uterus," he said, "she changes. The uterus becomes engorged with blood. She feels it and knows she's being bred. At that point, the oxytocin increases and soon she'll start leaking milk from the udder and you know you've gotten a response."

In swift movements, Ken removed the semen straw from his pocket, unwrapped it from the brown paper, snipped off one end with scissors, covered the straw with a clear plastic sheath, and loaded it into a slender, three-foot long metal tube called an inseminating gun. He held the gun in one hand while with the other he took another piece of brown paper—this one folded into a tight wedge about two inches square—and slid it down through the labia. The movement was similar to swiping a credit card.

Leaving the paper wedge, which he called a "vagina spreader," in the pink folds to hold an opening, he then reinserted his left hand up the cow's rectum. "I lean forward so the pressure straightens out the folds inside her vagina, so I don't get the gun caught in the folds and irritate her."

He then inserted the inseminating gun just above the vagina spreader, pushing in gently.

"Right at the end of the cervix is where you want to deposit the semen," he said. "You don't want to go up one horn or the other, you want to go right where the horns have common ground: at the end of the cervix."

Then he pushed with his thumb on the plunger of the inseminating gun; the cow was bred.

After Ken found and bred all nine Lawnel cows, we were ready to leave. Before we did, he brought a bucket and scrub brush from the back of his truck to an outside faucet near the herd office. In a ritual we repeated at every farm that day, Ken filled the bucket with hot water and disinfectant, and we scrubbed our boots. The spread of disease from farm to farm is a growing concern in the dairy industry. By my watch, Ken completely soaped, scrubbed, and rinsed each black boot— front, sides, back, and bottom—in seven seconds. "Your ankles get pretty flexible when you do this all the time," he said.

· · ·

We broke for lunch near the town of Mount Morris, site of a 790-foot-high concrete dam on the Genesee River. "Best Town by a Dam Site," boasts a billboard just outside the town.

Ken chose a scenic overlook in nearby Letchworth Park, a place he often stops for lunch with Buster. Here the Genesee River has carved a steep gorge in the soft shale rock. Locally, this natural vista is referred to proudly as "the Grand Canyon of the East."

We sat on a log about four feet from the canyon rim, eating sandwiches on a glorious late-September day in western New York: bright sun in a cloudless sky, seventy degrees, low humidity and a gentle wind just cool enough to hint at approaching autumn and make one appreciate the day even more. No one else was around, and except for the occasional muffled sound of a car on a country road across the canyon, it was as close to silent there as anywhere I have ever been.

I asked Ken if he'd ever seen feral cows, cows in the wild.

"Well, no," he said, "but I've seen moose up in Canada. You see them in herds.

I once saw thirty or forty cows and calves grazing up there. They stand around and look at you. They're just as curious as the cows I see on the farms."

I noted that of all the people I'd met on farms around here, Ken was the only one who didn't grow up in a rural area. I asked him what he made of that.

"I just prefer rural life," he said. "I always felt trapped on Long Island, like I didn't belong there. I wanted to be in wide-open spaces. I've also found that rural people are friendlier and easier to get close to."

Ken's parents and two brothers also have moved to small communities upstate; only his sister remains in the New York City area. He seldom sees her, he said, or any of his cousins in the city; neither is he in touch with any boyhood friends.

"I only go back to the city rarely—for funerals or weddings, if I can make it," he said. "When I do go back, I feel I have little in common with those people. It's difficult for me to connect with them. And they don't seem to have a whole lot of interest in what I do or where I live, or understand the differences in our lives."

City people, he said, tend to look down on farm people. "They think in terms of stereotypes: farmers are people with no education who work in dirty conditions, and are poorly paid. They don't realize what's involved in modern farming."

．　．　．

Our first stop after lunch was a seventy-cow herd. Ken checked the computer data for the first cow to be bred.

"She's had two lactations and been serviced twice already with no conception," said Ken, meaning two months in a row he bred her but she didn't get pregnant. "She's still milking good—seventy-seven pounds daily average—but this will be her third service. She's a good cow; we're going to keep trying. There's no bull here, so unless I can get her bred, she's probably going down the road."

"Down the road?"

"To the slaughterhouse."

Reproductive problems are often the reason cows are culled from dairy herds. For most cows, four AI services is the limit. After that, a farmer will milk her until she dries up and then cull her.

"I'll try a bull with a high conception rate, but not too expensive," said Ken. He chose a sire named Ambition whose semen is moderately priced at seventeen dollars a straw.

In an old barn we found the cow, a mostly black animal, lying in a stall. A hundred or more flies crawled across her back; she wagged her tail stump at them to little effect, then reached back to try to lick them off, also without success.

Ken squatted behind her.

"So, this cow's life may depend on you getting her pregnant?"

"Right! So she better treat me good and not kick. Hear that, girl?" he asked, performing the insemination. "Better be good."

·   ·   ·

Our last stop of the day was a small farm near the town of Avon. The only cow in heat was a virgin heifer, a young female that had not previously been bred. The owner had put her in a barn by herself, in a small holding pen. Ken prepared a straw of Bonanza's semen.

"I'm using Bonanza because he's known for easy calving." Offspring of Bonanza, he explained, tend to have small heads, so they are relatively easy for young heifers to deliver. Also, as Ken explained, virgin heifers have the highest conception rate, so he uses the more expensive bulls with these younger animals. "That way the farmer's got a better chance of getting something for his money," he said.

We entered the barn. The young heifer stood only chest-high to me, much smaller than most of the cows I'd seen. Heifers are kept separate from milking cows on most farms, so my exposure to them had been minimal, but I'd seen enough older cows to recognize how young and fresh this virgin heifer was. Her black and white patches of hair were clean and bright, her udder small and tight up against her underside.

She was jumpy. She moved her head up and down against the metal restraint of the stanchion, swinging her white rump back and forth. Ken stood back a bit so as not to be kicked.

"She doesn't know what I'm here for," said Ken. He inserted his gloved left hand into her anus and began feeling around. She quieted a bit. He inserted the vagina spreader and then the inseminating gun. In a few seconds it was over; she was calm.

·   ·   ·

Dusk was falling over the Genesee Valley as Ken drove me back to where I'd left my car. The opening fanfare of *All Things Considered* announced the six o'clock news. I asked Ken if he always listened to public radio.

"Commercial stations all sensationalize the news," he said. "NPR doesn't. It's the only unbiased news around. It's my radio and TV."

He also belongs to the Sierra Club, he confessed. "Some people think that since I'm environmentally conscious, it's a conflict with my job. It's true, the Sierra Club does believe in heavy regulations. They're concerned about waste disposal and whatnot, but, hey, I'm concerned, too, I have a well on my property."

He belongs to the Farm Bureau, too, a group considerably to the right of the Sierra Club.

I asked Ken if, when he ate at fast-food restaurants, he ever thought that some of the burger he was eating could have come from the same dairy cows he'd inseminated.

"I don't eat fast food too much because I'm pretty health-conscious. Occasionally I eat a steak, but, yeah, I guess I make the connection and I'm more appreciative. It's my industry. I know where it comes from. But, no, it doesn't make me sad to eat it. You saw that most of these cows looked pretty happy."

I wondered what the future might hold for Ken.

The AI industry keeps a running tally of how many cows every inseminator has bred, he explained. After twenty-five years, his total is about seventy thousand.

"When you get to one hundred thousand cows, they fly you out to Colorado for the annual convention of the National Association of Animal Breeders. They wine and dine you and take your picture and whatnot. They make a big deal of it, kind of giving you something to look forward to."

Ken does about six thousand inseminations a year, so he should be going to Colorado in another five or six years. After that, he said, he may take early retirement and move to California.

Of all the people I'd met around farms, Ken reminded me most of myself. He'd come to love rural life, yet in many ways he'd also retained the outlook of someone raised in a city.

3

Boarding and Banding

IT'S AROUND ELEVEN IN THE MORNING when Peter Vonglis's pickup pulls into the driveway of Lawnel Farms. In the back is a plywood crate about four feet square, with air holes drilled in one side.

"The calves go in that?" I ask.

"Yeah, I made it myself," Peter says. "I don't haul many calves. No sense buying an expensive hutch."

Peter, thirty-one, is of medium build with short brown hair. He has a thin face, blue eyes, and a bright smile under a long, straight mustache. The way he moves and talks suggests a lot of trapped energy: on the phone, my sober "Hello, Peter" is often greeted with "Hello, Peter!" as if he's calling to me excitedly from a distance.

I can't quite believe three seventy-five-pound calves will fit in that little box, but one by one Peter pulls them out of the superhutch, lifts them onto the truck, and shoves them into the crate. The first two he pushes in headfirst; the third he puts in backward, for a better fit.

. . . .

Before Thanksgiving, while waiting for the Bonanza-bred cows to give birth at Lawnel, I searched intently for a place to board the bull calf I hoped would be born. It wasn't easy. If you live in the suburbs, after all, whom do you know who boards calves? I found a few farms that raised dairy beef, but one didn't have room for more animals, and another wouldn't agree to let me visit freely and write about what I saw.

Finally, one farmer gave me the name of John Vonglis, who, in turn, suggested I talk with his son, Peter. John said his son worked full-time at a dairy farm, but raised about a dozen cattle—including dairy beef—on the side. Some of the meat he sold, and some he kept for his own family's consumption. In a lucky coincidence, the address John gave me for his son was on Route 36, just five miles south of Lawnel Farms.

Late one afternoon, in a heavy fog, I drove with my headlights on to meet Peter Vonglis. A gravel driveway sloped sharply down from the main road. At the bottom, a gutted deer carcass hung from a tree. I parked my car and walked back up the driveway toward an old barn near the road, when a slender, dark-haired young man suddenly appeared through the fog, loading pigs into a stock trailer to take to market. It was Peter.

Standing near the shoulder of the road, with traffic speeding by, our conversation was to the point. I told Peter I expected some calves to be born within a few days at Lawnel Farms, that I planned to buy them at auction, and then would need a place to board them. I explained I was writing a book about cows and farms, and that I'd want him to raise the calves for dairy beef in the normal way and that I'd need to come and visit often, but wouldn't interfere.

Peter said fine, he'd do it for $1.50 a day per calf, and I should call him when the calves were born.

Two weeks later I called Peter to arrange pickup. He wasn't home, so I spoke with his wife, Shelly. That was when I learned she used to be the calf manager at Lawnel—the position Jessica Treuthart now holds. She quit, she told me, because she disagreed with Sue Smith about how the animals were being treated. Shelly can be passionate on this subject, and in the same call she chastised me for my plan to run my calves through the livestock auction.

"You can't do that," she insisted. "Your calves'll be less than a week old. They're stressed enough in this cold weather. If you truck them to auction and make them go through the ring, they're likely to get sick or die."

Shelly seemed to know what she was talking about. I certainly didn't want my calves to die, so, yielding to her persuasiveness, I decided to skip the auction and instead buy the calves directly from Lawnel.

That was how it happened that just after Thanksgiving, I received the following invoice from Lawnel Farms:

SALE OF APPROXIMATELY ONE WEEK OLD CALVES:

1 Bull Twin - Approx. 75 Lbs. $25.00
1 Heifer Twin - Approx. 75 Lbs. 25.00
1 Bull - Approx. 75 Lbs 25.00

The bull and heifer twins were the calves I'd watched Andrew Smith pull from cow 4923 and that I'd helped Jessica Treuthart carry to the superhutch. Offspring of Bonanza, they were the calves I planned to observe from birth to slaughter.

The third calf, listed simply as "Bull," was another son of Bonanza born at Lawnel a day after my twins. I'd bought him as a backup, like an alternate juror, in case the others died.

Yet my conversation with Shelly had left me concerned. If there was ill will between her and Sue Smith, how would that affect my plan to visit back and forth between the two farms, and the two families? Also, would Shelly's passion for animals mean she and Peter would pamper my calves? I didn't want that. I wanted them treated in the normal way—no special handling.

·   ·   ·

Now, as I sit beside Peter in his pickup, I mention Shelly's earlier comments and my concern about how the calves will be handled.

"I'm the one who'll take care of them, not Shelly," he says. "Your calves'll be treated just like the others I raise."

Peter turns left off Route 36 and descends his sloping driveway. The dead deer is gone from the tree at the bottom. On one side of the driveway is a modest ranch house with pale yellow siding. On the other is an old barn and a smaller, three-sided structure that he calls a "running shed." Both the barn and the running shed open onto a fenced barnyard about half the size of a baseball infield. Electrified wire encircles the barn, running shed, and barnyard. About a dozen cattle, some lying in the running shed and others standing in the barnyard, quietly watch as Peter and I get out of the truck.

Peter unlocks the crate in the back, lifts out the calves, and one at a time pushes them toward hutches he's made behind the house. The hutches, about four feet high, are set three in a row. The sides and back are made of stacked hay bales; the front is open; a long wooden shutter lies across all three hutches as a common roof. Peter later tells me he found the shutter in a friend's old barn.

Peter puts my bull calf in the middle hutch, the bull's twin sister on the right, and the backup calf on the left. He ties a short length of yellow nylon twine around each of their necks, and fastens the other end to a rusty metal post in front of each hutch. Tethered so, the calves can take a step or two forward outside the hutch or a few steps back into the hutch. A section of metal fence separates the areas immediately in front of each hutch so the calves can see each other and even touch mouths through the wire, but otherwise they have no physical contact.

Using a sort of hole punch, Peter pierces each calf's right ear and inserts a short steel tag. My bull calf gets the number 7; the heifer, 8; and the backup, 6. In about eight weeks, when he moves them out of the hutches and up into the running shed, he'll fit each calf with a yellow ear tag that is bigger and easier to read from a distance. That's also when he'll wean and castrate them.

. . .

The calves quietly explore the area in front of the hutches, but seem reluctant to step inside. They sniff the ground; it is mostly mud, a little grass, stray pieces of straw. They lick the metal fencepost to which the tethers are tied. Through the wire fence mesh, the twins lick each other's faces and rub noses briefly. It's easy to tell the three calves apart: all have black faces with triangles of white on their foreheads, but only my bull calf's white hair extends down the nose. The backup's coat is more brown than the others; he's a little huskier, too. The heads of all three strike me as mostly ears: large, furry black wings sticking out to either side; the right one of each pair is adorned with the silver jewelry of an ear tag.

When I try to pet my bull calf, he shoves his head up against my palm. This is the same movement I saw the heifer twin make just after she was born at Lawnel and tried to nurse from her mother. It must be an instinctive movement against the udder to trigger a letdown reflex to start milk flowing. When I offer the calf my gloved finger or even my whole fist, he sucks forcefully.

. . .

A week later it is windy but still warm for early December, 40 degrees in midafternoon. No one's home at the Vonglises, only a black dog, some kind of Lab mix. It feels odd to come to a family's home when there's no one here, park my car, and walk all around wherever I want, but that's the deal I made with the Vonglises, and I'm grateful to them for trusting me and allowing me this kind of access.

The dog barks aggressively as I get out of the car and head for the calf hutches, but I find I can silence him with a hard stare.

My bull calf stands outside his hutch. He's put on some weight in the chest and shoulders. My notes describe him as "growing into his ears." Peter feeds the calves milk replacer, a formula of dried skim milk with additives, including antibiotics to help prevent diarrhea. A blue feed bucket hanging from the fence outside the bull calf's hutch is empty, so he must be drinking as much milk replacer as Peter gives him. Standing, the calf's rump is higher than his head and not quite up to my waist. His navel has dried but not yet fallen off; it hangs about four inches from his belly, black and twisted. There is just a bit of orange marker left on his white forehead. The black hair on his face, I see now, is not pure black but has an undercoat of brown, which softens his appearance. I notice some tiny black spots on the pink part of his nose above the nostrils.

The heifer, standing in front of her hutch, squats to pee in the mud, then steps toward the fence between her and her twin. The two lick each other's lips.

"Cross-sucking," as it is called, is common among calves and is of concern to dairy farmers because it can spread infection. It occurs, writes British calf expert John Webster, "almost invariably immediately after the calves have finished a large but short-lived meal of milk from a bucket. Kissing is not a fanciful term: I can think of no other word to describe an activity which involves two animals putting their lips together, sticking their tongues into each other's mouths and sucking. I think it is fair to conclude that . . . calves 'kiss' because they are deprived of the prolonged oral satisfaction of sucking."

The wind picks up, whipping clothes on the Vonglises' backyard laundry line. Nearby are a swing set and a children's climbing toy, a rusted oil drum, two garbage cans, a picnic table, a wooden doghouse, two girls' bikes with rusted frames, a brown Dumpster, a flat wagon piled with used lumber, a toy telephone on wheels, a red bike, a faded basketball, a snowplow blade, a naked Barbie, and a teddy bear.

Wrote the poet William Carlos Williams, "So much depends upon the red wheel barrow glazed with rain water beside the white chickens."

· · ·

Fatigue and a steady cough keep me home for a good part of December. A general antibiotic has no effect. After consulting a home medical reference book, I become convinced I am suffering from alveolitis—inflammation of the air sacs in the lungs caused by fungal spores that grow on hay or grain—a condition more commonly known as "farmer's lung." Sharing this discovery with my doctor earns me an expensive set of blood tests at a suburban clinic. The technician who draws my blood confides it is her first time testing for farmer's lung, and she has to look up in a reference manual how to color-code the blood vial for this disease.

I don't, of course, have farmer's lung. My conceit is in thinking I could get it from a few weeks hanging around cow barns and calf hutches. The medical book I had consulted lists conditions alphabetically; the one just before "farmer's lung" is "fantasy."

. . .

Drifting snow blows across Route 36 as I approach Lawnel Farms for my first visit in several weeks. I want to see how heifer calves are raised to become dairy cows.

Inside the greenhouse, where heifer calf 6717 has been housed since her birth just after Thanksgiving, the temperature is comfortably in the mid-forties.

The fifty or so calves in the greenhouse, all less than two months old, are arranged in the order of their births in individual wire-fence pens set in long rows on either side of a wide central aisle.

Calf 6717, daughter of Bonanza and cow 1523, is in a pen on the right side of the greenhouse, about two-thirds of the way down the center aisle. As I approach, she stands, rising first onto her front knees, then unfolding her back legs. Standing, the top of her head is about even with the top of the four-foot wire fencing that makes up her pen. She sticks her head through an opening in the wire mesh at the front of the pen to lick my gloved fist, then licks and sucks the knee of my jeans, then the top of my black rubber barn boot.

A patch of white in the middle of her black forehead is so tiny that if she'd hold still long enough, I could actually count the hairs. Her tail is still attached, though midway down it is beginning to curl and wither below a tight green rubber band I'd watched Jessica Treuthart apply on an earlier visit.

Two pens to the left, calf 6715 leaps once or twice around in a circle; that's about as much exercise as a calf can get in these four-by-five-foot enclosures. On the other side, 6718 and 6719 rub heads through the wire mesh and lick each other's necks.

The straw bedding in these pens is thick, and only lightly muddied with feces. Fresh straw is added twice a week, although the bedding will not be entirely changed until the calves are moved from here to a larger group pen when they are about two months old. The parts of the tails that have fallen off by then will get cleaned out with the straw.

Hay bales have been stacked in the middle of the aisle just across from 6717's pen. I sit on them to watch the calf, feeling for a moment like an indolent Li'l

Abner, lounging on straw in the middle of a cold day in the relative warmth of the Lawnel greenhouse.

Two plastic buckets—one black, one yellow—hang in a rubber frame on the wire front of each pen. By sticking her head through an opening in the wire, 6717 can eat grain from the yellow bucket and drink milk replacer from the black one.

As I watch, she stretches her neck and rubs its underside against the rim of the yellow bucket. Then, with lips and tongue, she raises the bucket's metal handle and licks it. Her lower front teeth gleam white against the jet black of her nose and lips. Like all cows, she has no upper front teeth. Cattle, being strictly plant eaters, have no need for upper incisors or canines; instead, the lower incisors tear and cut grasses and plants against a tough dental pad on the upper jaw. Now she reaches to her right and licks a star-shaped patch of white hair on the forehead of 6716, and then the metal ear tag in 6716's left ear.

6717's attention turns to the handle of the yellow bucket in front of her. She lifts the handle with her tongue, lets it drop, lifts it again.

Little metal clasps, about the size of clothespins, hold together the sections of fence wire on all the pens, but one clasp on the front of 6717's pen happens to be loose. She grabs it with her tongue, pulls it into her mouth, pushes it out, does it again, and again.

All she wants to do, it seems, is suck and lick things. Do these metal objects taste good, or is this play?

The bucket handle and this little metal clasp, it occurs to me, are the only objects she can manipulate. Indeed, it's remarkable what little her world consists of: three feet one way, five the other, the head and neck of the calf on the left, the same of the calf on the right, a yellow bucket, a black bucket, the handles on each, the straw underfoot, a metal clasp hanging from a fence wire.

The plastic sheeting lying loose over the greenhouse frame flaps loudly with each cold gust of wind.

This calf's huge eyes are dark, nearly black. I see myself reflected in one of them, rendered just a quarter of an inch high, standing in a brown parka and a ski cap, holding a notebook.

There is a place at Lawnel, just behind the office and in front of the greenhouse, where dead cows are put to be picked up by the renderer. I've come to think of it as "the dead pile." Often when I visit, a dead cow or two is lying here. I usually go over to look at them and see if I can figure out why they died.

This morning there is one cow in the dead pile, lying on its side. I go over to look at it, but this time the cow looks back at me. She is alive, though still; only her eyeball follows me as I circle around, and one ear rotates a bit.

Later, Sue Smith explains the cow had a displaced abomasum—a common nutritional disorder where part of the stomach shifts out of place—which Sue repaired through surgery, but now the cow has hoof problems, too, and cannot stand. Sue's left the cow here for the renderer.

. . .

It's late afternoon a few days before Christmas, when I next check on my calves at the Vonglises'. Winter has taken hold; it's 17 degrees today, with a strong wind.

I've finally bought myself a pair of coveralls. These not only help keep me warm, but also solve the problem of cow manure getting on my jeans and smelling up the car on my way home. I can wear the coveralls over my clothes, take them off after a farm visit, carry them home in the trunk of the car with my barn boots, and wash them.

I bought the coveralls at Davis' Trailer World and Country Mall, a store a few miles up Route 36 from York. Davis' sells everything from cowboy boots and belt buckles to wedding dresses. I'd looked at coveralls there last winter, but hadn't bought a pair, feeling—as I had earlier about barn boots—that I hadn't yet spent enough time on farms to earn the right to wear them. But this winter I feel entitled.

The tan coveralls—insulated Thermal Kings—zip and snap up the leg. There's Velcro at the cuffs so I can tighten them around my barn boots. Suspenders hold up the bib top, which has lots of pockets that are handy for holding pens, notebook, and camera. I expected the heavy coveralls to feel awkward, but actually they feel nicely snug, as if I'm wrapped in a sleeping bag.

. . .

In the Vonglises' backyard, snow covers the calf hutches, and the mud in front of the hutches has frozen. The blue feed buckets have tipped over and frozen to the ground on their sides. I bend to look inside my bull calf's hutch; he's hunched over with his face to the side wall, shivering, his legs and belly matted with mud, his ears hanging down, his eyes dull. I cannot coax him out even to suck my glove or lick the sleeve of my parka. In the snow in front of the hutch I see no hoof-prints; perhaps he has not been out even to cross-suck.

The heifer and the backup are more energetic. Both come out to lick my pants and coat, but even they don't seem to have the vigor they had a few weeks ago. After many minutes, my bull calf sticks his head out just far enough to lick weakly at one gloved finger.

The backs of the heifer's and backup's hutches, I notice, are hay bales, but the back of my bull calf's hutch is a plywood board with large cracks.

That night I phone Peter.

"Hello, Peter!" he calls. "I thought you'd been out today—saw your tire tracks in the snow on the driveway."

We talk about the cold weather. I ask him how often he changes the straw bedding inside the hutches.

"Every two or three days," he says.

"Peter," I say, "I know I told you I didn't want to interfere with how you treat the calves, but I noticed the back of the hutch where the bull calf is—the middle hutch—is just a plywood board. Would some hay bales back there keep it warmer?"

Peter says he'll put some hay bales back there, but assures me the calves are in no danger from the cold. "They love this weather. It's healthy for them—much healthier than hot weather."

I ask Peter when he'll be moving the calves into the barn, although he's already told me it will be toward the end of January, when they're about two months old. Still, I'm eager for the calves to get out of the cold, and have fallen into the anxious habit of watching the eleven o'clock news each night to see how cold it's expected to be in what the meteorologists on Rochester TV call "outlying areas."

"I'm gonna move 'em about a month from now, probably about the third week of January," he says. "I'll wean 'em, ear-tag 'em, and band 'em all at the same time."

Banding is the method Peter uses for castration.

· · ·

To accommodate as many employees, suppliers, and customers as possible, the Smith family this year has scheduled two dinner seatings—5:30 P.M. and 7:30 P.M.—for the annual Lawnel Farms Christmas party. The event is held at the Yard of Ale Canal House Inn, a party house in Geneseo, just a few minutes from York.

At the second-floor landing, Andrew and Sue Smith greet me with a warm "Merry Christmas." They look remarkably handsome; I've never seen either of them dressed in anything but coveralls. Andrew wears a brown suit and Sue a red sleeveless dress. The children, Kirsten, fifteen, and Amos, fourteen, are well scrubbed and neatly dressed. During cocktails, I ask each child if they might someday like to take over their family's farm. Kirsten says no, though someday she may want to teach veterinary medicine. Just now she's looking forward to visiting Australia next summer on a People-to-People student ambassador program. Amos says he would like to take over the farm.

The children's great-grandfather Nelson greets me in the bar with a smile and a firm handshake. I introduce myself and, in explaining about my book, try to favor the ear with a hearing aid, but I'm not sure he quite understands what I'm telling him.

Joan and Larry Alexander of York Landing restaurant also are here.

Helping greet the hundred or more guests are Andrew's parents, Larry and Catherine. Born in Chile to a family connected to the Standard Oil Company, Catherine was educated at private schools in New York City, and later attended Cornell, where she met Larry Smith.

Jessica Treuthart, who I normally see only in jeans and a flannel shirt, wears a slinky black dress. She's done up her long auburn hair in elaborate curls atop her head. Jessica introduces me to her boyfriend, Jason, who has just taken a job at Lawnel scraping manure from the barns and herding cows to the milking parlor.

Before dinner, Andrew Smith asks us all to stand and introduce ourselves. When it is his turn, Nelson Smith says, "Should I tell them about starting the farm with one borrowed cow?" Many guests chuckle, seemingly familiar with this family legend.

The buffet includes roast beef, meat lasagna, and filet of chicken.

It's been years since I've eaten roast beef, although as a child it was among my favorite dishes. I generally don't eat red meat these days. I do eat fish and eggs, and occasionally chicken. My diet mostly reflects the ambivalence I've felt since childhood about eating animals: sometimes I have; sometimes I haven't. My wife, a nutritionist, follows roughly the same diet, but mostly for health reasons. Still, I'm open to the possibility that after a year of following cows around, I'll be more comfortable eating them, and fill my plate not only with the chicken, but with the meat lasagna and roast beef, too.

After dinner, Andrew presents an award to Larry Wilkins for completing thirty years of work as feed manager and maintenance man at Lawnel.

•   •   •

At the Vonglises', on the afternoon of New Year's Eve, the temperature is 12 degrees. At night lately, it drops below zero. Inside the calves' water buckets, there is only snow. As promised, Peter has reinforced the back of the bull calf's hutch with a couple of hay bales.

The heifer warily comes out to lick my glove; so does the backup. But I cannot coax my bull calf out. Even when I reach into his hutch and hold my hand in front of his face, he won't suck. He must come out sometime because I see in the snow in front of the hutch a small pile of manure.

I bend sideways to see inside. He stares back at me, blankly. A *New Yorker* cartoon comes to mind: a man at the zoo stares at a monkey in a cage and thinks, "I wonder what he's thinking," and the monkey stares back at the man and thinks, "I wonder what he's thinking."

Two researchers at Oregon State University asked faculty and students whether they thought farm animals had minds and could think. Two out of three said yes. They ranked horses and pigs as smartest, then cows, then sheep, chickens, and turkeys.

All of which proves nothing.

If my calf is thinking, *what* is he thinking on this cold day? Does he recall his mother, 4923, licking his face? Does he long for her? I wonder how being removed from his mother and being raised for the first two months tethered by himself inside this hale bale hutch might affect his personality.

· · ·

In the first two weeks of January, nearly forty inches of snow falls on western New York. A break in the weather one Sunday—it is sunny and above freezing at noon—prompts Shelly Vonglis to call me at home. "We're going to move your calves today. How soon can you get here?"

Later, Shelly tells me she was impatient to move the calves because the cold weather was causing their nylon tethers to snap and they were getting loose—four times just in the past week. I ask her what the bull calf in the middle hutch does when he gets loose. She says he usually just goes into the hutch next door and lies down with the heifer.

I make it to the Vonglises' in an hour, arriving near dusk. Along the way, on the west side of Route 36, silos are silhouetted against the setting sun.

I drive down the sloping driveway as a young boy pulls two toddlers up on a sled. Behind them, Peter is walking toward the calf hutches in the backyard.

"Holy cow! There's a lot of snow!" Peter exclaims as I follow him. At the hutches, he pours two quarts of hot milk replacer into each calf's blue feed bucket.

"This is the last time they'll ever get milk," he says, reminding me he's weaning the calves today as well as moving, tagging, and castrating them.

Peter has a rough look about him. He seems not to have shaved in several days, and his insulated red plaid workshirt has a tear in the left elbow big enough for the lumpy cotton lining to show through.

He clips the bull calf's tether, leaving just a yellow collar of twine, and pushes the calf away from the hutch. I assume the calf's legs, matted with mud up to the belly, have grown weak from disuse after not taking more than a step or two in any direction since four days of age. Peter shoves my calf toward the driveway leading up to the barn, but then, like a deer leaping through the woods, the calf kicks out his hind legs and leaps off the driveway into a snowbank. Peter catches him and pulls him back onto the driveway. The calf takes a few more steps, but then balks in front of my car. Peter pushes him around it and on up toward the barn.

"You don't have to do that!" Shelly calls to Peter. She means pushing the calf. "They're hungry, Peter. They'll follow the bucket," she says, as she easily leads the heifer calf toward the barn by holding a blue bucket of milk replacer under its head.

"I'm doing just fine," says Peter, irritably. "You move yours and I'll move mine."

"I'm just trying to show you an easier way to do it," she rejoins. Shelly, thirty-three, is two years older than Peter. In cloth coat, hat, and gloves, she is also dressed more sensibly.

"I'm not asking to know another way to do it," he says.

They're arguing in front of me, and I make no effort to hide my note-taking. But I know how passionate Shelly is about treating animals gently, and how equally insistent Peter is about not babying them. I suspect what I'm hearing is a typical exchange when the two do anything together involving the animals.

The running shed's south side is open and faces onto the barnyard. Peter and Shelly move my three calves into a pen in the corner of the shed. There are already four other calves there, all about the same age as mine, and all black.

"These came out of a Holstein heifer bred to a beef bull, probably an Angus," Peter explains.

Shelly punches yellow plastic tags into the right ears of the three calves: numbers 6, 7, and 8, to match the numbers on the steel tags Peter put in their left ears earlier.

Then Peter slips a rope halter over my bull calf's face and around the back of its head. He ties the other end to a wooden post. The calf bawls and kicks. Earlier the calf's steel ear tag had fallen out, so before Peter does anything else, he needs to put it back in. He replaces it, but notices the steel tag says "7" and the yellow plastic tag Shelly just put in the left ear says "8."

"Shel, what number did you put in this one?" he asks.

"That's eight," she says. "The others are six and seven."

"I told you one of the steel tags had fallen out. Now you've got the numbers wrong!" he says angrily. "Honestly, you'd think you could put tags in three calves and get the numbers right!"

Shelly says nothing. She seems resigned to being criticized about the mix-up. The calf bawls and wriggles, trying to escape the harness.

"You can do that with them on the ground," Shelly offers. She's standing off to the side now among the other six calves in the pen. "Being tied up is more stressful for them than the banding."

"I know how to do this, Shel," says Peter. "If I need your advice I'll ask for it."

· · ·

A castrated bull is called a steer. Farmers castrate their animals to make them easier to handle and to reduce fighting among them. Bulls that fight, particularly just before slaughter, produce a darker meat due to depletion of energy and glycogen stores. (They're referred to as "dark cutters.") Steers also tend to be less aggressive with heifers.

"After they're nutted," Peter explains to me, "they won't show any interest in mounting females."

But castration has disadvantages, too: steers generally gain weight more slowly than bulls, and the stress of castration can temporarily slow growth and weaken an animal.

Still, today nearly all beef animals—including dairy bulls raised for beef—are castrated.

Farmers castrate bulls by cutting out the testes with a knife, crushing the spermatic cord and blood vessels with a pincer (called an emasculator), or cutting off circulation to the upper part of the scrotum with a tight rubber band. This last method, called banding, eventually causes the scrotum to dry up and fall off.

In a recent survey in one Midwestern state, the following percentage of beef producers used each of the three methods: banding (38 percent), surgical (36 percent), emasculator (24 percent). Animal scientists, concerned that stress slows weight gain and makes an animal more susceptible to illness, have tried to quantify and compare the amount of pain that might be caused by each of the three methods, but the studies have been inconclusive.

Peter stands over my calf's rump, facing forward, and reaches with both hands under its belly and between its legs.

"They don't really notice when you pull their sac down," he says. "You reach up inside and kind of bring each testicle down—" but he's interrupted as the calf backs up and kicks at him with its hind legs.

Traffic just outside the barn on Route 36 has picked up as people head home for the evening. Most cars have their lights on.

The banding rings Peter uses are green and about the diameter of the rubber bands my daughter uses with the braces on her teeth, but much thicker. I recognize them as the same bands Jessica Treuthart at Lawnel uses to dock the tails of heifer calves raised there to become dairy cows.

Peter fits one green band over two tiny prongs on either end of a pair of "banding pliers" and squeezes the handles. As the band opens wide, he slips it quickly over the calf's testicles then removes the halter from the calf's head. My calf walks quickly away from Peter, but otherwise shows no obvious response to the banding. Neither does it make any sound.

"The rubber band cuts off circulation to the sac," Peter explains. "It cuts through the skin, through the bottom of the sac, and then the testicles just dry up and fall off. When it's done, the whole sac is so thin it looks like a piece of paper."

·   ·   ·

Inside the house, Peter and Shelly's fourteen-month-old son, Colin, sits in a high chair at the kitchen table while Shelly feeds him oatmeal. Colin's three-year-old sister, Bridgette, sits in a regular chair, drinking from a plastic mug. When she pulls the mug away from her mouth, she has a milk mustache.

These are the two children I saw earlier, riding up the driveway on a sled. Pulling the sled was Billy, nine; he's seated in a reclining chair in the living room watching television. Billy is Shelly's child from a former marriage; he has a sister, Stephanie, eight, who is with their father tonight in Leroy, about ten miles to the northwest. Another child in the family, Kalie, twelve, is also in Leroy with her mother. Peter is Kalie's father.

Erin, the black Lab–springer mix, stands under Colin's high chair, waiting for food to fall. A brown cat curls around the table legs.

Public assistance, Shelly tells me later, has been a big help for the kids. "We're making it, we're getting by," she says. "We could have been getting it since Bridgette was born, and I wish I'd had enough backbone then to apply, 'cause my older two could have had the food that we have now. We're on food stamps and WIC—that's Women and Infant Nutrition—you get the peanut butter and the cheese and the milk. It's especially good with the formula Colin and Bridgette were on, because they were both allergic to the milk-based formula, and the formula they could tolerate was fifteen dollars a can."

While Shelly bathes Colin and Bridgette, Peter and I talk in the living room, where Billy continues to watch TV. On the wall near the TV is a framed Lion's Club certificate naming Peter 1998 "Lion of the Year." The club raises money for people in the community with hearing and vision problems. Above the certificate is a mounted deer head; the antlers have ten points. I remind Peter of the deer carcass hanging at the end of his driveway the first time I visited, but he says this is not the same deer.

"This one's about four and a half years old. I shot him in East Avon while Shelly and I were dating. We got about twenty deer that year—a group of friends and I."

Do the large antlers mean the deer was very old?

"No, that just means he had an easy life," says Peter. "He ate well."

"When I lived alone," he continues, "I used to keep deer meat and eat it all year, put it in a crock pot. It's better than a beef roast. But Shelly doesn't eat it, so I don't keep any of the meat anymore—I sell it all or give it away."

As we talk, Peter nurses a can of Genesee Beer, a regional brand.

Peter grew up on a farm in the town of Avon, just a few miles up the road. He was the youngest of ten children. The farm had animals, but Peter's father worked mainly at a machine tool company in Rochester. Peter attended Catholic elementary school. When he was seven years old, on the last day of school before Christmas break, his mother picked him up from school. "She took me home and told me to pack my clothes because we were moving," he recalls. "She already had the divorce papers, but hadn't told me."

That day Peter, his mother, and the five siblings still living at home moved in with an aunt in nearby Caledonia.

He had no quarrel with his mother's decision—"My mother left my father because they weren't getting along," Peter says—it was just the timing of the move that surprised him.

"While she was married, my mother was pretty much an old-fashioned girl," says Peter. "She had no marketable skills." After the divorce, his mother took a job at a local hamburger restaurant. Still, says Peter, "We were pretty much on welfare. We were getting food stamps—I remember I qualified for the free-lunch program at school. But some days, if I knew my mom had a break coming at work, I'd go over to the restaurant and we'd have lunch together."

At nine years old, Peter went to work at a farm that bred racehorses. "I was working after school, on weekends, and then all summer, and bringing home a couple of hundred dollars a week. It was illegal, of course, because of my age." By high school he was working fifty to seventy hours a week, earning nearly twelve thousand dollars a year.

"I don't regret it," Peter says of his childhood, "but I'm sure I missed things— like playing after school. Most kids didn't get out of school, get on their bikes, and go to work, or sit down at the kitchen table and ask their mother how much money she needed that week to keep living in their home."

In his senior year, Peter was made manager of the horse farm. About the same time, he began dating a girl a few years older than he. She became pregnant, and Peter agreed to support the child.

"We got engaged, moved in together, but it didn't work out. After some years we went our separate ways. I was about twenty-three."

Not long after, Peter took a job doing field work at a dairy farm in Avon. It was there he met Shelly, who was working with the calves and getting a divorce from her first husband.

On a sunny Saturday in the fall of 1994, they married. Peter's father attended, as did all nine of his brothers and sisters, including Michael, the fourth oldest, who was then in remission from cancer. Shelly made the wedding favors—tiny hay bales and steel milk cans—and her wedding dress, a white gown she patterned after a dress in the movie *The Little Mermaid*. The bridesmaids' dresses were Holstein black and white. Peter surprised Shelly by arranging for a John Deere combine to be delivered to the Presbyterian Church in Avon. "During the ceremony, I could hear it pull up," recalls Peter. "Shelly didn't know a thing."

Their wedding video shows a green combine tractor so large Peter and Shelly have to climb a thirteen-foot ladder to reach the cab. From there they wave to their family and friends, Shelly holding a corsage of white carnations and Peter in gray suit and ascot. Billy, five years old at the time, wears a tiny tux and clutches a teddy bear. He stands beside the combine, its massive black wheels much taller than he.

After taking a celebratory lap around the Avon town square, Peter drove his bride, at eighteen miles an hour, to a reception at a fire department lodge thirty miles away. There they danced and cut a white cake made by a friend from their church.

Soon after the wedding, Peter left the dairy farm in a dispute with one of the owners. For a time he drove an eighteen-wheel tractor-trailer, hauling salt and gravel. Bridgette was born, then Colin. Later, Peter worked for a construction company but quit when his boss insisted he work early one morning when he was home alone with the kids and had no baby-sitter available.

"That company and me had different opinions on family life," he says.

For a month or two, Peter stayed home with the children—the first time since he was nine years old that he was not employed. Peter speaks dismissively of "playing Mr. Mom," but mentions it often, and when he does his face softens, making me think the experience was more satisfying for him than he likes to admit.

These days, Peter's busy with a new venture: a "custom harvesting" business he's launched with an old friend, Scot, who owns a three-hundred-head dairy where Peter also works. "We're going to go in and chop everyone's hay and corn," he explains. They've leased a quarter-million-dollar, top-of-the-line, German-made chopper (with Mercedes-Benz engine), and Peter's already signed up enough customers to keep busy the first season. Scot's put up the cash and owns the stock, but Peter, who's done the selling and will do the chopping, intends over time to build his ownership share to 50 percent.

The harvesting business, with its focus on equipment and crops, appeals to Peter. "I'm not much interested in the animal part of farming," he concedes. But he'll continue to raise calves. He and Scot are partners in that enterprise, too. Scot pays for the feed, Peter raises the animals, and they split the profits.

I ask Peter if it ever feels weird to him to eat meat from an animal he's raised in his own yard.

"Not weird," he says. "I think it's great. I look forward to the day I can butcher an animal and put it in the freezer."

I ask if I can see the freezer. Together we go to a small storage room on the side of the house.

Peter opens the upright freezer. Nearly every shelf is stuffed with packages tightly wrapped in white paper, each labeled in blue stenciled capital letters: TOP ROUND STEAK, RIB STEAK, CHUCK STEAK, GROUND BEEF, SIRLOIN STEAK, CHUCK ROAST, SOUP BONE, PORTERHOUSE STEAK, BEEF LIVER, BEEF TONGUE. The sirloin steak packages are flat and long; the ground beef packages, which are the most plentiful, are round and fat.

"That's half a side of steer we grew," says Peter. "I sold the other half to friends."

•   •   •

Four days later I return to the Vonglises' to check on the calves. Western New York is enjoying a January thaw: sun floods the running shed through the open south side, and water drips off the roof from melting snow. Just outside the calves' pen, the ground has turned to mud. My barn boots make a sucking sound when I lift them. They leave a waffle impression where I step.

My bull calf—I don't know whether to call him 7 or 8, since he now wears both tags—lies in the sun in the middle of the pen. This is the warmest day he's known. He licks up a few straws from the bedding, chewing slowly. He reminds me of Ferdinand, the bull in the story by Munro Leaf, who would rather smell the flowers than fight.

My kids keep asking what I'm going to name the calves. I tell them I'm not going to name them anything; I'm going to call them by their numbers, just as the farmers do. Still, on a lovely day like this, when I'm sitting alone with the calves in the running shed, watching my bull calf lie in the sun, I think it would be nice to have a name to call him by, even just silently in my head. I really shouldn't, though; I should stick with my resolve to observe the normal process by which these animals are raised, and normally they are not named. I'm also a little concerned that if I name him I might start getting attached to him.

My bull calf rises and walks slowly toward the heifer, his twin sister. Squatting, I peer between his legs and can see the green castrating band still around his scrotum. His sister licks his left ear; he licks her right cheek, they switch. My third calf, the one I bought as a backup, approaches and the heifer licks his ear, too. My bull calf walks to a feed bucket hanging on the fence. He pushes in among three of Peter's black calves already there and licks up a mouthful of grain, assertive enough, apparently—despite the green band—to get what he needs.

The running shed is framed with steel girders covered with wood planks up to about four feet, and corrugated steel above that. On the east side, where my calves are penned, the planking has several large holes; wind and snow could whip through here, it seems to me, if we get any more nasty weather. But the running shed is in good shape compared with the barn, where Peter sometimes keeps calves, and pigs, too. The barn—Peter guesses it's at least one hundred years old— has gaps in the upper wooden walls large enough to throw a basketball through.

The barn has a sliding door over which is nailed a rusted horseshoe. Inside are stacked blue feed buckets, shovels, brooms, open bags of milk replacer, a wheel-barrow, a mousetrap, an orange and black COW X-ING sign, a boom box, a 110-volt electric fence charger, and a half-dozen empty Genesee Beer cans. On a narrow ledge near the window is a glass jar containing about fifty green castrat-ing bands. One veterinary supply house sells a bag of one hundred bands for $1.49, about a penny and a half apiece.

· · ·

I leave the barn and join Shelly in the house. She works three twelve-hour shifts as a patient-care technician on a cardiac floor at Strong Memorial Hospital in Rochester. Today's her day off. I've seen Shelly several times, but with Peter out and the kids napping, this is the first chance we've had to talk alone.

"When you called the first time," she begins, "and you wanted to board the calves, I figured you're just this city slicker coming out and you're writing a book and you're going to watch these little pretty baby cows. And it's like, you're a jour-nalist which is an interest I have—and you're Jewish, right? Anybody who has a different religious belief is of interest to me.

"And then this past week when you came out to move the calves, you saw Peter and me at a bad point and then you saw the rest of the family, and you've seen the house at its possible worst and everything, and its like—you're still com-ing back!"

We're in the playroom. As she speaks, Shelly crawls around the floor picking up toys. Her blue eyes are framed by thick, brownish red hair cut in bangs nearly to her eyebrows. She is thirty-three years old, of medium build, but broad-shouldered; I can easily imagine her turning over in bed patients much larger than herself.

The middle of five siblings, Shelly grew up on her family's eighty-five-head dairy farm in Caledonia, about eight miles north of York. "I milked cows for eighteen years," she recalls. "My earliest memories put me about three years old, watching cows being milked in a stanchion barn."

The farm was started by her grandfather, Carroll Bickford, now eighty-three. In separate farm accidents he lost both an arm and a leg, and is fitted now with both a hook and a plastic leg. "He still gets up every day," says Shelly, "and if his sciatica isn't bothering him or if his stump isn't bothering him, he's on a tractor. He's spreading manure, he's cultivating, he's planting, he's out there."

After the birth of Peter and Shelly's first child, Bridgette, Peter converted the garage into this playroom so Shelly could start a day-care center. She had more than a dozen children enrolled, but closed the venture after just over a year.

"The problem was I was getting attached to the kids to the point that I was bringing them clothes, sending packages of food home with them because I knew they weren't going to get anything to eat that night. My father said, 'Where do you find these people?' It wasn't that I was a sucker, but my heart was too big."

Shelly then earned certificates as a nursing assistant and an emergency medical technician, and began working at the hospital.

Her first marriage was to a boy she met soon after graduating from high school, "the first guy who told me he loved me," she recalls. The children of that marriage, Billy junior and Stephanie, attend school in nearby Leroy, where their father lives.

Shelly crawls over toward a Fisher-Price toy washing machine near the window, on the way picking up a plastic Barbie whose blond hair she strokes absently as she talks.

The earlier marriage unraveled gradually. "The reason for our split-up, indirectly, was Lawnel Farms," she says. "That's why when you said you were getting the calves from there, I'm thinking to myself, 'Oh my goodness! What is God intending for me now?'"

Colin cries, waking from his nap. Shelly brings him into the playroom. He stands at a coffee table, banging on a toy piano.

Shelly was calf manager at Lawnel. She sits in a child's yellow plastic play-chair, gesturing with a toddler's white sock in her right hand as she describes how jealous her first husband was of the men with whom she worked at Lawnel.

"I worked with all guys," she recalls. "So how was I gonna say, 'Matt did this, and Jim did this, and John did this, and another John did this, and Ken did this?' It's like, me and five guys? No way."

Colin crawls into his mother's lap.

Despite her husband's jealousy, Shelly enjoyed her work at Lawnel, except for her relationship with Sue Smith. Sue, who later would become herd manager, at that time still worked in the Lawnel office, learning the family business from her husband, Andrew, and her father-in-law, Larry Smith.

"During the whole time I was at Lawnel's, Sue did not want me there," says Shelly. "From the day I started, she was lookin' for a reason to get rid of me. Someone told me Sue didn't like me and I said, 'She's not going to push me out. She's not going to make me quit this place.'"

Shelly believes Sue was jealous of her. "Everyone got along with me. Everyone liked me," she recalls. "And I had a farming background. I was a farmer's daughter. She just married a farmer."

I point out that Sue also grew up on a dairy farm.

"Oh, did she?" Shelly asks. "Oh, okay, a small one?"

Shelly gives Colin, resting now in her arms, a pacifier.

I ask her about her disagreement with Sue over animal care.

"Lawnel had this guy working for them," she begins. "He was milking cows. Come to find out he was a drunk and he ended up treating a cow with antibiotics and put her back in the milking herd. He didn't separate her, and so when she got milked, the antibiotics went into the tank. Lawnel got fined. It happened twice, and from that point on, no antibiotics were allowed on the farm. So I had no antibiotics to treat my calves with. I had calves that the instant they were born you said a prayer because that's pretty much all you could do for them. And I was losing them left and right. And then Sue decided as soon as they were born I had to feed them five raw eggs and something else, and I'm thinking to myself, 'That's not going to cure pneumonia. That's not going to kill *E. coli*. That's not going to help dehydration.' It pissed me off. I watched cows that had freshened get uterine infections, then they'd get mastitis [bacterial infection of the udder], and I had to watch them die because Sue wasn't going to ship 'em [to slaughter] and she wasn't going to treat 'em. It was awful.

"One night," she continues, "I saw a cow totally sprawled out for at least twenty-four hours, and when we finally got her upright on her chest, she had calved. There's the dead calf underneath her. Nobody had even checked on these animals. And I called Sue—I got her out of bed—I was pissed. She came down and goes, 'Oh, well, at least the cow won't die right away.' Sue told me I was not allowed to call the vet anymore—if I had any concerns about the animals to go get the herdsman or go to her. It got to the point I was losing calves and I couldn't take it anymore."

Later I asked Sue Smith about Shelly's frustration in not being able to use antibiotics to treat the Lawnel cows. Sue said it was during a time when she had tried treating mastitis with fluids rather than with antibiotics, "to flush it out of the system. We didn't have any success with that program," Sue recalled.

After Sue Smith took over as herd manager, Shelly left Lawnel. She took a job at a dairy farm in Avon, and that was where she met Peter Vonglis.

Shelly remains passionate about the treatment of farm animals, cows in particular.

"A dairy farm is what my mom and dad have," she says. "They're milking two hundred and fifty cows. My dad and my brother-in-law know every single one. But you go to some of these big operations where they milk a thousand cows, the average life expectancy of a cow there is three lactations.

"My dad probably has ten-year-old cows that have had ten and eleven babies because it's a farm, it's not a milk factory.

"Cows deserve to have antibiotics," she continues. "They deserve to have dry environments. They deserve not to be crowded. They deserve—they're creatures; they're not a factory product."

I ask Shelly about her argument with Peter as they moved the calves from the hutches up to the running shed.

"Those animals don't deal well with stress," she says. "Pulling, pushing, tugging is stress. They can get sick from it. The ones I had were hungry, so they just trotted along behind me when I held the feed bucket. They didn't care that they were going by your car, but the ones Peter had stopped—they slid on the ice, and took off into the snow. Mine just walked by and went into the barn."

I'm curious what Shelly thinks of the nearly ten weeks my calves spent in the hay-bale hutches. Does keeping calves without exercise, play, or companionship affect them emotionally, make them timid or afraid?

"It might seem cruel, but it's more cruel to watch an animal die from pneumonia or an *E. coli* infection. That's what would happen if you allowed it to grow up with another calf. They do like being with each other, but they're not going to curl up in a corner and die if they don't."

I ask about eating meat.

Shelly says she eats meat, but only from beef animals, not from dairy cows. Partly for this reason, she avoids fast-food hamburgers.

"When I go to a restaurant, I'm assuming the meat is from a farm where they just raise beef animals and they're sold when they're healthy and vibrant and running around, not like a dairy cow when they can barely walk and are taking their last gasp of air."

Shelly says her sister—who, with her husband, is taking over the family dairy farm—won't touch hamburger.

"She will not touch it with her hands. When she makes meatballs, she uses a watermelon scoop."

Why?

"I don't know. My older sister doesn't eat beef at all. Plain doesn't eat it."

She's vegetarian?

"No, no, she'll eat turkey and some chicken and ham, but it's funny, we've all been raised on the farm and we've all got a little quirk about it."

I leave Shelly thinking the interview has been one of the easiest I've conducted: I turned on the tape recorder and for two hours just listened to her talk as she cleaned up the playroom and then held her son sweetly in her arms, rocking him to sleep.

Yet halfway home to Rochester, I suddenly feel sad.

What hits me is the contrast between Sue Smith and Shelly Vonglis. It's odd that the paths of these two women, raised on family dairy farms at opposite ends of the state, ever should have crossed at Lawnel Farms, Sue as owner and Shelly as calf manager; odder still that they should cross again through my boarding with Shelly and Peter the calves born at Lawnel. But today Sue successfully runs a nine-hundred-cow herd and hosts Christmas parties with two seatings, while four miles down the road Shelly, hurt by her first marriage, buys peanut butter and infant formula on a tight budget and tries yet another career. From direct observation, I know both women are hardworking, and both have been open and kind to me. I admire them both, Sue for her achievements and Shelly for her struggle; but their differing situations, I think, are like those recently of the heifer calves basking in the heated greenhouse at Lawnel, and my bull calf shivering in the Vonglises' outdoor hutch, the calves' genders alone—like Sue and Shelly's circumstances—dictating who shall be comfortable and who shall be cold.

· · ·

On a Thursday in early March I make a routine weekly visit to the Vonglises' to check on the calves. I hadn't expected anyone to be home, but Shelly's car is in the driveway. I knock and she calls for me to come in.

Erin, the dog, is lying beside the black, wood-burning stove in the kitchen; Shelly is seated on a sofa in the living room, under the deer head, folding laundry. She's not at work today because Colin is home with a cold.

"Your calf died," she says flatly. After all the emotion she had expressed about animal care, I'm struck by the matter-of-fact way in which she delivers this news. Maybe it's guilt for the calf having died on her watch.

Shelly explains, "Last weekend your calf was looking logy, so Peter gave him a shot of Micotil—that's an antibiotic—but the next day he was down." Then Saturday night, during a snowstorm, she and Peter moved all the calves from the running shed into the barn, where they'd be better protected from the weather. "We elevated your guy's head, put hot water bottles all around him, called the vet, but we lost him before the vet got here."

I asked her what caused his death.

"I think the weather. If he was having an intestinal bug he would have gotten dehydrated and then could have developed hypothermia."

What I want to know is to which "he" she is referring: my bull calf, or the backup?

"I think it's number seven," says Shelly. "Wasn't that the bull calf you're writing about?"

Since Shelly mixed up the ear tags, I'm not sure whether she means the bull or the heifer twin.

"It was definitely a bull calf that died," she says.

When I get to the barn, Peter is just coming out.

"Where's the calf that died?" I ask.

"Right there, Peter," he says firmly, gesturing to a place just inside the barn door.

Two dead calves lie in a heap next to the barn wall. One is all black, one of Peter's Angus-Holstein crosses; the other is a black-and-white Holstein. But the Holstein's head is twisted away from me. I can't see the calf's face or the ear tag. I step around the carcasses to look from the other side. This is a bull calf, but it's the backup.

I ask Peter why he didn't call to tell me the calf had died. "Well," he says, "I didn't call on Saturday because I remembered it was some kind of special day for you." I'd told Peter and Shelly I don't work on Saturday because it's the Jewish Sabbath. "I told Shelly to call you on Sunday," he continues, "but I don't think she wanted to give you the bad news."

Peter says snow and wind blowing into the running shed through cracks in the back and side walls may have stressed the calves and caused them to die of hypothermia, freezing. Either that, or it could have been a bug. Two other calves died the week before. Of fifteen calves Peter began raising in the fall, nine survive.

Peter will take the calves' bodies to a friend's farm that has a compost. He's already tied ropes around both their hind legs, and drags the black one out to a truck backed up to the barn door. I offer to pull the other carcass out. Peter hands me the rope. I tug hard, but can barely budge it.

"Heavier than you thought, huh?" Peter asks.

"What does he weigh, a hundred pounds?"

"More than that. Plus, being dead they feel heavier."

The carcass is stiff; the tail frozen in a sort of question mark. I bend the tail sideways and up and down to try to get the feel of a dead calf.

One of its eyes is still open. It's a glossy blue.

"What's with the eye?" I ask. I've never seen an eye that color.

"Oh, the eyes kind of glaze over when they die," says Peter.

While he drags the backup calf to the truck, I check on my remaining bull calf and his twin sister in the barn. Both seem okay, although the bull calf appears thin and bony. I wait until the calf faces away, and then squat to peer though his hind legs. I'm looking for the scrotum, but there is none; since my last visit it must have fallen off, completing the castration.

4

Friendship

THE SICKEST I'VE EVER BEEN was once in my twenties when I contracted salmonella, probably from an egg salad sandwich I bought at a cheap lunch carry-out. After a couple of feverish days, I was so dehydrated from vomiting and diarrhea, my physician sent me to the hospital. After five days of intravenous feeding, I was discharged and went to my parents' home to convalesce. When I felt well enough to eat, my mother asked what I would like, and without hesitating I answered, "Elbow macaroni and small-curd cottage cheese."

This didn't surprise her. Macaroni and cottage cheese had been my comfort food for many years; for whatever reason, it was what she used to feed me as a child whenever I was ill.

I was thinking about this after meeting the president of the milk cooperative that sells the Lawnel Farms milk. During our session he surprised me by remarking casually, "Lawnel milk never becomes fluid milk."

I'd always imagined schoolchildren drinking the Lawnel cows' milk out of half-pint containers. I'd even once calculated how many children could be supplied with half-pints of milk for how many weeks from one day's production of the Lawnel herd: with about 50,000 pounds of milk produced each day, and 8.6 pounds of milk to the gallon, that's about 5,800 gallons daily—enough to provide a half-pint of milk to each of 465 children every school day for a year.

It's not that there's anything wrong with the Lawnel milk, the co-op president explained. It could as easily be made into milk for drinking; it just happens that the processors who buy it make cheese. Each day the driver of the tanker truck that picks up the Lawnel milk alternates deliveries between two area cheese plants: on odd days he goes to Great Lakes Cheese in Cuba, New York, which makes mozzarella; on even days he goes to Friendship Dairies in Friendship, New York, which makes sour cream and cottage cheese.

That Lawnel milk is made into cheese turns out to be more typical than not. Only about 30 percent of milk produced in the United States is used as fluid milk; the rest becomes cheese, yogurt, ice cream, and other products. With consumption of fluid milk essentially flat—despite the popular "Milk Mustache" and "Got Milk?" ad campaigns—greater consumption of cheese and premium ice cream has been critical to the dairy industry.

"Thank God for pizza," the co-op president told me, a sentiment I'd heard expressed in the exact same words by others in the business.

Anyway, my conversation with the milk co-op president got me thinking about my old comfort foods. I easily recalled that the elbow macaroni my mother served was Mueller's brand, but I couldn't remember the brand of cottage cheese.

So I called my mom. She's eighty-four, and still sharp.

"Mom," I said, "the small-curd cottage cheese you used to give me with the elbow macaroni when I was sick—any chance you remember what brand it was?"

"Sure," she said. "It was Friendship."

. . .

A mid-April frost has left a haze hanging over the unplanted fields on my way to York today. At 6:00 A.M. the Lawnel milk parlor—the place where cows come to be milked—is hopping, as indeed it is twenty-four hours a day. Like a casino, the parlor lights are always on, the radio nearly always playing—country music—and always there are cows coming in, going out, vacuum pumps pumping.

Outside the parlor, the fourteen-wheel, stainless-steel milk truck is already backed up to the milk house, a room next to the parlor that houses three large "bulk tanks" in which fresh milk is stored. Even as I enter the building, milk is flowing from the tanks through a white plastic hose that runs through a hole in the wall and into the tanker truck.

Sue Smith looks wide awake and cheerful as she enters the parlor. Al, the morning milker, greets her warmly. It's just an hour into Sue's workday, but already she's been through the cow barns, and her blue coveralls are spotted with manure—behind the shoulder, along one sleeve, near the waist, and above the pocket on the right hip.

She carries into the parlor two red plastic buckets, one filled with white plastic syringes, the other empty. The syringes contain single doses of 500 mg of bovine somatotropin growth hormone, more commonly known as BST. She'll inject cows today as they're milked. The empty pail is for disposal of the syringes after use. "We have to account for every needle," she says, explaining that she's required to mail them back to the supplier in order to ensure control of their distribution.

In the cool, predawn air of the parlor, fourteen black-and-white cows stand in a row at the milking machine, their heads lowered, huffing out vapor like a long locomotive idling at the station.

In a holding area behind the parlor, cows wait to enter in a tightly packed group on a concrete ramp seventy-five feet long and twenty wide. The ramp is gently sloped so that manure and urine run backward toward a floor grate and from there to an outdoor storage lagoon. Despite some south-facing windows, it's dim in here. Four circular fans suspended from the low ceiling move the air. In the very last row of the group, the rumps of nine cows are pressed tightly against a five-foot-high metal gate—called the "crowd gate."

I stand behind the crowd gate, behind the last row of cows. From here, I can't even see the entrance to the parlor. It's like being so far back in a theater line you can't see the ticket booth. The hundred or so cows waiting in front of me stand quietly, bunched and facing forward.

In a natural state, a calf will nurse from its mother an average of six times a day. Many farms, particularly smaller ones, milk just twice a day, but even at large farms like Lawnel that milk three times daily, cows enter the parlor with heavy udders and generally are eager to be milked.

A motor starts up—a grinding, buzzing noise like an electric chain saw—and suddenly the crowd gate rolls forward, pushing the whole pack of cows ahead of it. One of the nine cows in the back falls to her front knees, then rights herself; another slips on the sloped, urine-slick surface, then regains her footing.

After fifteen seconds the motor stops. The gate rests some twenty feet closer to the parlor.

The purpose of the crowd gate is to position cows so they are ready to move into the parlor as soon as the group before them is done. The milker activates the gate from a control panel inside the parlor.

Animal scientists who study social relationships among cattle have found that when moving from barn to milk parlor, dairy cows tend to travel in a consistent order: dominant cows in the lead, subordinate cows in the rear. Compared with the cows in front, those in back are usually very young or very old, smaller and more timid. Interestingly, the studies show that "rearship" is more consistent than leadership; the leaders change sometimes, but the same cows tend always to be in the back, which means the most subordinate consistently end up with their rumps against the crowd gate.

One cow near the back—but not in the very last row—is 4923, the mother of my twin calves, the one with the reverse question mark on her forehead. She stands quietly. Her head hangs low, well below the stump tail of the cow in front of her.

The crowd gate buzzes again. Another cow in the rear falls to her knees but quickly rises. 4923 creeps forward. When the gate stops, the group is another ten feet closer to the parlor.

One employee told me a cow went down in the crowd gate in December and couldn't get up. "We had to kill it," he said. But that seems to happen rarely.

Sue's computer shows 4923's annual milk production is 24,600 pounds—2,860 gallons—a little better than the Lawnel herd average of 22,800 pounds, or about 2,650 gallons. Creeping up the ramp toward the parlor must be a familiar experience for her: by the end of this lactation—her third—she'll have made the trip nearly three thousand times.

The motor starts again, the gate moves forward; the mass of cows moves with it.

Nearby 4923 I spot an ear tag with a familiar number, 1423, but can't recall who it is. I flip back though my notes: it's Darla! Darla from whom Andrew pulled two dead calves, one of them in two pieces. I'm glad to see she's recovered enough to be back in the milking herd, but perhaps some lingering weakness has landed her toward the rear of the pack.

The next push of the gate puts us within earshot of the country music playing from the radio in the parlor.

Al, the morning milker, wades among the last fifteen or twenty cows left on the holding ramp. He slaps 4923 gently on her right hip. She walks into the parlor and enters the fourth stall on the left.

. . .

The modern milking parlor consists pretty much of just one enormous piece of equipment: the milking machine. Milking machines come in a variety of designs. Lawnel Farms has a "double-14 herringbone" machine, which means that on either side of a center aisle, fourteen cows stand in angled stalls to be milked. The center aisle, or "pit," where the milkers stand, is sunk about three feet below the level of stalls on either side. From the pit, a milker is at eye level with the cows' udders. Equipment like this, costing about a quarter-million dollars, allows one milker to milk one hundred cows in an hour.

Exactly how much milk a cow produces at any given milking depends in part on where the cow is in her lactation cycle. Cows produce more milk early in the cycle and taper off after some months. The peak period is about sixty days after calving, when in one milking a cow may produce as much as sixty or seventy pounds—more than seven gallons.

Many dairy farmers will freely admit they don't understand the complex formula by which the government sets the price of milk; they only know it changes monthly and is usually lower than they would like it to be. In general, farmers receive a market price—$13.50 per one hundred pounds of milk (just over eleven gallons)—with small premiums based on volume, fat, and protein content. That means cow 4923, which currently gives about 105 pounds of milk in three daily milkings of five to seven minutes each, produces about a dollar of milk per minute.

It is generally accepted that cows produce more milk in the presence of people who have what is called "cow sense"—that is, they are quiet, confident, and emotionally stable, and move easily and gently among the herd. This is consistent with the opinion of dairyman and publisher H. W. Hoard, who, in the early 1900s, urged farmers to treat cows gently in order to coax more milk from them. Sue Smith has posted on a bulletin board outside the parlor Hoard's well-known "Notice to the Help." It reads, in part, "Remember that this is the Home of Mothers. Treat each cow as a Mother should be treated. The giving of milk is a function of Motherhood, rough treatment lessens the flow."

I've also seen handwritten messages from Sue on the same board suggesting that the help doesn't always embrace Hoard's philosophy. In March, she wrote, "Please be gentle with these animals. We have had several bloody quarters lately [blood in the milk]. Do not hit cows on their udders."

When all fourteen cows on the left side of the parlor have backed into the milking position, the milker walks through the pit with a hose, giving each teat a quick spray of red, disinfecting iodine. Thirty seconds later he wipes them dry with brown paper towels, using a fresh towel for each cow. Disinfecting teats helps keep dirt and manure that may cling to them from spreading bacteria into the milk, or up into the cow herself through teat openings that dilate during milking, causing mastitis.

Mastitis—infection of the udder—is perhaps the most common ailment among modern dairy cows. Experts say that for every cow in a herd with clinical signs—head down; ears down; hot, swollen udder; watery or off-color milk—many more may have subclinical levels of infection. People who drink milk from cows with mastitis don't get sick, but the milk may spoil faster and not taste as good.

To a large extent, mastitis is a by-product of the living conditions of modern dairy cows. At the Herdsperson Training course I took, a veterinarian explained, "Cows in nature get mastitis less often because they eat in one place, shit in another, and graze on dry ground. It's the artificial environment and crowding and shit in dairy barns that creates a situation with high levels of mastitis."

Some dairy farmers try to prevent mastitis by clipping or singeing the hairs of their cows' udders to remove dirt or feces that might cling to the teats. Sue Smith says she tried this, but hasn't felt Lawnel has a serious enough mastitis problem to warrant it.

Fortunately, most mastitis clears up on its own with good hygiene in the barn and parlor. Serious cases usually respond to antibiotics, but chronic cases may require a cow to be sent to slaughter. As the vet who lectured to my class put it, "The best way to treat a cow with chronic mastitis who doesn't respond to repeated rounds of antibiotics is high-speed lead."

The milker now makes another pass down the aisle, attaching the milking unit—called a "claw"—and teat cups over the four teats on each cow's udder. Modern dairy cows are bred for good teat placement, meaning the teats are well spaced so the milking equipment can easily fit over them.

Farmers like an udder that is well attached, fits snugly against the abdominal wall, and extends high between the thighs in the rear. A heavy, pendulous udder can begin to break away from a cow's body if the supporting ligaments weaken or stretch. Udders continue to grow until cows are about six years of age, at which time they can weigh more than 150 pounds.

4923's udder seems about average, neither especially firm and high nor too heavy and sagging. Her teats, mottled black and pink, are about as long and thick as my thumb. The udder itself is covered with coarse white hair, ridged with prominent veins, and warm to the touch.

·　·　·

"Hi, Babe," says Sue Smith to 4923.

Sue's climbed a short ladder up from the pit and positioned herself behind the cow. 4923 seems calm, ruminating as she is milked.

Sue gives BST shots every other Wednesday morning. BST is absorbed into a cow's system over a fourteen-day period, so the animals need a new injection every two weeks.

"At five-fifty a shot," she says, "you want to make sure it's injected properly and given to the right animals." So she does it herself. "Personally, I don't like giving it; it's labor intensive and means a whole eight-hour shift in the parlor." But given the results—a 10 percent increase in the farm's milk production—she accepts it as an economic necessity.

"I just do it. I don't dread it anymore. If we're making more milk and it's profitable, it's something we should be doing."

BST is a form of a growth hormone occurring naturally in cows. Sold by the Monsanto Company under the trade name Posilac, it was first approved by the government for commercial use in 1994. Lawnel Farms was among its early users. The Smiths, in fact, are featured in a Monsanto promotional brochure. In the full-page spread, Andrew, Sue, and their daughter Kirsty stand in front of a wooden Lawnel Farms sign. "Using Posilac is an opportunity that we couldn't pass up," the brochure quotes Sue as saying.

Sue says Lawnel cows produce nine to eleven pounds—about 1.2 gallons—more milk per day on BST. Importantly, BST also lengthens a cow's lactation. Normally a cows begins to "dry off"—produce less milk—about ten months after calving. To lactate again, it must give birth. But some cows have trouble getting pregnant, or they miscarry. If they cannot give birth and lactate again, they are usually sold for beef. With BST, however, these cows keep lactating. Sue says she's had cows on BST giving milk for three years, "and I'm still milking them."

Use of BST has generated controversy among consumer advocates and foreign governments. Canada, for example, has declined to approve its use. Some distrust Monsanto-funded studies that found BST has no ill effects on milk drinkers. Nevertheless, about one-third of U.S. dairy farmers responding to an industry survey say they now use BST.

Sue begins giving BST about ten weeks after a cow has freshened, and keeps giving it throughout the lactation. She injects the hormone into the cow's fat. "You can also inject it subcutaneously—under the skin," she says, "but that increases the chances of twinning [giving birth to twins], although I don't know why."

Sue pokes the syringe into 4923 at a point just to the left of the point where the tail meets the cow's rump. The cow strains a moment, stretches her head forward, then relaxes.

Seven minutes and twenty seconds after 4923 began milking, the milking unit detaches from her udder, signaling that milk production has stopped. "Detachers," also called "automatic takeoffs," are among the most important labor-saving devices of the modern milking machine. Developed in the 1970s, detachers sense when a cow is done milking, disengage the teat cups, and swing the milking unit away from the udder and into position for the next cow.

The milker now makes another quick pass through the pit, respraying teats with disinfectant. He then pushes a button on a control panel and a metal bar—called a "rapid exit" bar—rises like the starting gate at a racetrack, releasing all fourteen cows at once.

The cows exit the parlor on a path that runs alongside the holding-area ramp and crowd gate, back toward the barn. Bringing up the rear of the pack going out, as she did coming in, is 4923.

. . .

Moments later, feed manager and maintenance man Larry Wilkins staggers against the parlor's sliding glass front door. Larry's the one who received a thirty-year recognition award at the Lawnel Christmas party. A heavy beard and shocks of white hair that stick out from under his farm cap make him look older than his fifty years.

Sue runs and catches him, but he doesn't look well. Holding him up, Sue calls to me to get a pail from the parlor for him to sit on. I look, but find none. She's having trouble holding Larry up.

"Call nine-one-one!" she says.

I run to the herd office and make the call. They want to know what the problem is.

"Possible heart attack," I guess, but then Sue rushes into the office, grabs some papers, and, on the way out, shouts to me, "No, chemical inhalation."

Outside, someone's parked a truck in front of the parlor and sat Larry on the tailgate.

"My lungs are burning," he groans. Larry also complains of chest pain. Between coughs and labored breaths, he says he inhaled a mixture of acid and chlorine while cleaning the milk storage tank.

A container he was holding when he collapsed reads: "Acid Dairy Cleanser. Caution: Irritant."

"The main thing is to get the air out of your lungs," says Andrew Smith, who as usual seems to have appeared from nowhere at just the time he's needed.

At 8:16 A.M., eight minutes by my watch since I called 911, the first volunteer medical technician arrives. He had been repairing farm equipment—his regular job—and picked up the 911 call to the ambulance on his car radio. The York Volunteer Fire Department ambulance arrives three minutes later. The driver, Dennis House, is the York town supervisor.

Someone puts an oxygen mask over Larry's face. I notice Sue biting the inside of her left cheek; it's the only time I've ever seen her show anxiety.

Larry coughs some more, and spits on the ground.

The next group of cows is being milked in the parlor, although they're missing their BST shots because Sue isn't there to give them.

The medical technician asks what happened.

"The system didn't work," says Sue, flatly.

No one's quite sure what did happen, but apparently in the process of cleaning one of the refrigerated milk storage tanks, Larry somehow mixed chlorine and hydrochloric acid and inhaled the fumes.

Chris, the office manager, says she's impressed Larry managed to hold on to the jar of acid and not drop it.

I'm impressed Sue had emergency instructions for both chemicals instantly at hand.

Larry's helped into the ambulance. They'll take him to a hospital in Rochester.

A sheriff's car arrives. The officer walks up the dirt driveway toward our little group standing around the pickup truck. I'm so used to seeing people on the farm—including myself—in drab, manure-spotted jeans and coveralls. It's startling to see this officer in a clean and neatly pressed black uniform.

"Who's injured?" the officer asks.

"The guy in the ambulance," Andrew deadpans.

"You the owner?" he asks Andrew.

I think of so much that had to have happened to make possible Andrew's simple answer: his grandfather Nelson Smith starting the farm, his father Larry Smith building it up, his two brothers deciding not to become farmers, Andrew leaving Cornell with a thyroid illness, starting again at another school, and finally earning a degree, then having the good fortune or good sense or both to marry Sue, and the two of them getting up every day for the last sixteen years at 4:30 A.M. and working as long and as hard as it takes.

"Yeah, I'm the owner," says Andrew.

"Name?"

"Smith, Andrew Smith," he says, James Bond–like.

Later, Sue explains to me what happened. "We have three bulk tanks. We use two, and one is always empty for cleaning. When the milk's been pumped out of the tank, we put soap and acid in a jar to wash it automatically. In the morning we put chlorine in the same jar and do another cleaning. But the acid must have been left in the jar—like when your dishwasher doesn't take all the soap powder out of the little dish. So when Larry put acid in the jar, the fumes mixed."

Larry was back at the farm by five that same afternoon, fixing a tractor. The doctors told him he shouldn't have any permanent damage; he'd just gotten a "sunburn" on his nasal passages and esophagus.

· · ·

Sue, Andrew, and Andrew's father, Larry Smith, meet at noon in the herd office to discuss plans for a new barn. Lunch is delivered from York Landing restaurant: ham and cheese sandwiches, potato chips, chocolate milk.

The veterinarian is supposed to be here, but he's late, so they start without him.

The goals for a new barn would be to increase milk volume, increase herd health, and ease management by housing more of the herd at the main farm.

On a picnic table, Larry lays out sheets of graph paper with drawings he's made of the barn—a structure the length of a football field, designed to house 350 cows, enough to bring Lawnel's total milking herd to one thousand animals. Larry, Andrew, and Sue discuss the merits of the design as to airflow, manure control, distance to the parlor, and snow removal between barns.

Builders' cost estimates have surprised Larry for being so high, especially compared with the cost of the last barn they put up a few years ago. Most now come in at five to seven hundred dollars a stall—over $200,000. And to milk the extra cows, they'd have to add at least four more stalls in the parlor, going from fourteen to sixteen on each side.

Sue says she'd use part of the barn to house dry cows—cows not being milked because they're within sixty days of calving—and maybe another part to segregate cows with Johne's (pronounced "YO-knees") disease.

Johne's is of increasing concern to U.S. dairy farmers, much as "mad cow" and hoof-and-mouth diseases have become concerns in Europe. An infectious cattle disease mostly affecting the intestine, Johne's causes cattle to develop diarrhea, poor digestion, and weight loss; ultimately it can lead to death. There is no cure.

I saw a Johne's cow in the parlor this morning. Without being told there was a sick cow in the group, I could tell it was ill: it appeared weak and thin, and avoided certain postures that seemed painful. I pointed it out to Sue, who told me it had Johne's and after this milking would be put on the "sick pack"—a section of barn close to the parlor for sick animals—and shipped off the farm next Monday.

Sue supports building the barn. "We've made small moves for the last five years and they've worked well, but we haven't done anything major. We're still milking the same number of cows. It's time to make a major move, develop a five-year plan and do it."

The meeting ends, but reconvenes a half hour later in the main office at Larry's desk when Dave Hale, the veterinarian, arrives. Dr. Hale, forty-two, is a graduate of Cornell Veterinary School. He treats Lawnel cows often, and is familiar with both the farm and the Smith family.

After Dr. Hale looks over Larry's designs, the conversation turns again to Johne's. Dr. Hale says statewide the chance any heifer has Johne's is about 20 percent. Sue says she's culling only about twenty cows a year for Johne's, or less than 3 percent of the herd.

There are some recent studies, Dr. Hale reports, in which the Johne's bacteria has been isolated in humans with Crohn's disease, a chronic intestinal disorder. Other studies, however, have been contradictory, so at present the possible risk to public health is uncertain. Pasteurization appears to deactivate the Johne's bacteria in milk, but concern persists that it could be spread through undercooked meat, unpasteurized milk products, and water.

Dr. Hale says that in designing a barn, the Smiths should also consider the likelihood of feed trucks picking up manure on their tires in one barn and contaminating calf areas in other barns.

Overall, Dr. Hale favors any steps that will help keep cows infected with Johne's away from calves and the rest of the herd. "If a one-hundred-percent relationship between Johne's and Crohn's disease is found," he warns, "the state will eventually require segregating cows, so you might as well plan for it."

The meeting breaks up with a consensus that a bigger barn makes sense. Larry will talk to more builders to see what can be done about the price.

. . .

Andrew had been quiet at both meetings. Later that afternoon, I ride with him while he plants corn, and ask what was really going on at the meetings. Who's for the barn and who's against it?

"Sue and my dad are for it, I'm against," he says. "My dad wants one thousand cows before he's done. That doesn't trip my trigger at all, but if Sue wants it, I'll make it happen. I'll stand by my woman."

For Andrew, more cows mean more headaches. "I'd rather milk twice a day than three times, with no BST, and with good employees—get rid of the ying-yangs."

He means employees who are not good workers.

He then goes into a funny bit, imitating all the reasons employees call to say they can't make it for work: "I got kicked by a cow! My car broke down! I'm sick! I'm in jail—can you bail me out?"

So, if they build the new barn and expand the herd, how will he find more employees?

"We'll just have to dip into the pool again and pull some more out," he says. "White trash is sometimes what you find. Maybe we can get some Kosovars, or Russians, or Hispanics, or Asians."

Of course it will be Sue, not he, who will have to manage additional employees to care for the extra cows, Andrew acknowledges, and he has full confidence in her.

"I know some of the guys in the barn think she's a real taskmaster, but few people are better organized. We're lucky to have her."

. . .

Shelly Vonglis and I sit on folding chairs in her backyard while Bridgette and Colin play in a sandbox. Just past where the lawn ends is a pen Peter has built for pigs, and hay bale hutches for a couple of new calves—my two calves are no longer the youngest ones here. Erin, the black Lab–springer mix, runs to me with a Winnie-the-Pooh doll in her mouth, wanting to play. The laundry line is heavy with shirts, pants, towels, and sheets hanging limp on this calm, sunny afternoon.

I'll return to Lawnel later today to observe cow 4923 go through the night milking, but first I've stopped at the Vonglis farm to check on my calves and to see how Shelly is doing. I'm concerned because when I spoke with her by phone recently, she said the calves were fine but that she herself had had a "nervous breakdown" and left her job at the hospital in Rochester. She added that Peter would be dehorning my calves soon, and if I wanted to see it I should come over this afternoon.

At about three months of age, a calf's horns begin to grow from little knobs of cartilage—called "buds"—on top of its head. Male and female calves both grow horns. Dairy farmers dehorn their animals because without horns they are less likely to injure people or one another; they're also thought to be quieter and generally easier to handle—much the same reasons used for castration.

In the barn, Peter already has my bull calf—now with the number 8 ear tag— tied to a fencepost with a halter and muzzle over its head. Shelly and the kids have come into the barn, too. Shelly seems tired. Her face is tight; she has circles under her eyes, and her hair is limp. I want to ask about her "breakdown," but this isn't the time or place to bring it up.

Shelly asks Peter if he isn't going to use a headlock.

He says no, the calves are too small and will just wriggle out of it. He'll hold them himself.

"They're going to fall over," she warns.

Shelly and Peter then joke whether I have a strong enough stomach for this. She asks Peter, "Is there anything in the way he can hurt himself on if he falls?"

"You mean the calf?" Peter asks.

"No, I mean Peter," she says, meaning me. "If he falls over."

Peter tells me it's going to smell bad—"not just the burning hair but the flesh." I remind him I can't smell.

Peter says my wife won't like the smell on my clothes when I get home. He suggests I take my coat off and put it in the car.

I'm wearing a light spring jacket.

"I'm leaving," Shelly announces. "I don't want to see this."

"You're going soft, Shel," Peter digs. "You're not much of a farmer."

Shelly leaves, but Bridgette and Colin remain in the barn with their father and me.

"We're just waiting for the dehorner to heat up," Peter explains. "I want to make sure it's hot enough, because it's old." He's plugged the device—a metal prong about nine inches long—into an outlet in a rafter.

While we wait, I reach over the fence to which my bull calf is tied, and pet him on the neck. I haven't been able to get close enough to touch him since he left the hay-bale hutch about a month ago; in the group pen, he moves away from me if I approach. He feels soft, especially the flesh that hangs under his neck, called the "dewlap," which is just developing.

To dehorn, as Peter does, using an electrically heated iron, the farmer presses one end of the hot iron over the calf's horn bud for fifteen to twenty seconds. This destroys the horn tissue and burns the hair and flesh surrounding it. It's said to be bloodless when done properly.

Other methods of dehorning include rubbing caustic potash on the horn bud. This prevents horn growth but does not actually remove the buds, and is used most often with very young calves, up to twenty days old. Another method is the dehorning spoon or tube, to gouge out the horns. These are also used with young calves. For older animals, those over three months of age, saws, shears, and clippers can be used to remove horns that have already begun to grow. I saw a cattle dealer do this on several older animals, and compared to that, burning the buds off a calf when young seems a good alternative.

Peter has gouged out horns, but prefers not to do so. "You have to pull out the veins," he says, "and you can clearly see things moving inside their skulls. It can get bloody." He may be exaggerating, but he points to bloodstains on the wooden fence against which I'm leaning.

I move away from the fence.

The electric dehorner glows red.

"Okay, here we go," says Peter.

Peter pushes the hot iron down against my calf's right horn bud. The calf's one eye that faces me bulges wide. He tries to bellow, but the muzzle holds his mouth shut and muffles the sound. His legs collapse and he falls to the floor.

Smoke billows around us.

I look behind to check on the kids. They seem not to react at all, perhaps because they've seen this so many times.

"You gotta do it till you can see red around the bud," says Peter.

My calf is lying on his side. I comment on how quickly he has quieted.

"He's in shock," says Peter.

Dehorning may be considered necessary, but no one argues it's a pretty sight. One of the farmers I visited when I was looking for a place to board my calves— before I met Peter and Shelly—was willing to take them but not to let me observe freely. "Gosh," he said, "you'll be writin' 'bout how I dehorn the calves, and people readin' your book'll get upset."

I admire Peter and Shelly for their openness. In fact, even at this moment, Peter encourages me to take a picture, which I do.

We have to wait a few minutes for the dehorner to heat up again. Bridgette, who left the barn when it became smoky, returns now with a dandelion she's picked for her father.

"It's yours," she says.

Peter thanks her.

"Okay," Peter says to his kids, "Daddy's got to do the other one now on the other side."

Peter brings the dehorner toward my calf's head again, but the calf moves backward and knocks him over.

"You better quiet down," Peter cautions the calf, rising and holding the animal more tightly. "You're making this harder than it has to be."

Peter pushes the dehorner against the calf's left bud. The calf jerks to the side and falls into a plastic bin filled with brown feed pellets.

I'm reminded of how, at Lawnel, just as Andrew Smith pulled this calf from his mother's womb, the calf fell into a bucket of soapy water before bouncing to the barn floor.

The burned, rust-colored ring around my calf's horn bud is about the size of a pocket watch. Peter says the calf may be "off his feed"—without much appetite—for a few days. The bud itself will fall off in three or four weeks; the hair will eventually grow back.

If dehorning is not done well, regardless of the method, sometimes the horn itself will grow back. I've seen cows with stunted horns, twisted horns, or horns fully regrown, but just on one side. Most cows' horns, though, do not grow back.

After he finishes with my bull calf, Peter dehorns the heifer twin. He does one side while she lies down, but has to apply the dehorner four times to get it burned right. The other side he does while she stands. When he applies the prong, she bellows and falls into the feed trough. My bull calf watches from about ten feet away.

As he puts away the dehorner, Peter comments on my ability to watch the process.

"This is what I signed on for," I reply.

I winced each time Peter applied the dehorner, but otherwise I'm surprised how little reaction I did have to seeing these calves—calves I own—being put in obvious pain. I suppose I've seen hundreds of cows at Lawnel, including these calves' own mother, without horns, so I figure they must have all gone through the same or similar process and survived.

But my tepid reaction, I think, also has something to do with the calves' own relatively subdued expression of pain. They did bellow and thrash a bit, and fall to the ground, but mostly they kept quiet. I've seen this many times on farms: cows kicked, jabbed, twisted around, even given electric shocks, show minimal reaction, if any at all.

Veterinary experts A. F. Fraser and D. M. Broom, in their book *Farm Animal Behavior and Welfare,* suggest that prey species, such as cattle, may have evolved very good reasons for not showing pain. "A [wounded] animal which is very close to a dangerous predator might do best to keep quiet. . . . For species which are very vulnerable to predation . . . dramatic displays associated with feeling pain might be wholly disadvantageous."

In other words, if cows and other prey animals show pain from an injury, they may invite even more danger, because the predator might sense their vulnerability and finish them off. Better to hide the pain.

· · ·

Later that afternoon, Shelly sits on a folding chair in her backyard, arms and legs crossed, watching her kids play. Her bright red nail polish does little to off-set her obvious tiredness.

I ask about her breakdown.

"One morning," she begins, "I woke up and was just trembling from top to bottom. I was scared to death and couldn't hold myself tight enough. It was a total loss of emotional control."

The breakdown—a panic attack, actually—was triggered, she believes, by an event two weeks earlier at the hospital. A patient had stopped breathing, and Shelly had responded by trying to save the woman's life. "I'm doing chest compressions," she recalls, "and only then I find she's a DNR" (meaning the family had left the instruction "do not resuscitate").

"I felt guilty 'cause I'm the one who was pumping her heart back," recalls Shelly. Days later the patient died, apparently of a heart attack.

"I brought this woman back to life on Tuesday and then bagged her on Friday," she says.

Shelly's on disability now, and continuing with antianxiety medication that she began about a year ago.

Ironically, the same day she experienced the panic attack, she received a letter of acceptance into a two-year nursing program at Alfred State College, about a one-hour drive from her home.

"There's about a gazillion opportunities out there for nurses," she says confidently.

Shelly will begin classes in the fall. In the meantime she's glad to be able to stay home with the kids, and is looking only for part-time work over the summer.

"I need a no-brainer job *not* dealing with people having heart attacks and respiratory problems. I need a stress-free life for a while," she says.

Shelly says Peter handled the panic attack "much better than I thought he'd be able to," and supports her current desire to stay home with the kids. She says his new business of chopping hay and other crops for area farmers is off to a good start.

As we talk, Colin and Bridgette ask Shelly lots of questions, bring her toys and other objects, knock over drinking glasses, fight, cry—they are lovely and sweet children, but they are toddlers and I wonder how Shelly handles even this amount of stress.

I ask why she left the barn when Peter dehorned my calves.

"I have a hard time attending something when I know it's going to inflict pain—unless I'm doing it myself," she says. "I'm not going to put down my husband's technique, but when I dehorned at Lawnel, we put the calves in a head-lock and numbed them with Novocain, and they didn't move at all."

. . .

At 6:00 P.M. at Lawnel, lame cows enter the milking parlor. Lameness is so common among dairy animals that there is a special place, called the "lame pack," for cows who have trouble walking. The lame pack is a well-bedded area located near the parlor so that the cows housed there have to walk just a short distance to be milked. To further reduce their walking, lame cows are milked just twice daily rather than three times.

Joe Krenzer herds the group in. Joe, fifty-five, is stocky, with a full head of gray-ing hair. He came to Lawnel just eight months ago after working many years at a sawmill. After three days of training he was made a herder, which means he moves cows back and forth from barn to parlor, and helps with other chores. Joe is good company; at the slightest quip, he breaks into a huge grin and laughs.

About a dozen animals rouse themselves to begin a slow, labored parade. Many are matted on their sides with mud and straw from lying so long. One, nearly all white except for the mud, takes the lead. Her head bobs up and down as she hobbles toward the parlor. A very large cow behind her takes tiny steps, seemingly hesitant to put weight on any foot. A third cow walks with the toes on her back hooves spread far apart.

"C'mon, let's go," calls Joe. A cow stops for a drink at a water trough. Joe gives her a minute, then urges, "Hurry up, c'mon."

"She got a pinched nerve," says Joe of the cow who just drank. "I don't think she's gonna get better."

Of another cow, he says, "She's only got two tits, not producing much milk."

It is poignant to see Joe herd these tottering animals because he himself walks with a noticeable limp, swaying from side to side as he moves.

Many cases of bovine lameness involve inflammation or injury to the hoof or the skin between the hooves. Hind feet tend to be affected more often than front feet. Other afflictions include swollen knees and joints.

Experts attribute some of the problem to genetic manipulation designed to increase milk yield by producing larger udders. "It is impossible to escape the conclusion," writes the British veterinarian John Webster in *Understanding the Dairy Cow,* "that the abnormally large udder of the modern dairy cow has distorted the posture and gait of her hind limbs in such a way as to predispose to foot damage." Inspection of cull cows at slaughter, he reports, shows nearly every animal affected by some form of foot damage.

Other factors that contribute to lameness include living on concrete floors, which tends to affect the sole of the foot, and eating too rich a diet. Dietary lameness, called laminitis, usually results from excess intake of starchy, concentrated foods, which, though they can help increase milk yield, can also create too much lactic acid in the bloodstream and soften foot tissues.

Regular hoof trimming, careful attention to rations, and even foot baths are among the ways dairy farmers try to prevent or cure lameness. Lawnel, for example, employs a hoof trimmer who comes to the farm two mornings every week.

The lame cows move into the parlor, the first taking their places in the milking stalls. I point out to the milker one cow with an uncut tail, and ask his opinion on tail-docking. Is it really necessary to protect milkers from having manure flung at them?

"Yeah, those tails can swat you right in the face, even behind your eyeglasses," he says, "and that can really burn.

"On the other hand," he continues, "it's cruel to cut the tails 'cause the cows need 'em to swat flies, but we ain't got many flies around here anyway."

The milking done, the crippled cows begin their slow trek back to the lame pack. The cow with just two teats is last out of the parlor. She rests between steps, holding her head close to the ground.

.   .   .

At 9:30 P.M., just a touch of natural light remains as 4923, the mother of my calves, and the rest of the hundred or so cows in her group head toward the parlor for their third milking of the day. They had first been milked at around 6:00 A.M.

Lawnel is quiet now, empty of people except the two-man night milking crew. Night milkers can be a weak link in the milking chain. Morning and afternoon milkers tend to be middle-aged men and women with families, but the people Sue Smith is able to hire for the night crew are mostly young men with little experience, willing to milk cows only until something better comes along.

That few of the daytime Lawnel employees ever even see the night milkers only adds to their mystery and the tales told of them. The afternoon milker, for example, swears one of the night milkers once told someone milk was blue inside a cow and only turned white when it hit the air. Night milkers also make handy scapegoats when things go wrong. Any cow mistreatment is often attributed— with or without evidence—to the night guys.

On duty tonight are B.J. and Dave, both in their early twenties. Dave milks while B.J. herds cows into the parlor.

B.J., twenty-two, practices rodeo riding during the day, something he would like to do professionally when he "figures out his life." Though he's been at Lawnel only four months, he easily herds and whistles the groups of cows toward the parlor. By the time the cows reach the holding ramp, 4923 is in the middle of a very tight pack. The scene reminds me of a crush of cars trying to exit a thruway at night through just two open toll gates.

A large halogen light over the ramp bathes the jammed-up cows in a dull gray light.

"Let's go, let's go, get up!" calls Dave, standing at the entrance to the parlor. A red and blue Budweiser Beer scarf on his head covers most of his long blond hair, but not the scruffy mustache and beard. He wears jeans and a sleeveless blue sweat-shirt without coveralls.

4923 enters the fourth stall on the right side of the parlor. She stands with her head low, almost touching the floor. Crouching beside her, I note that her head is about as large as the entire upper part of my body.

Dave sprays and wipes her teats, then hooks her up to the milking machine.

The parlor feels different at night, more industrial. Maybe it's the contrast between the utter pitch blackness outside and the bright fluorescent lights within. The lights make the steel milking machine shine. In the quiet of the night, one better hears the hissing of the air-pressure hoses and vacuum pumps. The country music playing on the radio seems louder, too.

After five minutes or so, the milking units begin to detach automatically from the udders of the cows on her right and left, but 4923's milk continues to flow. This may be another hundred-pound day for her. After seven minutes, she's done. Dave sprays her teats. The exit bar rises.

As I watch 4923 and the rest of the group head back to the barn, I thank Dave for letting me watch the milking and say good night.

"Hey," he says, "you want to come with me to check for fresh cows?"

One of the night milkers' jobs is to check the maternity barns at one of the Lawnel farms down the road a few times during the night, to see if any cows have calved or need help. In fact, when I made my first middle-of-the-night drive to York to watch calves being born, it was a night milker who sounded the false alarm.

Dave says once in a while he does find a freshening cow who needs help. "I've called Sue and Andrew a couple of times at two or three A.M.," he says, "but sometimes we just wake up one of the other milkers to come." He says this with a laugh, suggesting the night milkers see the day crew as easy marks, people they can rouse from bed so they don't have to disturb the bosses.

I get in Dave's truck to drive with him to the Hanna Farm. It's nearly midnight and the ride takes only a couple of minutes.

There are about twenty-five pregnant cows in the maternity barn. We get out of the truck and walk among them. Dave shines a flashlight on the straw bedding, looking for newborns. We find two. He lifts their legs to see if they are bulls or heifers, and says the cow's number out loud to help remember it until we get back to the parlor, where he'll record it on his nightly report. Then we drive back to the road, toward an open pasture behind the Hanna Farm, and get out to have a look at a dozen or so cows lying there.

"This is an electric fence," cautions Dave. "You'll wanna duck."

I tell him to go ahead; I'll watch from the road.

Dave crouches under the fence and walks into the pasture, shining the flashlight on the grass ahead of him.

"I've got one," he calls back softly. The quiet, almost maternal tenderness of his tone, surprises me.

In the narrow beam from his flashlight, I can see a newborn calf lying on the ground, its mother standing beside it. Dave lifts the leg. He says quietly, "It's a boy."

•   •   •

Across the street from my office in Rochester is a strip mall anchored at one end by a supermarket. I stop in at the end of the workday and locate the refrigerated dairy case in the back. Cottage cheese occupies about ten feet of shelf space, between fluid milk and yogurt. The Friendship products are stacked three high on a shelf at eye level. Their plastic containers, each showing a stenciled white dove in flight, all contain one pound of cottage cheese. None of the packages says "small curd"—the kind my mom used to mix in with the elbow macaroni for my "comfort" food—but by process of elimination I figure the one called "California style" must be the small curd.

In the express lane, a high school girl rings up my purchase for $1.99.

Back at the office, seated at my desk, I remove the container's plastic lid and peel back the foil inner liner. I guessed right; it's small curd. A new container of cottage cheese, like a fresh jar of peanut butter, offers an irresistibly smooth surface. I dip in with a plastic spoon, and taste. It's exactly right; these creamy white curds taste like another day off from school, a sore throat still on the mend.

And yet, after all my time in the milk parlor, is there nothing new in this container? I dip my spoon in again. It's now 6:00 P.M.; I can imagine, at Lawnel, Joe Krenzer moving the lame cows up the holding ramp into the milking parlor; later, 4923 will come in for milking. The night milkers will activate the crowd gate and move her up the holding ramp and into the parlor, nearly her three-thousandth trip.

I can't exactly taste these things in the cottage cheese, but now I know they're in there.

5

Pasture

IT IS FOR JUST A FEW MINUTES, not more, that I stand in the long, verdant pasture to the side of Peter and Shelly Vonglis's house late on a sunny afternoon in June and intently watch the wrong calf. This is the first time I've seen my bull calf on pasture, so I'm not used to spotting him from a distance. It is some comfort later to read that naturalist Dian Fossey, in her initial visit to Africa to watch mountain gorillas, spent her first hour in the field with her binoculars trained on what turned out to be a log.

But soon I correct my error and pick out my calf from among the two dozen cattle grazing. I recognize the distinctive marking of white hair on his face: an upside-down triangle on the forehead tapering and connecting to an upright triangle on the bridge of his nose. My calf and his twin sister walk in the rear of this small herd as it moves slowly across the field.

Peter Vonglis has put my calves in the pasture along with a group of older heifer calves. After a few months of grazing, he'll move the heifers back to a dairy farm owned by his friend and employer, Scot Batzing, where they'll be bred and then become milk cows.

It is a lovely thing to see cows on pasture, especially Holsteins, whose black-and-white bodies stand out so sharply against the green of the field and the blue sky. My calf's hair has lost the brown tint it developed at around two months of age; now, at seven months, he is vividly black and white.

These calves move slowly and as a group, walking, standing to eat grass, lying down in the sun or the shade of a tree. Studies show that cattle on pasture spend between five and eight hours a day grazing—eating grass and other plants—and another two hours walking. There are two major grazing periods, one just after sunrise and the other—like this one—during late afternoon until sunset; between, they rest.

My calf is smaller than the older heifers, but already stands chest-high to me and weighs, I'd guess, nearly six hundred pounds. It is both arresting and calming to watch animals of such mass stand still and silent. To watch them move, when they do, almost as if in slow motion, mesmerizes. I imagine God playing chess, silently pondering the board, then slowly and deliberately moving one black-and-white piece, then another.

Perhaps this pasture is my calf's reward for enduring the cold and isolation in the hay-bale hutch last winter, and then the snow and wind in the running shed, to which the bull calf I'd bought as a backup succumbed.

To get a photo of my calf, I sit in the pasture, too. My coveralls protect me from dung and thorns. I lay an apple on the ground to entice him closer. Since he retreated inside the hay-bale hutch last winter, he has been skittish and won't come close. The nearest he'll let me approach without fleeing—his "flight distance"—is about four feet.

The apple, bright red against the grass, seems to intrigue my calf. He approaches within a few feet and lowers his head to sniff, but as I raise the camera, he turns and walks away.

I didn't know it then, but this would be the last day I'd see him on pasture.

.   .   .

It's a hot, sunny July day, in a long string of such days; for weeks, western New York—indeed, the whole Northeast and Atlantic coast—has had little rain. TV meteorologists are beginning to call it a drought.

But inside the cab of Peter Vonglis's new harvester—he calls it a "chopper"—it's pleasantly cool. "You wouldn't want to be in this chopper without air conditioning," Peter exclaims. "These windows let in all the sun, and you can't open them." The cab's front windows extend from floor to ceiling, framing forty acres of alfalfa.

Since weaning my calves at about ten weeks, Peter's fed them chopped alfalfa and corn—a standard diet for dairy bulls being raised for beef. He brings most of the feed home from the Batzing Farm, where he works as field and crop manager. This being the growing season, I decide to visit the Batzing Farm and hitch a ride with Peter on his chopper to see where my calves' food comes from.

Peter and Scot lease the chopper not only for use on the Batzing Farm, but also in the "custom chopping" business they've formed to harvest crops for other farmers. Their business card includes an inch-high black-and-white photo of the German-made Claas harvester: engine in the back and cab in the front over front tires nearly six feet tall. A chopper like this can swallow a whole plant—top to bottom and all the stem in between—and in a fraction of a second reduce it to pieces about the size of your thumbnail.

Purchased rather than leased, the chopper would cost about $250,000.

I mention to Peter that I rode recently on a similar chopper with Andrew Smith at Lawnel Farms.

"I know Andy just bought a New Holland chopper," he says. New Holland and Claas are competing farm equipment companies. "But this one's more expensive. It's better built. Got a Mercedes-Benz engine."

Peter's tendency to speak loudly and in short sentences serves him well when trying to be heard over the noise of the chopper's engine.

The chopper has onboard computer electronics and wall-mounted radio speakers. Peter, in work boots, jeans, short-sleeved shirt, farm cap, and sunglasses, sits comfortably on the gray cloth driver's seat.

This farm, set between Route 36 and the Genesee River, has been in the Batzing family for generations; in fact, the road it sits on is called Batzing Road. With about three hundred milking cows and eight employees, it's about one-third the size of Lawnel Farms. Like many dairy farms, including Lawnel, the Batzings grow as much of their own feed as they can.

Cows readily digest alfalfa, a nutritious legume, whether fed fresh, dried as hay, or preserved in a silo and fed in fermented form. As with a lawn, if you cut alfalfa, it grows back. Today Peter chops this season's third cutting of alfalfa. A fourth cutting, late in the summer, would be typical, but this year that may depend on rainfall. Chopping is actually the third step in harvesting alfalfa. First it must be mowed, or cut, and then mechanically raked into long piles called windrows. Now the piled cuttings are ready to be chopped into smaller pieces and removed from the field.

The length of the cut is important, as it can affect cows' productivity and health: too short and cows can become ill; too long and they'll expend their energy digesting food rather than making milk.

As a prey species and a vegetarian, the cow has evolved to ingest quickly a huge quantity of plants on pasture and then slowly digest them later, out of the way of predators.

To do this, the cow has developed a four-part stomach. The first part, the reticulum, is where food goes after it's eaten. Later the cow regurgitates the food, chews it again—this is called ruminating or "chewing the cud"—mixes it with saliva, and reswallows it back into the second part of the stomach, the rumen.

The rumen, a hollow chamber that can hold forty to sixty gallons of food at a temperature above 100 degrees, acts as a fermentation chamber.

"When you left the farm today, you thought you were feeding cows," explained a veterinarian who taught my Herdsperson Training class. "But what were you really feeding? The rumen—that fifty-gallon can filled with bugs, juice, and feed. The rumen," he continued, reducing a cow to the largest part of its stomach, "ingests feed and produces milk and meat."

The mechanics of the rumen is what makes the size of alfalfa and other food particles so important. If you decrease fiber by chopping the plant too small, fiber-digesting bacteria will decline and other types of bacteria, such as starch-digesters, will increase. Too many of these, in turn, can cause lactic acid to enter the blood-stream and soften foot tissue, causing the cow not only to produce less milk, but also to become lame.

Peter has set the chopper at 17 millimeters; each piece of alfalfa will be cut to about three-quarters of an inch, within the range recommended by most animal nutritionists.

From the rumen, food moves into the third part of the stomach, called the omasum, where water is removed, and finally into the fourth part, the abomasum—sometimes called the "true stomach" because it works like our own—where secreted enzymes further break down particles.

We're moving along at about nine miles an hour, which sounds slow but seems a lot faster when you're riding fifteen feet off the ground on top of a powerful diesel engine. Immediately to our right, a dump truck, a ten-wheeler, keeps pace. The chopper blows a torrent of green bits through a long chute into the open back of the truck; though the truck can hold ten tons of chopped alfalfa, it fills quickly. From the chopper's cab, Peter can see when the dump truck is filled better than its driver can.

"Head on back, Dave," Peter calls on a CB radio to the driver. The truck turns back toward the Batzing Farm and another moves up to take its place. To lease this chopper, Peter and Scot pay one hundred dollars per running hour, so it's cheaper to keep several trucks running alongside in rotation than to idle the chopper and wait for a single truck to empty its load and return to the field.

Peter radios the driver of the next truck to turn left at the end of the field, and as the two vehicles make a synchronized turn, Peter electronically swivels the chute forward and then back so the blizzard of green bits of alfalfa continues to fall into the truck's open back.

I ask Peter whether he'll bring any of today's alfalfa harvest back to his farm to feed my calves.

"When were your calves born?" he asks.

Thanksgiving week last year, I remind him. They're just under eight months old.

"Then they won't get any of this feed," he says. "I'm switching 'em to shell corn and pellets as soon as I get a chance."

Shell corn is whole kernels of corn without any green matter mixed in; pellets are a manufactured feed supplement that includes minerals, vitamins, and often an antibiotic that acts as a growth enhancer. Together they make a high-fat, high-protein "finishing" diet aimed at maximizing weight gain before slaughter. A large commercial feedlot, or a small, private feedlot—essentially what Peter operates on his farm—will typically start finishing calves at six to eight months of age so they reach a slaughter weight of about 1,200 pounds at around sixteen months.

A mechanical counter next to Peter's seat indicates he's filled twenty-three truckloads so far in this one field. It's about four in the afternoon, and this is the third field he's chopped since early this morning. Hour after hour he drives the chopper in a straight row, keeps an eye out for stray items in the field, and keeps the chute aimed at the dump truck.

What does he think about while chopping?

"I daydream about the farm, the kids," he says. "I also listen to the chopper, because I can tell by the sound if everything's all right."

How's Shelly doing?

"She's fine. Starts nursing classes next week."

How'd the golf tournament go?

"Good turnout this year. We had 111 golfers and raised over two thousand dollars."

Each year Peter's family sponsors a golf tournament in memory of his older brother, Mike, who died of cancer several years ago. They give the money to local charities.

Suddenly there's a "beep-beep" and the chopper's engine stops. The dump truck next to us idles. The chopper's metal detector has shut down the engine. Its purpose is not only to protect the chopper, but also to keep bits of stray metal out of the feed. "Sometimes it gives a false reading," says Peter, restarting the engine.

Stray metal—nails, fence wire, gear shavings—is hazardous to dairy cows. Ingested with feed or licked up off the barn floor, it can seriously injure an animal's internal organs. To prevent this, farmers give their cows magnets.

At Lawnel, for example, all heifers have magnets inserted into the reticulum, the first stomach, at about six months of age. The magnets, cigar-shaped and about three and a half inches long, are heavy and powerful: I once laid two next to each other and had a hard time pulling them apart. The farmer inserts the magnet down the cow's throat with a metal plunger, called a "balling gun." The magnet rests in the bottom of the reticulum where it grabs any stray metal, preventing it from moving farther through the digestive tract.

I once asked a farmer what happens to the magnets when dairy cows are slaughtered. He said he wasn't sure, but had always suspected that slaughterhouse workers cleaned up the good ones—those that were not heavily corroded—and resold them to dairy farms.

Peter and I are about halfway through chopping the alfalfa field when Peter reveals his news: Scot has invited him to become a partner in the Batzing Farm. Scot's father is ill with cancer, and Scot is buying out his share. He's proposed giving Peter a small percentage in exchange for work already done, and gradually increasing Peter's share in exchange for continued work. Moreover, none of Scot's three daughters—all in their teens and early twenties—has shown an interest in the farm. "So when Scot retires, I could have a buyout and end up owning the whole farm," says Peter.

Peter and Scot, who is in his early forties, have known each other for fifteen years.

This is an enormous development for Peter. His father worked for a machine-tool company in Rochester and then, before he retired, for the state conservation agency. His mother worked as a waitress. Peter, the youngest of ten children, would become only the second family member to own his own business; one sister owns a frame shop.

"I've dreamed about it all my life," he says.

When I note that Shelly must be excited about the news, Peter says he's not so sure. "She's afraid I'm going to have to work too hard and have trouble finding good help. She says, 'You'll never find anyone like you'—she means anyone who works as hard as me.

"Shelly thinks I'm a workaholic. She doesn't understand why I stay until a job is done and do it right every time, even if no one's watching. Shel wasn't raised that way. She milked cows, that's all. Milkers milk their shift and leave.

"I'm not a lazy person, and I don't like lazy people. I make sure I stay at a job as long as I need to, to get it done."

.   .   .

It's nearly dinnertime when I arrive at the Vonglis farm. Shelly's in the kitchen, preparing to take the kids to McDonald's. We sit a moment at the dining room table. Bridgette pulls up a chair and draws me a picture of a cat. Billy shows me a scrapbook he's filled with pictures of farm equipment cut from magazines.

Shelly sends the kids to wash up. When they've gone, she confesses she's not thrilled about Scot's offer to make Peter a partner in the Batzing Farm. In fact, she doesn't like the idea much at all. She's concerned they'd have to live in one of the Batzing farmhouses, and she doesn't want to move again, "especially to a house I don't own." She also fears she'd feel compelled to help with the herd, abandoning the nursing career she's just about to start.

But mostly she's concerned for the kids.

"Unlike Peter," Shelly explains, "I grew up on a dairy farm, and I'm not sure I want that for my kids. Already I see Colin and Billy into tractors and stuff. If we move, they'll be drawn into working the farm—I know it. That's how it happens.

"Don't get me wrong," she says. "I liked my childhood on the farm, playing in the hayloft, in the barns, and being close to my grandparents.

"But farming's just not a wonderful way of life. It's a hard life. Chasing cows when they get out—like we chased yours when it got loose. Running a rope from the house to the barn so you can find your way there in a blizzard. Digging the barn door out of a snow drift. You work hard, there are injuries"—I think of Shelly's grandfather with both a hook arm and a prosthetic leg—"and you don't necessarily go to college or experience life off the farm. You don't become a millionaire."

.   .   .

Outdoors, to the side of the Vonglis driveway, my calves stand under a shade tree. With his tail, 8, the bull calf, switches flies from his rump, then, with a quiver of the muscles along his back, shakes more off his belly. He rubs his face against the neck of his sister, 7. Even in a herd of two dozen, these two often stay close.

Coming nearer, I notice that both of 8's eyes are tearing and half shut. He lowers his head and reaches it back toward his hind leg, then raises the leg as if to rub his face, but doesn't—he's too stiff or just can't make the stretch. His sister's eyes are tearing and a little cloudy, too.

It's pinkeye, says Shelly. Bacterial pinkeye (infectious bovine keratoconjunctivitis), I learn later, is a common ailment among cattle, especially young calves in the summer. It's transmitted from calf to calf mainly by flies feeding on eye discharges of infected animals. Left untreated, pinkeye can cause blindness.

Shelly says Peter usually treats pinkeye with an antibiotic powder that he puffs directly onto the eye. When he gets home this evening, she'll have him look at the calves. "He'll have to move them into the barn to treat them," she says, "but that's just as well because with pinkeye they're more comfortable out of the sun."

. . .

The following Thursday when I visit Lawnel, Sue Smith tells me that the previous Monday night a cow went "over the edge" in the milk parlor. The cow, 4482, was entering the first position on the left side of the parlor at around 3:00 A.M., when her left hind leg slipped off the platform and in toward the pit. The night milkers, unable to move her, called Sue and Andrew at home. They came to the farm, and Andrew, using a board, managed to push the cow back up onto the milking platform. The cow "kind of crawled out of the parlor on all fours," says Sue, but she must have hurt or broken a hip, because as soon as she got back on concrete, "she split right out," meaning her back legs did a split. "I tried to hoist her with straps," Sue says, "but she's too big an animal. She's been a good cow. I was hoping she'd be okay."

"Downers"—cows that become unable to stand—are a regular problem for dairy farmers. Often the cause is weakness or nerve damage after a difficult calving, severe illness from diseases such as mastitis, or fractures to the pelvis or hind limbs—as is the case, apparently, with 4482. Often a farmer doesn't know why a cow has gone down, but regardless, it is important to get it up as soon as possible, because if a cow lies on a limb for more than a few hours, the limb's nerves and muscles can be further damaged by the animal's great weight.

Getting a down cow back up is no easy matter. Private companies offer a variety of solutions. You can float her up in a sort of portable mini-bathtub, or raise her with an inflatable lifting bag, or hoist her up with a harness and sling ("Get your animal up on its feet . . . FAST!" promises one maker of livestock slings.) Recently I'd seen a Lawnel farmhand tighten brackets around the protruding hipbones of an older, downed cow and hoist her with a forklift. The forklift carried her out of the barn, her hips eight feet in the air, her face and front hooves dragging on the ground behind.

I've also seen Sue try to raise a cow that wouldn't get up from its stall. She tried to coax it up with gentle words, then twisted its stump tail and yelled, "C'mon, get up, sweetie!" then jabbed her knee into the cow's side and, placing her mouth within inches of the cow's ear, screamed like an enraged drill sergeant: "Get up, you! Get up! Get up!" It didn't work. Neither did twisting the cow's ear, or jabbing it in the ribs a half-dozen times with an electric prod.

The cow that fell off the milking platform is on the sick pack, the area of the barn where downers and other ill cows are kept while they recover or wait to be removed. Eleven cows occupy the sick pack this morning; all lie quietly on the floor, which is thickly bedded with straw. Next to 4482 is a twelfth cow, 4490, but she's dead: her head, eyes open, is curled back against her side.

Sue is correct: 4482 is a huge animal—maybe one-third larger than a normal cow. She lies with her front legs folded under her chest, head up, eyes wide and slightly bulging.

A container truck pulls into Lawnel and parks just outside the barn. A heavyset man gets out. He looks to be in his late forties, has a double chin and maybe a couple days' growth of beard.

"Which one is she?" he asks, looking toward the sick pack. "Dead ahead?"

Bill Mest once owned a small dairy himself, but now operates Mest Bros., a custom slaughterhouse for downed cows. Fittingly, for someone in his line of work, he is dressed all in black: black boots, black jeans, black sweatshirt, black hat.

"What'll it take to get her up, a cattle prod?" he asks.

"She's not going to get up," says Andrew Smith, who has suddenly appeared in the barn. He'd been working in the machine shop, but must have seen Bill Mest arrive and come over to the barn to help. Andrew gets on a small tractor and backs it through the barn door while Bill ties a sling around 4482's front right hoof. When the sling is attached to the tractor, Andrew reverses direction, dragging the downed cow thirty or forty feet across the barn floor, her useless back feet spread wide, her left front hoof kind of paddling along to keep up.

"Damn, that's a big cow!" Bill says to Andrew, walking alongside the tractor. "What'd'ya have planted?"

"Oh, we got one hundred and fifty acres in corn," says Andrew, "'bout two hundred in—" and then I lose his voice in the noise of the tractor engine.

As she slides across the mud, manure, and straw of the barn floor, 4482 doesn't bellow, or even moo. The only change I see in her face is an increased bulging in the eyes.

When 4482 clears the barn's side door, Bill removes the sling from the cow's right front hoof. Five or six cows on the sick pack come over to the door and look at 4482 where she lies in the dirt.

"I'll reposition the truck," Bill says to Andrew.

"That other one," says Andrew, motioning to the dead cow on the sick pack, "you don't have to worry about."

"Dead and gone," says Bill.

"Now, how do you get a cow that weighs maybe sixteen hundred pounds into the truck?" asks Bill.

"Or out of the pit?" adds Andrew. "I put two-by-fours under her legs. Saving her the other night took around two hours."

"Oh my Lord," says Bill.

Andrew returns to the machine shop, and Bill pulls down the six-foot-high back panel of his truck. Another downed but still-alive Holstein cow lies inside. He lowers the outer edge of the heavy panel to the ground, so it becomes a steeply inclined ramp leading into the truck. Then he ties two heavy cloth straps, like handcuffs, around 4482's front hooves. From inside the truck, he activates a mechanical winch: a wheel turns and slowly pulls 4482 up the ramp by the front hooves until she's lying in the back of the truck with her nose to the rear of the other cow that's still alive.

As Bill prepares to close up the truck, 4482 pees. The urine puddles on the truck floor where she lies, then snakes down the loading ramp.

Bill is headed forty minutes west, to the town of Strykersville, where 4482 will likely be slaughtered by the end of the day. He says downed cows at the plant are euthanized before they are hoisted for slaughter. Federal inspectors, he says, condemn about one-third of the animals he brings in due to disease or injury, so their meat cannot be used for human consumption.

Later I asked Sue Smith if she'd ever considered euthanizing downed animals on the farm. She said they'd actually done it once, but the procedure was expensive. "Anyway," she said, "I couldn't do it myself. I couldn't bear to watch."

As quickly as he came, Bill Mest is gone. The other cows on the sick pack have resumed their positions, standing or lying on the thick bedding. That cow 4482 ever was here is evidenced only by a forty-foot smear of manure, mud, and straw running along the floor from the middle of the barn to the side door.

•   •   •

Later that day I stop back at the Vonglis farm to see how my calves are doing with pinkeye. It's breezy today and not so hot, but inside the barn it is stifling and stale. Number 8's left eye is half-shut, and in the right eye there's a cloudy spot. He looks thin and listless. As his sister, 7, walks by, he defecates, leaving feces on the side of her head and flank. Her left eye tears. When Peter gets home, I'll ask him to give the calves another treatment of antibiotics. Curiously, the infection seems not to have spread to the five black steers with whom my two calves share the barn.

But why are they all confined in the barn, and not on pasture with the heifers Peter is raising for Scot Batzing?

On the floor, yellowish corn kernels are visible in the small piles of dung. I suppose this means Peter has switched the calves to a "finishing" diet of shell corn.

My calf still won't let me pet him, and he won't eat from my hand, but today at least he's not running away. Maybe his flight distance with me has narrowed. I want to get to know him, and to do that, I feel I need to get close enough to touch him.

Taking advantage of his willingness to stand still, I shoot a roll of film, mostly close-ups of the white pattern on his forehead and the random markings on his sides. Through the lens, he appears without the usual context of barn and fellow animals, and what I notice is his hide. When he's dead, I could own this hide—put it up on the wall of my office, or drape it over the front seat of my car, or walk on it like a rug.

It's odd this thought has never occurred to me before, but since his birth seven months ago, I've been so focused on keeping up with his growth I haven't thought much about actually owning him, or what I'll do with him.

If I keep to my original plan—to observe him raised in the normal, commercial way, without interfering—I should have him slaughtered about six months from now. Lately, though, I'm not so sure. It's not that he's a pet; I haven't named him, and actually I've never petted him. And when I'm home and thinking of York, as I often do, my thoughts of calf number 8 are mostly fleeting. I'm more likely to think of the lame cows coming through the parlor at Lawnel, or of

Andrew and Sue up each morning at four-thirty, or of Shelly working hard to finish her courses so she can become a nurse.

Still, I rubbed orange chalk on his forehead when he was still wet from birth, and paid Lawnel for him. In effect, I plucked him off the transport to slaughter. I put my mark on him. And after observing him for so long, I'm starting to feel confused about whether I can continue to watch him without interfering, and about what I'll ultimately do with him.

Over by the house, Shelly, just home from nursing class, is trying to weed a flower bed, but Colin and Bridgette keep interrupting. I know she needs to leave soon to work the night shift—a new part-time job—at the hospital in Rochester, so I try to move the kids out of her way by playing with them on the swing set. I'm totally focused on their play, pushing Bridgette on the swing and catching Colin as he jumps from the slide, when Peter's pickup rolls down the driveway. He's been at the Batzing Farm since early morning.

Peter, who doesn't like people not working, has come home to find me pushing his kids on the swing set and chatting up his wife. I am working, of course, but I'm pretty sure it doesn't look that way to him. I wonder if what I see in his eyes is resentment, but I don't ask.

What I do ask is how the drought is affecting his crops. The federal government has just declared Livingston County—and thirty-three other New York counties—agricultural disaster areas.

Peter walks me out to the forty acres he has planted in corn behind the house, and unhusks a few ears. "These are half the size they should be," he says tersely. He says he's heard a rumor that Lawnel is buying corn, the implication being that Lawnel's own crop is so bad they don't have enough to feed their herd.

In the pasture beside the cornfield, the dozen or so heifers stand with heads lowered, ripping grass from the dry soil. They look lovely against the reddening sky. This may not be the richest pastureland, given the drought, but it's pleasant to see the heifers with space to roam. I want my calves to enjoy that, too, and ask Peter if he plans to put 7 and 8 back on pasture soon.

"No," he says, "I just switched 'em onto shell corn and pellets. That'll bulk 'em up. That's how you raise beef. If I put 'em out on pasture, they won't gain as much and it'll build muscle where you don't want it. It'll toughen the meat."

How much less weight would the calves gain if they were on pasture?

"How long are you planning to keep 'em before you butcher 'em?" he asks.

About six more months, I say, not mentioning a slow-growing uncertainty about that plan.

"Well, six months on pasture, I'd guess the exercise and what they eat would cost you about a hundred to a hundred and fifty pounds of gain."

Maybe we could put them on pasture for just a couple of weeks during this nice weather, I suggest, and then put them back in the barn later.

Even as I say this, I can hear myself deviating from the original plan: to observe but not to interfere. Still, I want the calves to enjoy the pasture and the good weather. What else have they got? The barn is dark and often muddy, and though bigger than a pen, it still seems a small space for seven large animals.

"Oh, go ahead and put them on pasture," I tell Peter, assuming it is a request he'll honor. "Let's do it for a few weeks, anyway. We can always put them back in the barn later."

Peter says he'll take care of it in the morning, and I leave the farm, relieved that my calves will again enjoy the pasture.

．　．　．

Alfalfa and corn are the main crops that dairy farmers in Livingston County grow, but some farms, Lawnel among them, also grow wheat. They sell the grain as a cash crop and keep the straw to bed the cows. At current prices, it actually costs Lawnel more to grow the wheat than they get for selling it, but it's still cheaper than buying straw.

Andrew Smith is combining wheat today, and I'm along for the ride. The cab seats just one, so I sit on a metal platform outside the cab, in front of a red fire extinguisher and a sign that says DANGER—NEVER ALLOW RIDERS ON THIS MACHINE. I climbed up a narrow four-step ladder to get here; if I fall, I get mangled.

"Any bumps likely I should know about?" I ask.

Andrew says it's usually a pretty smooth ride.

We talk through the open door of the cab.

The combine is about twenty-five feet long and rides on two front tires that are at least my own height and two back ones about four feet tall. The power of the engine feels like that of an airliner taking off. We're moving at only three miles an hour, but, as on Peter Vonglis's chopper, when you're seated high off the ground with so much power under you, it seems faster.

This is a big piece of equipment, but Andrew Smith is a big man. Seated in the cab at the combine's controls, he fits the machinery: thick, broad-chested, muscular as he must have been when he wrestled in high school; black T-shirt and jeans; sunglasses across his ruddy, round face, full mustache, shaggy brown hair.

With a little bit of concern for my own safety, I ask Andrew if anyone else has ridden on the combine with him.

His kids did when they were little, he says.

"Amos and Kirsty used to ride with me in the cab doing their ABCs and one-two-threes. Amos'd sit right there next to the clutch, near the front window, and Kirsty would sit near the gear shift."

The wheat planted in this field is a soft-kerneled pastry wheat used for making cakes and other baked goods. Bread wheat has a hard kernel.

When the wheat is ready to harvest, Andrew has little control over his schedule. Yesterday he began harvesting at 4:30 A.M., went until ten at night, ate an ice cream bar, and went to bed. A phone call woke him at 11:30 P.M.—the new night milker left a gate open and the cows got loose. Andrew rounded up the cows in a field behind the barn, then went back to bed. He was up again at four-thirty this morning, and has been going all day.

The machine is called a combine because it combines several functions: it cuts the wheat stalks—which are about three feet tall—threshes them (knocks the grains off the heads), and then windrows them (deposits the chaff and straw in a narrow row on the ground). It drops the seeds in a bin behind the cab, and later pushes them through a chute into a dump truck. The windrows of chaff and straw will later be rolled up by another machine into enormous round bales.

Like a hungry cow on pasture that gathers up grass with its tongue and cuts it across its lower front teeth, the combine gathers sixteen-foot swaths of wheat, bends the stalks toward the center, and cuts them across a bar fitted with 125 razorlike blades.

"Do your neighbors know what we do here?" Andrew asks me. "There's a degree of ignorance about where their food comes from. There's negativity. Agriculture isn't a part of their lives."

He pauses.

"I don't think they understand the enormous amount of work it takes to produce the food—the hours, the knowledge."

He pauses again.

"Farmers have to know a lot, but if we go to a meeting we're considered stupid."

What kind of meeting?

"School meetings, you know, that's what they think."

Even in a farming community like York?

"Sure. Most people don't farm anymore. They've got jobs in the city or some-where."

That must be demoralizing, I offer.

"It doesn't demoralize me," he says. "It annoys me."

At around 5:00 P.M., Andrew pulls a sandwich wrapped in clear plastic from the floor under the combine's steering wheel. He studies the sandwich and then, unasked, announces its contents, half-shouting over the roar of the engine: "German bologna, muenster cheese, and jalapeño hot mustard on white bread."

His hands are black with grease from working on the combine.

I ask if he's going to wash his hands.

"Where am I gonna wash 'em? I just hold the sandwich with the plastic."

He takes a bite.

"Now, I guess that wouldn't be kosher—the bologna and cheese," he says. "You could eat a bologna sandwich and a cheese sandwich, but not bologna and cheese in the same sandwich. Is that right?"

"That's right," I say, "but even if you put them in two separate sandwiches, you can't eat both sandwiches at the same meal."

I'm surprised Andrew knows about the Jewish dietary laws. Later he tells me his roommate at Cornell was Jewish.

"What's the reason for that?" he asks, meaning separating the meat and cheese. "They end up in the same place."

If you need to explain something complicated simply and quickly, it helps if you're forced to do it over the roar of a combine's engine: "If you eat according to the rules, it makes eating special or sacred, instead of ordinary."

"I see," he says. "You keep these rules?"

I say generally I don't, although there are some foods prohibited by the dietary laws that I don't eat at all, such as pork.

Just then a phone in the cab rings. It's Sue. She'll stop in a few minutes to pick Andrew up on her way home for dinner.

Since Andrew's opened the door on matters spiritual, I ask him a question in return: Does harvesting wheat—in essence, making food—feel important and special, even when you do it day after day?

"It does," he says. "It is important and it is special, and I think about that—I don't think about it all the time, of course, maybe twenty percent of the time."

We're heading west now, away from the Genesee River. The sky above the wheatfield is brilliantly blue, and at just after 5:00 P.M., the sun remains well above the horizon.

•   •   •

We spot Sue in the family's sport utility vehicle, and Andrew stops the combine. Sue pulls up alongside us in the field. She has already changed out of her Lawnel work clothes, so except for Andrew's coveralls, which are flecked with wheat chaff and straw, Sue and Andrew could be any suburban couple heading home at the end of the day.

Alone in the field, I make my way over to a round bale of wheat straw. A thin netting of black plastic mesh holds it together. The bale is nearly five feet tall and weighs hundreds of pounds. I lean into it and push with my shoulder; as it moves a few inches on the stubbled field, it makes a loud crunching noise, like a giant snowball being rolled across the ground on a very cold day.

Once I grew wheat in my backyard in the suburbs. My wife and I wanted to show our kids where food comes from, so we ripped up a small plot of lawn and planted wheat seeds. The local paper ran a story about it, with a photo of our daughters, then eight and five, exploring "the tiny wheatfield behind their home." Late in the summer we cut the three-foot stalks with a scythe. They lay on the ground for a couple of days, and then one afternoon I gathered the stalks into sheaves and tied them around the middle with kite string to keep them together. There were six sheaves.

To further dry the wheat before threshing, I'd prepared a little space at the top of a covered wooden platform attached to the kids' swing set. I figured that would be a good place to keep the wheat safe from squirrels and birds.

As I bent to lift the first sheaf, I was struck with a powerful sense of having done this before, even though I hadn't. Then I realized the motion of bending and lifting the sheaf is the same motion as lifting a Torah scroll. A Torah scroll is similar in size and shape to a sheaf of wheat and, like a sheaf, is bound around the middle with a sash or belt.

The connection struck me as an epiphany, but I wasn't sure then what it meant, and I'm still not sure. Maybe the ancient Israelites, most of them farmers, would have seen the sacred scrolls as a symbol of a sheaf of wheat, itself a symbol of sustenance. Or maybe a sheaf, like scripture, contains some fundamental truth.

• • •

With a few breaks during war years, Livingston County residents have enjoyed a summer agricultural fair each year since 1793. In recent decades the fair has been held just up the road from York, in Caledonia, a town bearing the Latin name for Scotland and so reflecting the ancestry of many of the earliest settlers of this region.

"Ebrell's Exotics," the first exhibit I encounter at the fair this lovely August day, features a penned emu, miniature donkeys, and a Vietnamese potbellied pig. A white-haired woman who may be connected with the exhibit asks about my hat.

"'Ben and Jerry's,'" she reads aloud. "Whose dairy farm is that?"

My oldest daughter biked through Vermont this summer and got me the hat.

"They make ice cream in Vermont," I tell her.

"Oh, ice cream, is it?" she says. "Don't know either of them."

In a building marked WOMEN'S BARN there are dimly lit displays of vegetables, canned fruits, jam, quilts, and other crafts, many with prize ribbons laid beside them.

In the animal barns, cows, calves, pigs, and goats fill dozens of pens. The cows look remarkably clean, their coats gleaming. Then I see they have been shaved so that their hair is cut to just a fraction of an inch in length.

In one pen, a man swabs out his cow's ears.

Some of the young people exhibiting animals sleep overnight in the pens—they bring their own folding chairs and cots—so they can tend to their animals and also avoid the round-trips home during the four or five days of the fair.

Outside the barns, on the midway, is a man who for two dollars will guess your weight; there's also a Ferris wheel and an inflated plastic ship called *Titanic,* with a steeply angled deck that children climb up and then slide down.

This evening a "Bullriders Rodeo" will be held in the main arena, in front of the grandstand. The only evidence of it this afternoon, however, is a dozen beige Brahmin bulls lying quietly in a small corral, most with their eyes shut. A young man in a cowboy hat, sitting on a fence nearby, sees me eyeing the bulls. "You get in there with 'em, they won't be so gentle," he warns.

A man in a trailer sells ostrich burgers; THE BETTER RED MEAT, says a sign.

Nearby is an ice cream stand run by the New York Farm Bureau. Its sign says,

"We believe everyone who eats benefits from agriculture." Farm Bureau members volunteer to work in shifts during the fair, scooping ice cream. This afternoon the stand is staffed by Andrew and Sue Smith and their sixteen-year-old son, Amos.

While Sue talks with a woman customer, Andrew, in white Lawnel cap and sunglasses, discusses the drought with another man helping on this shift. Amos scoops vanilla ice cream into a tumbler, pours in milk, and turns on the shaker.

Earlier that afternoon at Lawnel, I'd noticed four ears of corn lying on a counter in the office. One, unhusked and shriveled, showed a few kernels at its end.

On a scale of one to ten, I ask Andrew, with ten being a disaster, how would he rate the drought in terms of its effect on Lawnel?

"I'd give it a seven," he says. He says the drought has already cost Lawnel $40,000 worth of feed they'll have to buy, "but we'll make it up on the price of milk." The base price recently has been twelve to thirteen dollars per hundred pounds, and he expects it to rise to between seventeen and eighteen dollars. "So it'll be a wash," he says.

I'm so used to seeing Sue Smith managing the Lawnel herd, moving 1,500-pound animals around, overseeing three shifts of more than a dozen employees, and directing the work of hoof trimmers, cattle haulers, and renderers, that it's curious to see her here, at the ice cream stand, deferring to her husband and son on how to make milkshakes and how many scoops go in each size cone. Sue seems content just leaning on the counter and chatting with customers—most of whom she appears to know by name.

After a while, Sue agrees to take a break and tour the animal barns with me.

We visit the pig and cow barns, but skip the chicken barn. When she was little, Sue says, she had to help a friend raise chickens, and ever since has had no interest in them.

In the goat barn, we stop at a pen with baby goats for sale. "Oh, they're so cute!" she gushes. "Look at their eyes! I'd love to have one—just to keep outside the house as a pet." Sue asks the goats' owner, "Can you bring them in the house?" The woman says you can. "Oh, my husband would never let me have one," says Sue. As we leave the barn, she gives the owner her first name and phone number and says to call when the goats are old enough to buy. "But I know my husband won't let me have one," she repeats.

Sue says she probably won't go to the rodeo tonight. "I don't care for it," she says with a slight grimace. "I think they put the bulls in those chutes just to get them upset."

Back at the ice cream stand, a slender young girl in a silver tiara, with a white sash across her blue dress, hands out "Got Milk?" stickers to passersby. She is Katie Clymo, the Livingston County Dairy Princess. Most rural counties in the state have a dairy princess. She is chosen in an annual competition to help promote consumption of dairy products at events such as store openings, school picnics, and fairs. A high school junior, Katie says she has a 97.8 grade-point average and wants to be a doctor.

Suddenly, I want my own kids to be here, to see the fair. The whole thing—the ice cream stand, the goats and cows and prize-winning vegetables—is straight out of *Charlotte's Web,* a book I've read lovingly to all three of them. My girls are fifteen and twelve. I want them to appreciate the simplicity and richness of rural life. My six-year-old son would love the animals and rides. I want my kids to be inspired by the young people who sleep overnight on cots in the pens with the animals they've brought to exhibit.

The only phone is way across the midway, in a trailer that serves as the fair office. When I explain to the woman at the desk why I want to have my wife and kids join me at the fair, she lets me make the long-distance call to Rochester. It's four-thirty on this spectacularly beautiful late-summer afternoon; if they leave right now, they could be here in plenty of time for dinner.

My wife answers, and I, a little too desperately, describe the wonders of the fair and ask if she'll put the kids in the van and join me. We can eat dinner on the midway. Oh, and there's an added bonus: the Smiths are here, and their son Amos, too! You can finally meet the people I've been writing about and talking about at dinner for the past year.

I can feel the woman at the desk listening, trying to figure out what I'm up to.

My wife says a friend just came over for a planned play-date with our son, and she and the other boy's mom are planning dinner together. Our girls are watching a movie they've rented; they've been active all day and need some down time. Maybe they could all come tomorrow or the next day, she says.

But the Smiths won't be here then.

My wife wishes I had let her know about the fair sooner, so they could have made some plans.

I wish it, too. But how could I have known how taken I'd be with the Livingston County Fair?

Frustrated, I walk back through the midway and over to the cattle-judging competition.

Under a small tent, a blond boy maybe five or six years old stands beside a tiny Holstein calf. The calf's little tail ends in a pretty tuft of white hair. The boy, in white shirt and short white pants, holds the calf's halter firmly against its cheek and leads it slowly around the tiny, sawdust-covered ring.

Two little girls in matching black-and-white cow-pattern dresses then parade their calves around the ring.

All the children wear "Got Milk?" stickers on their shirts.

The judge, a woman in her late teens or early twenties, must assess the animals for "strength, style, and balance." "Style" means an animal's overall appearance.

"You have to admire the angularity," she says of a two-year-old heifer. "Also, she's straight and strong over the top line."

Later, of an older calf, she observes, "This one's tight in the shoulder, and stronger over the chime." The "chime" is part of a cow's back just behind the shoulders. A third-place winner, she notes, "was sharpest and most angular, but doesn't have the style to place higher today."

Even from a bench in the first row, it's difficult to catch all the judge's words because of noise from the amusement rides nearby. The closest ride, the Scrambler, has giant teacups that spin with a loud mechanical whir. But just as the Scrambler interferes with the cattle show, I imagine the nearness of the cattle show must temper the fantasy of riding the Scrambler, grounding riders, as they whirl about, with recurring glimpses of their real lives.

As the judging continues, I try to imagine how 8, my bull calf at the Vonglis farm, would rate at a show like this. I'd have to shave him and clear up his pinkeye. Yet I haven't paid much attention to his overall appearance; I don't know if he's angular or strong over the chime, or whether he has much style.

"Hey, I didn't know you'd be here!"

Swiveling on the bench, I see Shelly Vonglis.

"Peter!" calls Bridgette, running to give me a hug.

It never occurred to me that the Vonglises would be here, but of course why wouldn't they? It's the county fair. Shelly and Peter and all their children are here, and so is Shelly's brother, her three sisters, and her parents.

Now I'm even more frustrated my family couldn't come.

Shelly and I chat quietly as the judge continues: "tightness through the shoulders" . . . "high, wide rear-udder attachment" . . . "lots of style and balance, I admire her angularity throughout."

Then the crowd gasps. People gather around a young girl. She's thirteen. Her cow stepped on her as she was leaving the ring. Emergency medical technicians come to treat her. Later, when I tell Sue Smith about the incident, she says she already heard about it because the Dairy Princess stopped by the Farm Bureau stand to buy the injured girl an ice cream cone.

Milking cows now parade around the ring. "Best udder even though dry . . . best front-end and best set of teats in class."

One of the last competitions, called "dam and daughter," has milk cows standing alongside their six-week-old calves. As I watch several mother-daughter pairs paraded around the ring, it strikes me that in all the time I've spent on dairy farms, I've never seen a mother and her calf together except for those first few minutes after birth, before the calf is taken away. To see them together seems both natural and odd.

When the cattle judging ends, I'm unsure whether to stay with Shelly and the Vonglis family or return to the ice cream stand with Sue and the Smith family. Since Shelly quit her job as calf manager at Lawnel Farms several years ago—one step ahead of being fired by Sue—the two haven't spoken. Shelly claims Sue allowed the animals to suffer; Sue says Shelly was inefficient and unreliable in caring for the herd. I've been up-front with both: Shelly knows I visit with Sue, and Sue knows I visit with Shelly—and occasionally each asks me about the other— but as far as meeting or speaking together, they don't.

Now they're both here at the fair. I feel as though I've been dating two women and they've both shown up at the same movie.

For many years I worked professionally as a mediator; maybe I can help make peace between them.

I tell Shelly that Sue and Andrew are at the ice cream stand, and offer to take her over to see them.

She says no thanks.

And Sue doesn't want to see Shelly. Earlier I'd asked her about Shelly's work at Lawnel. "That was a tough time in my life, that period with Shelly," she said. "I try to forgive and forget. Sometimes it's hard, though."

"Which one is hardest?" I asked.

"Both," said Sue.

• • •

The "Rawhide Rodeo Bullriding Blitz" begins at 8:00 P.M. The master of ceremonies, in cowboy hat, fringed vest, and wireless microphone headset, rides a pale horse back and forth in the main arena, welcoming a crowd of several hundred. He begins by saluting "our men and women in the armed forces" as a woman with long blond hair circles the ring on horseback, carrying a large American flag. We stand and remove farm caps, and two little boys—they may have been twins—sing "The Star-Spangled Banner." Now the MC prays: "God make us all worthy of going to heaven, and help us live according to His rules so that when we approach the Heavenly gates, we find we've already paid our entry fee. Amen."

I'm seated with Sue, Andrew, and Amos in the grandstand. Just after the show begins, Shelly and Peter Vonglis and their kids cross in front on the way to their seats; I can't tell whether they notice the Smiths and me or not.

This is the first time Sue's been to a rodeo, although in the 1970s, when she and Andrew were dating and mechanical-bull riding was the craze, they used to go to a bar near York, where Andrew and his friends would ride the bull.

What's the purpose for the hump on a Brahmin bull's back, Sue wonders. To hold water, like a camel's hump? To make it look fierce? She asks people seated nearby, but no one knows.

Sue and I try but can't quite see what is done to the bulls as they stand in the chutes with the riders on their backs, waiting to enter the ring. Do the leather cinches press against their genitals? Are they electrically prodded? Clearly something encourages these otherwise sleepy animals, when released from the chute, to buck wildly and race about.

Of the first ten riders, only two manage to stay on for the required eight seconds. Curiously, though, when the bulls are done, most head straight to the exit gate, as if they know exactly what their role is and when their gig is over.

Sue points out that the bulls look old, maybe fifteen years or older. I've never seen a dairy cow more than eight or nine years old; most don't make it past five. So, compared with the other possible lives these bulls might lead—and for most that would be the slaughterhouse at an early age—these old fellows don't seem to have it so bad: eight seconds in the ring, a ride to the next county fair, an afternoon snooze, and then another eight seconds. And they must be fed well to look so good in the ring: they're filled out, tight through the shoulders, strong over the chime, good angularity throughout. I admire their balance and style.

I'm beginning to enjoy the show.

A bull charges out of the chute and races toward the side of the arena, slamming his rider against the perimeter fence. Sue clutches my arm and hides her head behind my shoulder as the bull brings his back hooves down hard on the fallen rider. A man dressed as a clown runs toward the fence, waving his arms to distract the bull. The injured man crawls out of the ring through an opening under the fence, while from the far end of the field, an ambulance moves toward the ring.

Andrew recognizes the next rider as someone he wrestled against on the varsity team in high school. "He looks older than me, doesn't he?" he asks Sue. In fact, the rider does appear much older than Andrew.

"Looks like he's had a rough ride in life," Andrew says quietly.

The Smiths stay until a former Lawnel employee, B.J.—one of the night milkers I'd met just a few weeks earlier—has his turn to ride. Even though B.J. recently gave notice and left Lawnel, we all clap and cheer him on.

It's after 10:00 P.M. when the rodeo ends. I scan the crowd as the grandstand clears, but do not see Shelly or any of the Vonglis family; they must have left the fair earlier. All will be up early tomorrow for another day of work.

Across the midway, in the cattle, sheep, and goat barns, most of the youngsters have already bedded down next to their animals for the night.

*   *   *

A couple of weeks after the County Fair, I sit one afternoon in Peter Vonglis's barn. Just outside, on Route 36, trucks roar by. Some are loaded with corn—not chopped corn, but corn in husks—sweet corn, corn for people. A car carries a canoe and pulls a small trailer; it's the first of September—must be people heading home from summer vacation.

I don't understand why my calves are still in this barn. Peter told me he would move them back onto pasture. But no one's home now to ask, Peter's at work at the Batzing Farm and Shelly's at nursing school.

Number 8 is still tearing a bit from the left eye, and now there's a round, grayish patch of skin on his right cheek that I recognize as ringworm. Bovine ringworm is a skin disease caused by molds or fungi, and can be contagious to humans.

I've tried these past months to find something my bull calf will eat from my hand so I can get close enough to pet him. Apples, cauliflower, and broccoli haven't worked. On the recommendation of Ken Schaeffer, the artificial inseminator who bred 8's mother with semen from Bonanza, I've made what is called a "sweet feed," a mixture of rolled oats, granola, and molasses.

My calf approaches within a few feet to sniff at the green-lidded plastic container holding the sweet feed. He doesn't seem too interested, though, and when I move closer with the mix, he backs off. So much for sweet feed.

It's hot in this hundred-year-old barn, and dim. The dehorning iron sits enshrouded in cobwebs on a rafter, just where Peter left it four months ago after burning off my calves' horn buds.

A gray metal folding chair leans against a wall. I set it up just outside the far end of the barn, where a door opens onto a little exercise yard. At least it's sunny here; I can sit comfortably and watch the calves.

Mostly they don't do anything, but just huddle together with their backs to me around the corner of the barn near the plastic water tub. A green garden hose feeds the tub, refilling it continuously as the calves drink. There are seven in the herd: my two Holsteins and five smaller black steers. After twenty minutes they move to the yard. Number 8 keeps near the rear, perhaps more timid than the rest. This small area has been pretty much stripped of grass and other plants, and with so little rain there's not much new growth. Still, they stand in the sun and pull at the odd tuft of grass.

The black-and-white markings on 8's middle and back have never seemed distinctive to me, but today I see patterns: on the right side, a boy and a jumping dog silhouetted in black against white; on the left side, a man in a hat silhouetted in white against black.

Twenty minutes later the calves move back to the water tub. All seven just stand at the tub, facing in the same direction, crowded together, hooves black with mud. One of the black steers momentarily gets his front feet tangled in the hose. He untangles them, takes a quick drink, glances back at me.

There are bits of grass and weeds, and dung, and pieces of undigested corn on the dry ground around my chair; a few feathers, too. A fly crawls up over a clump of dung and then down the other side; a butterfly with orange wings flits by, half a foot above the ground.

From behind a foundation cinder block next to the barn door, a brown mouse the length of my finger pops up and chews a clump of dried straw.

As I leave the barn, my bull calf walks toward the folding metal chair. He nudges it, rubs his neck against it, and licks the back, legs, and seat.

. . .

Substantial rain has raised hopes that the drought is easing. For several days now, Peter's been chopping corn on the Batzing Farm, and the yield, if not great, is acceptable.

He's invited me to ride on the chopper with him.

This is the same machine Peter used to cut alfalfa, but now fitted with a different cutting edge for corn. The chopper takes down six rows of corn at once. Peter's set the blades to 13 millimeters, smaller than the chop-size for alfalfa. A thick stream of green particles blows into the dump truck running alongside. It's not until you see corn plants six feet tall reduced to half-inch bits that you realize how much of a corn plant is plant and how little is corn.

This time Peter's got the radio on. We're chopping to "And the Beat Goes On"—Sonny and Cher.

Of nearly 61,000 acres in Livingston County planted in corn, 54,000 are feed corn—corn for cows, mostly; some for pigs and other animals. Only seven thousand acres are planted in sweet corn—corn for people. Peter explains how to tell the difference: feed corn tassels are darker than sweet corn tassels. He can drive along Route 36 at sixty miles an hour and instantly know which kind of corn is planted in a field. I've tried, but still can't tell the difference.

How's Shelly doing in nursing school?

Real well, says Peter. She's in her second week already.

I saw Shelly briefly a few days ago. She seemed busy and energized, a big change from just a few months ago.

And what's new with him and Scot and the partnership plans?

"Nothing will happen on that till the harvest is done," he says. "Probably not till December."

Our small talk's going nowhere. I might as well say what's on my mind; Peter certainly would.

"Why didn't you put my calves back on pasture?" I ask.

"I decided not to," he says bluntly. "Right after you left last time, I asked Shelly if she put you up to asking me to move 'em back, but she said no, it was your idea."

"It *was* my idea," I say. "Shelly had nothing to do with it. So why didn't you do it?"

"Because you told me originally 'no special treatment,' and you weren't going to interfere," he says. "If you put 'em on pasture, they're gonna exercise and not gain weight, like I told you. Look, if you're writing about raising a calf for beef, it should be in the barn. If you want to raise it organically or something, that would be a different book."

His tone is assertive, but not angry.

"I've got 'em in the barn now on shell corn and pellets," he continues. "That's a good finishing program. It'll bring 'em up fast to slaughter weight, and I'm gonna keep 'em on it till you eat 'em or whatever you're gonna do with 'em.

"What *are* you gonna do with 'em?" he asks.

"I'm still planning to have them slaughtered six months from now," I say. This still doesn't feel like the time to discuss my doubts about what to do with the calves.

As the chopper consumes row after row of corn, Peter and I both study the field in silence.

"I know people can get attached to animals," Peter says suddenly. "But you told me originally this is how you wanted me to raise 'em."

Apparently I'm easy to read.

"Have you ever gotten attached to a farm animal?" I ask.

"I haven't," he says quickly, but then tells me a story.

"There was this one bull calf—we named him Mikey 'cause he was born just a couple of days after my brother Michael died. He got to be a little like a pet, I guess. Bridgette used to ride around on his back like a horse.

"Anyway, we eventually sold him to a guy as a breeding bull to run with his heifers."

"If you still owned Mikey, would you be able to have him butchered and eat him?" I ask.

"Oh sure," Peter says. "No problem. I know what it's here for."

We've reached the end of the field. As we turn and start back in the other direction, Peter electronically swivels the chopper's chute to keep the torrent of green bits aimed toward the dump truck as it makes the turn next to us.

What's he going to do with the other five steers in the barn, the black ones?

Peter says those belong to the Batzing Farm. He's raising them for Scot. "Every year they offer their employees a side of beef. It's like a holiday gift," he says. "When each steer's ready, I take it to a custom butcher and then the employee can pick up a side when he's ready."

Suddenly the chopper stops. An automatic shut-off has kicked in. The cutting blades are poised six inches from the next row of corn. Peter climbs down from the cab to see what's wrong. It seems he ran the chopper too deeply into a furrow and bent the leading edge.

I also climb down and inspect the damage. Our conversation may have diverted Peter's attention. If so, I think it's the first time I've accompanied him on a farm chore where my presence distracted him to his detriment. Now he has to stop chopping, take the chopper back to the barn, and spend the afternoon repairing it. Whether deserved or not, I feel guilty. There's an awkward silence while Peter assesses the loss.

"Did our conversation distract you?" I ask.

"No, you didn't distract me," he says tersely.

Peter will drive to the machine shop at the Batzing Farm to fix the chopper, and finish harvesting the corn tomorrow.

. . .

Three silos, one blue and two silver, tower over the cow barns at Lawnel. During the second week of September, if you stand in the middle of the farm at dawn and face east, the sun will rise within the sliver of space between the two silver silos, as if they were constructed by Stonehenge astronomers to reckon the end of the growing season in western New York.

These silos, however, which for city dwellers tend to symbolize farm life, in fact hold a relatively small portion of a dairy farm's feed. Indeed, at Lawnel all three silos hold only one type of feed: shell corn—whole corn kernels.

Just across from the silos stands a commodity shed about the size of a two-car garage, open in both front and back. It has three bays, each of which holds a different feed component.

The first bay contains a protein mix, the second contains a cornmeal mix, and the third contains bagels.

I first saw the bagels when I visited Lawnel with Ken Schaeffer, the artificial inseminator. We mistook them for rolls, and Ken commented, "Hey, next time you order a hamburger, tell them to hold the bun—it's already in the meat!"

What makes the bagels difficult to recognize is that many dozens are crushed and flattened together, and covered with yellow and green mold. Only a few bagels retain their individual forms, which vary considerably: one, covered with white powder and round patches of green, is crushed flat like a slice of dried fruit; another is yellowed and puffy.

Even on this cool, overcast day, flies swarm over the bagels; a mouse peers at me from under one large, congealed clump, then disappears into hay bales stacked behind.

The bagel pile, when full, measures about five feet high, four wide, and maybe ten deep. If you took out all the seats from a family minivan, the bagels would just about fill the interior.

"They love bagels," says Lawnel feed manager Larry Wilkins. "They go right after it. Brings 'em right to the feed."

The bagels, which provide starch for the cows, are not store returns, but manufacturers' waste. Explains Larry, "Sometimes they may make a batch with too much dough, not uniform in size, baked too much or not enough."

On a previous visit, a stray wrapper in the bagel bay revealed the contents' origin: plain, presliced kosher bagels shipped from Weis Markets in Sudbury, Pennsylvania. Today, a wrapper fragment shows that the bagels are Lender's.

• • •

The commodity shed, like the silos, holds just a small portion of what the Lawnel cows eat. The main meal is found behind the shed in four huge mounds that rise over the farm like a landfill.

The mounds—each about twenty-five feet high, one hundred yards long, and twenty-five yards wide—offer a way to store large amounts of feed horizontally as opposed to silos, which store small amounts vertically. Lawnel maintains four mounds, two of alfalfa and two of corn. Each has a concrete floor and concrete walls separating one from another.

For several hours after being placed on the mound, the chopped corn or alfalfa—now called silage—continues to respire, often heating up to 100 degrees Fahrenheit. But as oxygen is depleted, bacteria acidifies the mass; the plant matter, in effect, gets pickled. Within about two weeks, fermentation stops and the silage becomes stable: an enormous outdoor storehouse of animal feed. When completed, the mound is covered with black plastic tarp held down with old tires; only a working face on one end is left exposed.

Standing in front of the uncovered, open end of a corn mound is like standing at the bottom of a river gorge, only here, rising before me to a height nearly four times my own, are not striations of shale rock, but layers of chopped corn. The color of each layer reflects the age of the crop: browns and tans of older cuttings near the bottom; dark greens toward the middle; bright greens—fresh, like a salad—of recent cuttings near the top; a rim of gray is visible at the surface, where exposure to air has caused some of the silage to rot.

I touch the face, expecting the bits of corn husk, stalk, and flattened yellow kernels to be soft and to give, but they do not. The face is compacted and hard; with a hammer, you couldn't do much more than chip at it.

As I watch, a farmhand drives a yellow front loader toward the mound. He's collecting ingredients to mix into this afternoon's feed. Dairy farms used to feed cows grain in the morning and hay in the afternoon, or vice versa, but today most farms feed a "total mix ration"—TMR, for short—all the ingredients mixed together in the same ration and fed at every meal.

As if cutting slices off a long loaf of bread, the front loader moves to the leading edge of the mound and cuts a half foot off the face. A mini-rockslide of silage falls to the concrete surface.

I touch the newly exposed face; it's warm, like your forehead with a fever, but cools quickly.

The driver then swivels the front loader around and dumps the shovelful of corn silage into the back of a feed truck. An auger—a large metal screw—inside the truck slowly turns, blending all the ingredients. Later he'll drive the truck down the center of each barn, laying feed along the aisles. When the Lawnel cows return from the milk parlor, their next meal will be waiting.

•   •   •

I've come to the Vonglis farm this late-September afternoon with a new enticement: beet tops. A textbook on dairy cattle science says that "beet tops and crowns are relished by cattle." That's what I've been searching for, something my calves will relish and eat from my hand.

I enter the barn, where all seven calves are standing around, with two large bunches of fresh beets, their leafy, green-purplish tops intact. Several of the calves, including 8, approach the fence. Through it, I offer my calf a leafy beet top. He reaches with his neck, sniffs, leans his head closer, then curls his tongue around the stem and yanks it from my hand. I offer another, and another. There's a slight crunch as he bites each firm stem before swallowing.

As he pulls at more leaves, he lets me stroke his neck. I stroke on the side without ringworm. This is the first time I've petted him since he was born at Lawnel, nearly a year ago.

His neck is firm and warm, and soft—like fur, not leather. It's handsome, too, even though the black hair is flecked with dirt and straw. Up close, I can see there's still some cloudiness in his dark eyes; both continue to tear. I'll probably never know if the pinkeye permanently damaged his sight.

After the fifth leaf, he briefly licks my jeans and barn boots, then backs away.

•   •   •

The calves move to the small yard outside the barn and gather near the fence facing the road. Rush-hour traffic, what there is of it, races by. Most of the yard has been picked clean of grass; two of the calves, sticking their heads through broken wires in the fence, reach with their tongues toward grass and weeds on the other side.

They move as a tiny herd, these seven calves, around the little yard. I see the five black ones now as holiday gifts, walking sides of beef, heading for the freezers of Batzing Farm employees.

The herd passes me without a look as it heads for the water trough. My heifer twin, 7, has circles of ringworm on her left cheek, above her nose and over her right eye.

A black calf stops, hunching slightly to urinate. Another lowers its head to drink the urine as it is expelled, the way you'd drink water from a hose. Urine drinking is an abnormal behavior in cattle. It's rare in cows, but more common in calves, particularly males reared in confinement. In his book *Understanding the Dairy Cow*, professor of animal husbandry John Webster says a calf drinks urine when it doesn't have "enough useful things to do with the mouth, which is not only the organ that eats but also the one that investigates."

All the calves' tails swish constantly; if I had one, I'd use it, too, to keep all these flies away.

The feed trough is empty. Peter feeds the herd just once a day now, usually in the evening when he gets home from work. On shell corn, 8 should gain nearly three pounds a day, up to a slaughter weight of around 1,200 pounds by early spring.

The patterns I'd imagined recently on my calf's sides are still there: a boy and a dog in black against white on the right side; a man in a hat in white against black on the left. As 8 bulks up, I suppose the images will gradually expand, like pictures on a balloon.

.   .   .

On an earlier visit, I'd shot a roll of film and later brought the photos home to show my wife. One of the pictures, a close-up of my bull calf taken straight on, shows the pattern of white hair on his forehead and down the bridge of his nose. I had always seen this pattern as two triangles: an upside-down triangle on top connecting to an upright triangle on the bottom. I pointed this out to my wife, with some pride in the keenness of my observation.

My wife looked at the photo and said, "It doesn't look like triangles to me, it looks like a chalice."

I looked at the photo again, and in an instant my focus shifted; the triangles disappeared and instead I saw on my bull calf's black forehead and nose a white goblet, a chalice.

A thousand years ago, Crusaders invaded the Holy Land searching for a particular chalice: the wine cup used by Jesus at the Last Supper, what medieval legends call the Holy Grail.

Sometimes I wonder, in following this calf so intently, exactly what grail I seek.

6

Kneeling in a Barnyard

As THE MORNING SUN RISES behind him, Andrew Smith power-washes a broken tractor. Clouds of mist swell over his stout silhouette. When it's working, the small tractor pulls a five-foot-wide truck tire—cut in half and laid on its side—through the aisles of the cow barns to scrape manure.

"Some guys last night ran it into a concrete wall," says Andrew, referring to the tractor. They busted the back tire and rim. "No one will 'fess up who did it," he says.

Finished spraying, Andrew starts up the engine. The tractor, hobbling like a lame cow on its way to the milk parlor, limps toward the machine shop. There, Andrew lies on a "creeper"—a dolly—and disappears under the back end of the tractor.

In a minute he rolls out again. His blue coveralls, previously wet with spray, now are also spotted with grease.

"I read a book last week," he says, looking up at me. "Probably only the fourth book I've read since college. I just don't read books much."

I don't recall ever discussing a book with Andrew.

"It's called *A Day No Pigs Would Die*," he says. "I can't remember who wrote it."

Andrew pronounces *A Day No Pigs Would Die* with the slow, exaggerated diction I've noticed he often uses when he's either very pleased or very angry, as when he's telling me something about his kids that he's obviously proud of, or when he's complaining about an employee. Maybe he's uncomfortable being open with those emotions, so he puts a little ironic twist on it. I think he is pleased, or even proud, to have read the book.

He says his wife, Sue, bought the book at the grocery store for their sixteen-year-old son, Amos. "But I figured Amos'll never read it, so I did," he says.

I ask Andrew to tell me about the book.

"There's this Shaker boy who grows up on a farm in New England—Vermont or New Hampshire—I forget exactly where," he begins. "Anyway, his dad's a pig butcher—that's what he does for a living, butchers all the pigs in the village. Well, a neighbor gives the boy a pig as a present for helping him with something, and the boy raises the pig like a pet. He feeds it and plays with it, you know, like a pet. Then the father gets sick and dies, and I forget exactly what happens, but at the end the boy has to take over his father's butchering work, and the first pig he's got to kill is his own, his pet."

I'm riveted.

Andrew continues, "I guess it's supposed to show that a boy grows up when he sees there's things in the world he's got to do, not just do the things he wants to do."

Is he telling me this because he knows I'm struggling with what to do with my calves?

"Sounds like an interesting book," I say.

"Pass me that ratchet wrench, will you?" he asks, motioning toward his workbench. I have no idea what a ratchet wrench is. He points to the one he wants, and I hand it to him.

I ask Andrew if he ever read *The Yearling,* by Marjorie Kinnan Rawlings. I read it at fifteen. It's about a boy in rural Florida and his pet deer. The deer starts eating the family's corn crop and so the boy has to kill it, symbolically ending his own childhood and becoming a man.

"No, never heard of that one," says Andrew, kneeling on the floor as he puzzles over a dent in the tractor's scraper attachment, "but this pig book's pretty good. You might like to read it."

. . .

It's 65 degrees this first day of November, a lovely Indian summer morning in western New York. Leaves cover all the lawns in York, and line the roads.

"Nice shades," I say to Peter Vonglis as I climb up the side of the green John Deere combine to join him in the cab. Peter turns aside the compliment. He says he only wears sunglasses because when he was twelve years old he accidentally burned the outer layer of his eyes with a welding torch.

"Ever since, my eyes hurt in bright sun," he says.

The acres before us on the Batzing Farm where Peter works hold the last of this season's corn crop. These plants, allowed to dry completely, stand brown and gray, so shrunken you can pretty well see between the rows. The hard, dry kernels they yield will be used as cattle feed.

The combine pulls down six rows of stalks at a time, pops off the ears, pushes the ears into a holding bin under the engine, then knocks the yellow-red kernels off and into a bin behind the cab. Stalks and husks blow out the back onto the field.

I ask Peter about the effects of the summer drought. "These ears are pretty good," he says. "The plants aren't as tall as last year and the yields aren't as high, but it could have been a lot worse."

In a really good year, he says, corn stalks can be "as tall as the cab on this machine"—which would be about twelve feet high. Today they're about half that size.

I ask how Shelly's doing at nursing school.

Peter says she's doing well. In fact, she was just elected president of her class. "The letter announcing the results is up on our refrigerator," he says.

"She may have found her calling," I offer.

"I hope so," he says.

How about his plans for becoming a partner in the Batzing Farm with his friend Scot?

Peter says he's met with a Farm Credit consultant, and that Scot will sign shares over to him either just before or after New Year's. He and Shelly will sell their house and move closer to Batzing's. "The farm's only ten miles from where we live now, but still that's a long way," he explains. He's heard that a house just down the road may soon be for sale.

A large brown rabbit hops away from us off to the side as the combine roars on.

"Shelly doesn't like the idea of moving," says Peter, "but she knows it's gotta happen. I'd like to do it before Bridgette starts school in a couple of years."

Does he think Billy and Colin will become farmers someday?

"They both love farming already," says Peter. "It's nothing I'd push on 'em— either you like farming or you don't."

As we continue to mow down rows of corn, there's a pause in the conversation. Peter takes over the questioning.

"So, have you decided what you're gonna do with your steers?" he asks. "You gonna send 'em through the auction, or you gonna slaughter 'em yourself?"

Peter's asking if I'll send them to the livestock auction in the nearby town of Pavilion, and let one of the large, national slaughterhouses buy them, or if I'll take them to one of the small, custom slaughterhouses near York that will butcher the animals and pack the meat for me to take home, sell, or give away.

But there's a third option: whether I'm going to slaughter the calves at all.

I've told Peter all along that my plan is simply to observe these animals without interfering as they go through the normal commercial process. But as they're getting closer to slaughter weight, I'm not so sure. I'm just not ready to decide whether to slaughter them and, if so, how. Fortunately, my calf is just eleven months old. Most cattle finished for beef are not slaughtered until sixteen months, so I've got time left to figure out what to do.

"Would any of the local places actually let me slaughter the steer myself?" I ask. "I mean, actually pull the trigger, or whatever?"

Peter doesn't know.

"Have you ever slaughtered an animal yourself?" I ask.

"No, I never slaughtered an animal," he says. "I've shot 'em—like I've shot a cow on the farm if it was dying."

He continues, "As a kid, I used to have rabbits, and I did kill them. Probably had a hundred and fifty, two hundred rabbits at a time. I had one guy buying 'em to feed his snakes. Other people'd buy 'em for other things. I used to give my grandmother one every year—to hear her, you'd swear to God I'd given her a million dollars. She loved gettin' those rabbits."

"How'd you kill the rabbits?" I ask.

"Club 'em behind the neck. Then skin 'em and cut 'em up."

There's a rifle lying over the rafters in Peter's barn I've always meant to ask him about. I ask about it now.

"Oh, that's a BB gun," he says. "I used it a couple of times to shoot pigeons in the running shed."

"Pull the lever there, right under your seat, will ya?" asks Peter. "Pull it slowly."

I reach to the side of my seat and grasp a metal handle. The lever has the feel and resistance of a car's emergency break. As I pull it forward slowly, a torrent of yellow kernels from the bin behind us pours through a chute into a dump truck running alongside. Thousands of delicate, dried hulls from the kernels—Peter calls them "bees' wings"—blow away behind us in a cloud of golden chaff.

· · ·

It's a cold, wet Veterans Day when I next visit at Peter and Shelly's. It rained yesterday and the barnyard—about half the size of the infield on a baseball diamond—is mud. My bull calf, 8, lies in the running shed next to his twin sister, 7. The five other black calves lie there, too. It's below freezing today; tonight it's supposed to drop into the low twenties.

I park my car at the end of the Vonglises' sloped driveway, take my barn boots from the trunk and begin pulling them on over my shoes, and then my bull calf—and he alone among all the calves—rises and walks quickly to the fence near me. Before I open the gate and enter the barnyard, I lean over the fence. He licks my gloved hand, the sleeve of my jacket, and then the bare spot on my wrist between the jacket sleeve and the glove.

His pinkeye seems finally to have cleared up, and I don't see any spots of ringworm on his face or head. He looks well, filled out and taller—his back is as high as my chest, and though he often stands with his head lowered, if he held it up, he'd be taller than I am. Though I still think of him as a calf, he's really become a large animal; if this were two years ago and I hadn't yet visited any farms and become familiar with cattle, I'd be afraid to get close to him, just for his size. The wound where Peter burned off his left horn bud last spring is still visible as a circle of pink, but the wound on the right side is mostly covered with black hair. His coat looks good—I think I've read that a corn diet will do that. It looks cleaner (other than mud on the legs and flanks) and brighter than it did in the summer.

Today I forgot to bring beet tops, but maybe he'd like some of the grass that grows outside the barnyard fence, just beyond his reach. If he can't be on pasture and is eating mostly dried corn, a little fresh grass may appeal. I pull up a couple of handfuls—the green blades are five or six inches long—and hold them out to him. He reaches across the fence, extends his thick tongue, and yanks the grass out of my hand, swallowing quickly. I pull up some more, and he devours that, too. A third and fourth handful follow. I don't need beet tops; he's ravenous for grass.

By the fifth handful, he's become calmer, and as I feed him with my right hand, he lets me stroke him under his neck with my left. This is the first time he's stood still to let me pet his neck. The skin is heavy and warm, and oddly loose; I can bunch it and kind of waggle it back and forth. He tolerates my petting him as long as I have grass to offer, so I hold on to the grass more tightly, forcing him to work harder to pull it from my grip.

The six other calves have gathered near us at the fence.

My calf coughs, and extends his tongue upward first into his left nostril and then his right, licking each.

I open the gate and enter the barnyard. Across the yard in the running shed is an orange metal wagon, about the size of a U-Haul trailer, covered with a silver tarp. That wasn't here the last time I visited. I walk over to the shed through mud so thick in some spots it sucks my boots down four to five inches. There's a ladder attached to one side of the wagon. I climb up and peer inside. The whole thing is filled with corn kernels, clearly the winter feed supply for the corn diet on which Peter is "finishing" the calves.

In a corner of the barnyard is a large, flat-topped rock. I sit on it to watch the calves, and soon mine comes over. I suppose he wants more grass, and I'd like to pet him some more, so I get up and go to the fence nearby. There's an electric wire that runs along here, so I have to be careful. I squat down, reach through an opening in the fence, and pull up a few handfuls of grass. Back on the rock, I take my gloves off. My calf eats the grass, then begins licking my bare right hand. As he does so, with my left hand I rub and scratch under his neck. Even though I have no more grass to offer, he lets me continue scratching, so much so that my left arm tires and I have to support it with my right.

He takes a few steps away, and I go back to the fence and carefully pull up more grass. This time I hold the grass stems tightly so he has to rip them from my hand with his tongue and lower teeth, the way he would on pasture. I like the sound and feel of his tugging and ripping, and imagine he does, too, though I can't be sure.

His dark eyes used to look blank to me, but they don't anymore.

The other calves have gathered in the middle of the barnyard. Most were watching as I petted 8. He leaves me now and joins them.

I rise from the rock and stand just off to the side of the group.

This whole barnyard is mud. Do the calves' hooves ever dry out?

A cold wind whips across the yard. It's sunny now, but there is no warmth in the sun.

I stand without moving to see if my calf or any of the others will approach me. After about ten minutes, 8 comes over. He licks the spiral metal wire on my notebook. I move to pet him, but he walks away, then pees. One of the black calves drinks his urine as it comes out. Peering underneath 8's rump from behind, I can see two pink male nipples among the white hair, each about a half-inch long. I assume hair hides two other nipples. With my notebook, I push his tail to one side, then grasp it lightly. I've never held a calf's tail; it feels like a girl's pony tail but with a strong muscle inside.

I'm freezing.

Has a person ever stood still in this barnyard—just stood as still as the calves do? I can't imagine Peter or even Shelly or their kids ever doing so. The people these animals see are always moving: opening fences, closing gates, filling feed troughs, changing straw bedding, emptying feed bags, herding the calves from place to place, catching them to insert ear tags, burn off horns, vaccinate, castrate. But has anyone ever come here and just stood still?

I stand for twenty minutes, twenty-five minutes; despite the cold, it's not that hard to do.

A few yards away, 8 reaches backward and licks five or six patches of hair near the top of his back. Licking against the grain, he makes the black hair stand up. Cowlicks are what he's made.

Standing in the middle of this barren barnyard, I have no grass to offer him. I wonder what would make him come over to me.

I've read that cattle are less afraid of people when they reduce their size by kneeling or lying down.

Has anyone ever knelt in this barnyard? Made himself small enough not to appear threatening to these animals?

I kneel. Cold mud soaks through the knees of my dark blue coveralls. But almost at once, 8 turns around and walks slowly toward me. With each step, mud oozes through the clefts of his hooves. When he's nearly on top of me, he lowers his head and licks my jeans, then the sleeve of my jacket.

Then he puts his head in front of mine and licks me under the chin.

His tongue is warm and rough, like my father's cheek when I was three and he would carry me, piggyback, up to bed. As he climbed the stairs I would lean forward over his shoulder and press my cheek against his, rough with a day's growth of beard.

In my room, there was a wooden floor and a single bed with a high wooden frame. I don't recall other furniture, not even a nightstand, although I suppose there must have been some. The room was cold, or seemed cold. My father would put me to bed and sing a lullaby, and then go back downstairs to join my mother and brother, who was a teenager, and my sister, who was ten. It wasn't so much frightening to be in that room as it was lonely—it felt as if the family downstairs was complete and content to carry on without me. I would call my father, and sometimes he would come back up and sing to me again. Once he brought up a small record player. He placed it on the floor in a corner of the room and put on a 78-rpm record of a man singing the same lullaby he sang to me, and then went back downstairs. But the record played for only a couple of minutes.

Last winter I thought of being alone in that room every time I came to the Vonglis farm and saw my calf, then just weeks old, tied inside the hay-bale hutch. I remember sensing—or imagining—how alone he must have felt in the cold and dark, as I had.

Some mornings when my father would leave for work, I would stand on a window seat overlooking the driveway. As he drove away, I would kick and pound on the window and cry for him to stay. Looking back, I think what I was trying to say was "Choose me!" But he had to go to work.

When I was four, my parents began building a house in the suburbs, and because there were many dogs in the new neighborhood, they decided to get a puppy so I could become accustomed to dogs before we moved. One Sunday morning my parents took me—just me—into the car and sat me on the front seat between them. I asked where we were going but, teasingly, they wouldn't say. Then a song, popular at the time, came on the radio: "Lollypop, lollypop, oh, lolly, lolly, lolly . . ." and they said the song was a clue. I guessed right away we were going to the local animal shelter, called "Lollypop Farm," to buy a dog. We looked at dogs that day but didn't buy one, yet I remember the day clearly as the only time in my early childhood when my parents did something alone with me.

Some time later, it might have been the next Sunday, our whole family drove out to the country, to a place where a man and his wife bred collies. A dog had just had a litter. All the puppies were tricolor—a little brown on the nose and maybe a paw, but otherwise their bodies were black and white. My parents let me pick out the one I wanted. I picked the one who seemed the shyest.

The dog vomited in the car on the way home, and my father cleaned it up. That night he put the dog in the basement with a ticking clock to keep it company. I remember lying in bed thinking how sad and afraid the puppy must feel at having been taken from his mother and siblings.

My parents said I could name the dog, and I named him Fella. By the time we moved later that year, Fella had become my closest friend, a companion close to my own size and glad for my company.

When I was eight, a man from the Humane Society came to a school assembly. He brought with him some farm animals—chickens and roosters, as I recall. At one point he let them out of their cages to fly around the auditorium. Many children tried to grab legs and wings as the birds flew low over the seats. I was relieved when the animals finally perched safely on exit signs over the doors. Then the man told us about some of the cruelty cases he had worked on: people whipping dogs, burning cats alive, starving their horses. When I got home I cried and told my mother what I'd seen and heard. She called the school to complain, but said the principal told her it appeared I was the only child out of hundreds in the second grade to have become upset.

With my chin still wet from where my calf has licked me, I reach up and put my hand and forearm under his huge head and feel its weight.

The wetness from the mud has seeped through my coveralls and into my jeans. It's cold, and time to go. As I stand, my calves and the others scatter toward the barn.

Nailed to the wall around the barn, like wainscoting, are plastic feed troughs—tubs, really. Their color—almost a neon blue—contrasts sharply with the straw-covered dirt floor and wooden wallboards. The troughs hold dried yellow corn kernels mixed with brown pellets; the ratio of kernels to pellets is about a hundred to one. My calf bends his head to the trough, like a dog eating from a food bowl, and licks at the hardened kernels. As he does, the kernels slide and bounce around against the plastic, making a clickety-clack sound, like hail against a window. The sound startles me, and I realize for the first time how unnatural a diet these animals are eating. Peter said he was feeding them corn, but it just didn't register with me that corn is *all* he's feeding them—corn plus those little pellets of minerals, vitamins, and an antibiotic growth enhancer. There's no hay, alfalfa, or other roughage, no plant material or grass. Just corn kernels that they lick from a plastic tub.

So this is what "corn-fed beef" means. But now I wonder: Is this a healthy diet? If my calf eats nothing but corn, how does that affect his rumen, which I know is designed to break down roughage? I never thought to ask Peter about this.

 . . .

"That's not a healthy diet for a ruminant," veterinarian Dave Hale says when I describe to him what my calves are eating. "It's just not designed to keep an animal alive for very long."

Over the past year, I've spent considerable time with Dr. Hale tromping through cow barns at Lawnel Farms on his regular weekly visits. Given our acquaintance, I didn't hesitate to call to ask his opinion.

A corn diet, explains Dr. Hale, can cause metabolic disorders and disease such as acidosis (increased lactic acid in the rumen, leading to lameness); bloat (increased gas that distends the paunch); and, most dangerous, liver abscess, a bacterial infection that can destroy the liver.

He asks how long my calves have been on corn. I think Peter started it in August, so that would be three months already. Dr. Hale says it's possible to take them off corn and "make them ruminants again."

I suggest I could put them back on pasture, but Dr. Hale says it's too late in the year to pasture animals. Instead, he suggests I feed the calves a small amount of hay and a total mix ration, the mixture of roughage and minerals commonly fed to dairy cows.

"You can feed a steer on total mix ration," he says. "It'll head you toward the finish line just like corn. It'll just take a little longer to get there." Finishing a steer on roughage used to be the standard, he says, and would get an animal to slaughter weight between eighteen months and two years. "Now, with corn and other high-concentrate feeds, we've pushed it to as little as thirteen months."

But even if I switch the calves back to roughage, says Dr. Hale, they already may be permanently damaged. "A liver abscess is only fatal if it ruptures, but if an animal's already started to form an abscess—which would be possible in a couple months of corn feeding—the damage can't be undone." He says there's no way of knowing if an abscess has started except possibly through an ultrasound.

"You can't undo the damage," he repeats. "The animals can go down at any time. Sometimes you'll see them, a day before slaughter, they just drop dead."

He continues, "A finishing diet like this is like a human eating just candy bars—you can live on it for a month or so, but eventually you're going to get sick."

I confide to Dr. Hale that I'm not yet sure what I'm going to do with my calves, if I'll slaughter them or not.

"In that case," he says, "I suggest a maintenance diet of grass hay with trace minerals added in a salt block. If you're not sure what you're going to do with them, it'll buy you some time."

       •   •   •

Images of my calves suddenly dying from liver abscess fill my thoughts after my talk with Dr. Hale. Perhaps the issue of what to do with them has become moot; it may already be too late to save them. I'm angry with myself for not having paid close enough attention to how Peter was going to finish the calves. He told me all along he'd feed them corn, but I never thought much about it.

Saying the calves would be fed a corn diet sounded harmless. How can corn be a bad thing?

I feel like a student who has failed to read far enough ahead in the textbook. In fact, the book I usually consult, *Dairy Cattle Science,* by M. E. Ensminger, doesn't cover finishing diets because dairy cows aren't put on finishing diets the way beef animals are. Before the day's out, I order by phone the 1,100-page illustrated companion volume, *Beef Cattle Science,* by M. E. Ensminger and R. C. Perry, for one hundred dollars from Interstate Publishers in Danville, Illinois. This book has a whole section on finishing diets. It says, "Several metabolic disorders, or diseases, in feed-lot cattle are attributable wholly or in part to the feeding regimen. Among the more prevalent ones are: acidosis, bloat, liver abscesses, and urinary calculi (kidney stones)"—Dr. Hale hadn't even mentioned kidney stones, which the book says are particularly common in castrated male cattle.

So yesterday my bull calf is licking me and I'm thinking maybe I'll save him, and today it seems the decision may be out of my control. Even if somehow I were to keep him from going to slaughter, he might already have irreversible liver damage. Would I be saving a sick animal? And how could I ask Peter to change the diet or add roughage? It would be more work for him, and I know he'd resent it because I'd be reneging on our original agreement—that he'd raise my calves exactly as he raises other animals for beef—no special treatment. Even if he did agree, which is unlikely, I don't see how practically he could do it. There's no easy way to segregate my two calves from the other five that share the barn and barnyard.

I need more information about this before I talk to Peter, but the longer I delay, the sicker the calves may get.

• • •

The next evening I telephone Shelly Vonglis at home. She did above average on her midterm exams at nursing school, she says, and has started rotations at a nearby hospital. She has already qualified, she says proudly, to "give out meds."

What's been Peter's experience, I ask her, raising calves on this corn diet? Has he lost any to liver abscesses or other disease? Shelly says that although Peter's raised steers for beef many times, this is actually the first time he's tried this special corn diet—it's his father, John Vonglis, who's been doing it for a long time. If I have questions about the program, I should call John.

"You know," says Shelly, "the calves look so good—their coats are really full and shiny. Peter and I were saying the other night if you don't have any plans for them, maybe we'd buy them from you and put 'em in the freezer—'cause we know where they came from and how they've been raised."

I tell her I'll keep it in mind.

. . .

When I call John Vonglis at his home, he's already heard from Shelly that I have some concerns about the finishing diet.

"So tell me about this corn diet," I begin. "Shelly says this is Peter's first time using it, but that you've got a lot of experience."

John says that twenty-five years ago a company developed what they called the "Tender Lean" program for finishing beef steers.

"I was impressed with it right away," he says. "They were able to grow steers to one thousand pounds at one year old—no roughage, no hay, just shell corn. See, with a regular Holstein steer on pasture in the summer and on hay in the winter, it might take two years to get 'im to a thousand pounds, but with Tender Lean you get there in one year. That was the whole purpose.

"When I started on the program, I couldn't believe these calves were just a year old. I used to eat four of them a year. They'd grade right under prime—very little fat."

The company that developed Tender Lean went out of business, says John, but he liked the program so much he's continued it on his own. Currently he's raising thirty-one steers on it.

Shell corn is the secret, he says. Though feedlots usually grind corn before feeding, Tender Lean uses the whole kernel.

"You'll see, the kernels are not in the droppings. It's all been digested. They crunch it up with their teeth. Only thing is, you can't run out of feed even for one day, because they'll gorge themselves next day and bloat."

I ask John if he's ever had a problem with liver disease.

"Occasionally I've seen a liver abscess, a little pus on the liver," he says. "You can't eat the liver if you get that."

But he doesn't recall a steer ever dying before the year was up.

I tell John my concerns based on my conversation with Dr. Hale, and ask him what he would think of Peter adding a little hay or other roughage to the calves' diet.

"No, you can't feed 'em hay," he says emphatically. "Hay would defeat the purpose. The hay with the roughage would push the corn right through 'em. They wouldn't be gaining weight.

"It'd be like feeding a guy meat and potatoes," he continues, "and then put 'im on lettuce. He'd have to eat like crazy. He'd starve."

.   .   .

A half mile down Craig Road and across Route 36 from Lawnel Farms, York Memorial Post 634 (Veterans of Foreign Wars) shares a clubhouse with the York Sportsmen's Club. The clubhouse sits between the field where I rode with Andrew Smith last summer as he cut wheat and the barns where Lawnel heifers are housed until they're ready to be bred.

Today's Veterans Day ceremony is being held outside the clubhouse in a wood-frame pavilion. A large crowd is expected for the dedication of a new veterans' memorial. Organizers have hung blue plastic tarps across three sides of the pavilion to help cut a brisk afternoon wind. Inside are about one hundred folding metal chairs, but when I arrive fifteen minutes before the ceremony is set to begin, nearly all the chairs are taken. Many people stand; some older people sit in wheelchairs around the periphery. Many wear winter coats, but most are still trying to get by with fall jackets.

I want to attend this ceremony today because I feel I'm getting a little obsessed about the fate of my calves. Standing among local residents as they honor their war dead, I'm thinking, might help put the issue in perspective. In light of the long record of human sacrifice for freedom, the question of what to do with two Holstein calves ought to seem insignificant, and therefore maybe easier to resolve.

I've never seen so many people in one place in York.

A dozen members of the York High School band begin tuning their instruments.

We all stand for the Pledge of Allegiance, "The Star-Spangled Banner," and a prayer offered by the VFW post chaplain. Then a gray-haired woman in black, introduced as Shirley Schlaffer, the mother of a recently deceased veteran, stands and slowly walks toward the newly built memorial. The rope hanging on a nearby flagpole flaps in the breeze; it makes a pinging, clanging noise against the pole. Mrs. Schlaffer pulls a green cloth tarp off the memorial. It's a black metal monument, five feet tall, like an oversized tombstone.

John Generaux, president of the York Sportsmen's Club, is the first speaker. Although not a veteran himself, he says there have been veterans in his family since the War of 1812. A schoolteacher for twenty-six years, Generaux observes, "I have watched the patriotism of the young diminish." He concludes, holding back tears, "It is because American veterans have performed their service so well, that the young have no personal knowledge of war and sacrifice."

Another speaker notes that "the lives of 2.8 million American servicemen and women have been lost in sixty-nine wars and actions since 1775."

Concludes the final speaker, "God bless each and every one of you here today. God bless our veterans, and God bless these United States of America."

The high school trumpeter plays taps. The clear sound, rising above an accompanying snare drum, floats over the cow barns and empty fields of the Genesee Valley. In the silence that follows, a man dressed in a tartan kilt emerges with a bagpipe from behind the pavilion and plays "Amazing Grace."

After the ceremony, salt potatoes, roast beef slices, and soda are available for free inside the clubhouse. The walls of this one-story building are covered with photos and award plaques honoring not just the veterans but also members of the York Sportsmen's Club, with whom the vets share the building. On one wall, for example, military ribbons share space with a typed report on the annual "Deer Harvest" ("Number of Deer taken: 84—72 with gun; 12 with bow"). A folding table displays both a disarmed World War II mortar shell and a stuffed deer head surrounded by photos of hunters posing with their other kills.

During the ceremony, my thoughts were focused on the men and women to whom I owe a debt for my freedom—including the freedom to write—but the deer heads and hunting photos have brought me back to the same unresolved question I came with: What to do with two calves in a barn four miles down the road?

• • •

On a Saturday evening, from the lobby of a Rochester hotel where my wife and I are attending a party, I call Peter Vonglis at home. I hope to arrange to visit him and Shelly tomorrow to settle this matter of my calves' diet.

"Peter, hello. It's Peter Lovenheim."

"Hello, Peter!" he calls back.

There's a band playing behind me, and suddenly it seems awkward to be calling Peter at home while I'm out partying. He answered the phone, so I suppose Shelly's working at the hospital tonight and he's watching the kids.

When I ask what's new, however, he tells me he and Scot Batzing returned last night from their annual fall gambling trip to Atlantic City, New Jersey. Peter says he came back with a little more than he took, and had a great time.

I'm not so concerned about the band music now.

"Peter," I begin, "I've been asking around about this shell-corn diet."

He says he knows I spoke with his father.

"I also talked with Dave Hale, the vet who comes to Lawnel. What I'm hearing is that without any roughage the calves can get liver abscesses and other problems, and could die at any time, so I'm a little concerned."

Peter says his father's been raising calves on this program for years without a problem.

"Well, I was just wondering if we can add some hay or other roughage—you know, to improve the odds so the animals are less likely to get ill."

"When are you gonna send 'em to slaughter?" he asks. "I mean, how long do you have to keep 'em going?"

I realize I haven't leveled yet with Peter about my uncertainty over what, finally, to do with my calves.

Rather than answer his question directly, I suggest it would be better to talk about this in person. Will he and Shelly be home tomorrow?

He says they're all going to Shelly's parents' house at noon, but if I come by around eleven, we should have time to talk.

"I can tell you, though," he says, "you can't add hay to this shell-corn diet. It won't work. It'll push the corn right through 'em and they won't gain any weight. But you can come by tomorrow."

．　．　．

"I'm going to tell Peter to just forget this hay business and feed the calves whatever he wants. That was our original deal, and I should live up to it," I tell my wife as I dress Sunday morning to drive to York. I pull on jeans and button a heavy, western-style blue flannel shirt I bought at Davis' Trailer World and Country Mall. "My calves are probably already sick, so even if I could find a way to save them from the slaughterhouse, what would be the point?"

She seems interested, but our son, Ben, needs breakfast and his teenage sisters, Sarah and Val, are asking who can drive them to various activities planned during the day. So my wife is not available just now to further discuss my calves' future. As to what ultimately I do with my calves, I don't think she cares, so long as it's a decision I can live with.

During the forty-minute drive to York, I turn the question over again: I need to honor my commitment to Peter that the calves receive no special treatment. Also, I know that even if he were willing, there's no practical way to segregate my calves from the others he's raising.

Peter and Shelly are in the kitchen when I arrive. Peter has the beginnings of a beard.

"I started it last week," he says. "It grows in pretty fast."

Shelly looks tired. She worked at the hospital from three yesterday afternoon until eleven last night, is due back today at 1:00 P.M., and is struggling now to get Bridgette and Colin dressed for lunch at her parents' house.

We sit at the dining room table. The kids were watching TV, but now Bridgette runs over to show me a picture she's drawn. Colin, with a runny nose, sits on Shelly's lap.

I can tell that Peter has told Shelly about my phone call last night and my concerns about the calves' diet, because I can feel the tension in the room. I want to resolve this quickly.

"Look," I begin, "after our conversation last night, I've thought about this thing with the calves' diet. You're doing a good job, so just go ahead with it. I'm not going to make an issue of the roughage."

"Good," Peter says, "'cause I wasn't gonna put 'em on hay, anyway."

"Oh, thank you, thank you," says Shelly in response to what I'd said. "I am so relieved."

Peter leans forward. "This Tender Lean program is a short-term feeding program—they're not meant to live on it for a long time. You sure you understand that?"

I tell him I understand.

"Anyway," he says, "if you put 'em back on roughage now, they'd lose weight."

"They'd die!" says Shelly. "They'd just die. They'd never make it through the winter."

"No. They wouldn't die, Shel," says Peter, "but they'd lose weight."

Peter once again repeats what his father told me on the phone, that once on the corn diet, if the calves eat roughage, it will "push the corn right through 'em" so they get no nourishment.

"You can see when I change the bedding in the barn and put down fresh straw," he says, "they eat the straw right away and the next day you can see it in the manure—whole kernels of corn—they haven't digested it, so they don't get any nutrients from it."

I explain again to Peter and Shelly about my conversation with Dr. Hale, that calves on a corn diet can get liver abscesses and die at any time.

To my surprise, they say they know Dr. Hale—he's also the vet at the Batzing Farm, where Peter works. Even though I'm resolved to let Peter continue on the Tender Lean program, I suggest we talk to Dr. Hale together so we can both hear what he has to say. Peter agrees. We'll meet at the Batzing Farm on Tuesday at 7:00 A.M., when Dr. Hale makes his next regular visit.

Shelly says, "You know, Peter and I were talking and I don't know what you plan to do with the meat after you have the calves butchered, but—maybe I mentioned this already—we'd be interested in buying the meat."

I don't respond immediately.

"So do you know what you're going to do with them yet?" she asks.

"No, I don't," I say. "To be honest, I'm just getting used to the idea of actually having these calves slaughtered, so I hope you're okay with my being a little uncertain yet about what I'm going to do."

They say that's fine with them; they understand.

I'm relieved.

Tomorrow is opening day of deer-hunting season, I mention as I get up to leave.

Peter says he's not sure he'll hunt this year. He hasn't bought a license yet.

"I'll be at the farm," he says. "Everyone else there takes off for the week—someone's got to be there to work."

He's starting to sound like an owner, I comment.

"Oh, please!" says Shelly.

"Oh, Shel!" says Peter.

Before I go, I ask Peter to show me how he feeds the calves. He says he usually feeds them at night when he gets home from work, but he'll give them a little extra today so I can see how he does it.

We enter the barnyard and walk toward the running shed, the small, open-sided barn. The calves are all in there, and so is the feed wagon. The corn comes from the Batzing Farm, he confirms; it could be some of the same corn he cut when I rode with him on the combine in September.

As Peter climbs on the feed wagon to scoop out a bucket of corn, the herd, except 8, backs out of the running shed and moves to the middle of the barn-yard. Only 8 walks over to me, where I've taken a seat on the flat rock in the cor-ner of the barnyard. He's used to getting a couple of handfuls of grass or hay from me, but I don't have any today. I offer him my bare hand, and he steps closer. I move my hand up to his head, over the white chalice, and down his nose. He licks my finger. I look back at the running shed and see Peter watching.

"See?" I say to Peter, but I'm not sure what I mean to convey. I'm a little embarrassed the calf is licking me—obviously I've done some petting here in my visits when Peter has not been around.

Peter smiles, but I'm not sure what his smile means. Is he thinking, "Oh, that's nice. You've gotten close enough to your calf so it goes right over and licks you," or "I have to feed and water this dumb steer every day and here you've gone and made a pet out of him!"

Peter pours a bucket of corn into a plastic-lined feed trough, then rips open a bag of brown food pellets and adds those, too.

I leave my calf and follow Peter toward the barn.

A water tank just outside the door refills automatically from a hose, he explains, but in the winter he fills it manually because otherwise it will freeze.

Inside, the barn is thinly bedded with straw. He changes the straw weekly, in the winter sometimes twice a week, when the calves spend more time indoors.

I'd like to come by at night to observe the calves sleeping, I tell Peter. What time do they tend to lie down for the night?

"I don't know if they sleep at night or during the day," he says dismissively.

Cattle tend to sleep an average of about four hours a night, according to ani-mal behaviorists whose work I've read, and to drowse for another six hours or so during the day. Their nighttime sleep looks identical to sleep in humans, includ-ing periods of deep sleep and rapid eye movement, or REM. During deep sleep, a cow usually lies with its head resting on the ground and turned back into its flank, or side; twitching of the ears and facial muscles is common. In one study, cattle kept in a corral chose the same spots to sleep in night after night.

As I prepare to leave, I ask Peter again to bear with me as the calves get toward what Dr. Hale calls "the finish line" and I have to deal with slaughtering them.

"That's okay," he says. "I just wonder how you'll be when I take 'em out of the barn and load 'em on the truck—or whoever you're gonna have do it—if you'll have tears in your eyes, or whatever."

. . .

On Tuesday morning I arrive at the Batzing Farm just before sunrise. It's a cold, frosty morning, two days before Thanksgiving. A full moon hangs over the barren fields. On a narrow gravel road leading to the farm, I pass an old man walking a dog on a leash and wearing a bright orange vest, which reminds me deer season has begun.

Peter Vonglis arrives a few minutes later and joins me in the small, somewhat shabby farm office. There are four or five other men here: Scot Batzing, the herd manager, and a few farmhands. They sip coffee from Styrofoam cups and talk about who hunted yesterday and what they got. Peter hunted in the afternoon, after buying a license at Wal-Mart, but didn't get anything. The Batzing Farm feels a lot rougher than Lawnel Farms. It's definitely more of a "guy" place—lots of grunting.

When Dr. Hale arrives, Peter and I explain why I'm here and follow him into the barns to talk as he examines cows.

"My father's raised calves on this program for twenty-five years," begins Peter, filling Dr. Hale in on the background of the Tender Lean feeding program.

Dr. Hale listens as he inserts his sheathed arm up one of the Batzing cows to check for pregnancy.

"How many of your dad's steers made it through to the finish line?" he asks.

"He's had good results," says Peter, not quite answering.

"Well, he probably loses some along the way," says Dr. Hale.

The vet repeats his earlier assessment to me: there is a danger of acidosis and liver abscess.

Are the calves ruminating at all on this diet? I ask Dr. Hale.

"They have a rumen functioning at very low efficiency, maybe ten percent," he says. "There's still a population of bacteria that are wanting to digest fiber and forage, but they're not being fed that, so the calf becomes more like a simple-stomached animal. Fortunately, the Lasalocid [an antibiotic] in the feed pellets discourages rumination, so it does help some."

I'm curious whether an inability to ruminate would cause a calf any stress. Dr. Hale says he doubts it would.

"I'm more concerned with clostridium," he says. He describes this as an "overeating" disease where bacteria that thrive on high-concentrate feeding take over the gastrointestinal tract. "It can be fatal in one big hurry. I mean eight to ten hours. Baby sheep, lambs, and calves get it."

He asks Peter if he's vaccinated the calves against clostridium, but Peter says he hasn't. Dr. Hale says he'll bring some vaccine next week. I offer to pay for it, but Dr. Hale says each dose costs only about forty-five cents.

Dr. Hale finishes examining another cow, then turns to me in the aisle of the barn.

"What Peter's doing here is standard for raising beef cattle," he says. "This is how beef animals are finished on a feedlot, and although there is some risk the calves could go down before they're finished, given Peter's father's record with the program, it's probably a reasonable risk to take.

"But the longer the calves go," he continues, "the greater the risk. Keeping them till May is riskier than keeping them till April. You're okay with this calf finishing in April?"

This feels like the moment of truth.

Peter looks at me.

"Yeah," I say.

"'Cause this is a short-term feeding program," he repeats. "The calf can't survive on it much beyond that."

"The problem is," says Peter, "he's getting attached to the calf."

.   .   .

This late-November day that began so bleak and cold has turned remarkably warm and sunny. Yesterday's high of 71 tied a record, and today feels nearly as warm. (If I'm going to have my calves slaughtered in April, this may be the last really warm day they experience.) At lunch at York Landing restaurant, hunters traded tips for keeping deer meat from spoiling in the heat.

I pull to my usual spot at the bottom of the Vonglises' driveway, open the car trunk, and pull on my barn boots. All seven calves are resting in the barn; 8 alone gets up and walks quickly across the barnyard toward me. The others soon follow. He's looking for hay, I know, but the tiny bit I usually keep in my trunk has run out, and I forgot to pick up some more.

It's over for this guy, anyway. I need to accept that.

A dozen gray pigeons and, oddly, one perfectly white one fly out of the running shed.

My calf's twin sister, 7, defecates; the pie is mustard yellow with little bits of corn kernels.

The calves mill about the barnyard, pulling at the tiniest bits of grass that grow around fenceposts and a few large rocks. The rest of the ground is bare. In a few more weeks, what little grass there is here will be covered by snow.

A cattle buyer visited here with me last week to give me his opinion of how the calves are doing. He estimated 8 weighs about 650 pounds and should be up to 1,100 by April. That's just over four months from now, which means he's gaining more than three pounds a day on the corn diet. I can see him expanding week by week.

I sit on the flat rock in the corner of the barnyard. My bull calf comes over. I remain still as he licks my boots, jeans, shirt, neck, chin, cheek, and hair.

He walks to the running shed and eats some corn from the trough. I'm sorry I'm going to have to slaughter him, but not killing him would feel as though I were betraying the Smiths and the Vonglises and all the other people I've met who labor to make food for the rest of us.

When I started this, all I wanted was to be able to follow an animal from birth to slaughter—conception to consumption—and now I'm doing exactly that. If I can't save the calves, at least I have calves and have been able to observe their lives and all the people who have cared for them. That should be enough.

So I'll be like the Shaker boy in the book Andrew Smith told me about, the one who had to slaughter his own pet pig. I'll go and watch my calves be killed; maybe I'll even grow somehow by the experience.

Two gunshots sound from the woods beyond the cornfield behind Peter and Shelly's house.

I can feel 8's saliva drying where he licked me on the side of my neck.

The warm sun feels so good, but it's time to head home. I get up from the flat rock and leave the barnyard, locking the gate behind me. At my car, I open the trunk and take off my barn boots. Turning to look back at the barnyard, however, I see that my bull calf, and he alone, has left the running shed and is standing at the fence. I walk back to the gate. My calf lowers his head and licks my shoe—my leather shoe. It's the first time I've stood near him without boots.

Two more gunshots sound from the woods. Then another, and another. Then five more. Pop, pop, pop, pop, pop. Three small deer run from Peter's cornfield into the woods.

What does it feel like, I wonder, to be a calf and to lick a leather shoe.

7

Thinning the Herd

A CHRISTMAS WREATH HANGS OUTSIDE the window of the herd office at Lawnel Farms this cold, damp Friday afternoon. Inside, Sue Smith sits at her desk studying a computer printout, what she calls a "look-at" report. It's a list, based on this morning's milking, of every cow who is producing less than thirty-two pounds—just under four gallons—of milk a day, a figure Sue calculates is break-even.

"There are animals out there who are not paying for themselves," she says.

That's why Sue has to cull unprofitable cows and replace them with younger, higher-producing animals.

Sixty-seven cows have come up on the list. Not all will be culled. Sue will consider each one, and make her decision. The cows she selects for culling will continue to be milked over the weekend, and then be picked up Monday morning by Joe Hopper, the livestock hauler. He'll take them to the livestock auction in the nearby town of Pavilion, and from there they'll go to slaughter.

I'll try to follow these culled cows all the way to the slaughterhouse. It's not something I'm eager to do, but it will be useful as a kind of "dry run" to see if that's where I'd want to send my own calves if I decide to have them slaughtered.

. . . .

"For each cow," Sue explains, "I ask myself: Is she sick or ready to dry off, or is she a dog—a low producer?"

I recognize just one number on the list: 4923, the mother of my two calves. She gave just twelve pounds of milk.

Lawnel's cull rate is 35 to 40 percent. This means Sue sends about three hundred of her cows to slaughter each year. Put another way, 80 percent of the cows I saw here on my first visit nearly two years ago are already dead, replaced by other animals. Sue would like the cull rate to be lower. Dairy organizations recommend a rate of 25 to 30 percent.

Some culling choices are clear-cut, as with seriously ill, lame, or injured cows, but others can be close calls that rely less on milk-weight than on Sue's intuitive sense of a cow's potential. Timing is important. Should she milk a marginally profitable cow for six more months and risk selling it when its body condition has deteriorated, or cull it today and get a better price at auction? This question was addressed recently by a comment in *Hoard's Dairyman:* "We all know we have some of those bottom 5 percent cows that would make us all more money under the Golden Arches."

Some cows have low milk-weights because they're pregnant and close to giving birth. That's when they naturally "dry off," reducing their lactation to conserve energy.

Other cows have trouble getting pregnant, and that's why they're giving less milk. With BST—bovine growth hormone—Sue can extend a cow's lactation beyond the normal 305 days, sometimes beyond 400 days, but eventually a cow who doesn't have another calf is going to give too little milk to stay in the herd.

If Sue is unsure about a cow's health or whether it's pregnant, she'll mark it down for a "vet check" the next time Dave Hale comes to the farm.

I ask Sue how she feels about culling cows she's known for years.

"You get hardened," she says. "It's a business. You have to see it as a payback—you can't put money into a cow you're not going to get back."

Then she tells me about Wart, a cow she came to know because as a calf it was unusually friendly. She named it for a prominent wart next to its eye. Years later, Wart developed a digestive virus and her production dropped. "I should have culled her, but couldn't," says Sue. "I didn't have the heart to send her to market. That's why it's not a good idea to get attached to cows."

Sue concludes, "We kept Wart four to five days and then she died.

"On the other hand," Sue continues, "there are some cows I'm glad to put on the beef list—they are genuine pains in the neck."

Sue works through the look-at report, one cow at a time.

"I know every cow on this list," she says.

Every cow? Just by their number?

"Sure, I can picture them. I've seen them freshen three or four times, or at least checked them right after they freshened."

I marvel at how Sue can know hundreds of cows by number.

"It's sort of a gift," she says. "You have to be a real cow person. I've been doing it all my life."

She points to one four-digit number. "This one recently aborted," she says. "That can really throw a cow off. I'll let her breed back and see what happens."

Of another she says, "This one's a definite beef animal. She's already in her fourth lactation and has got a terrible udder. I won't breed her. She's gone."

Four cows on the list she knows are in heat. "Cows in heat won't let down"—give milk—"for one or two milkings, so I'll let it pass. But after that, they've got to make milk—that's the bottom line."

She comes to 4923.

"This is your cow, isn't it?" she asks. "She's pregnant. We had to rebreed her"—artifically inseminate her—"a couple of times, but Dave Hale checked her last month and she's definitely bred."

So 4923 is safe for now. Sue will take her out of the milking herd and move her to Valley View Farm until she's ready to give birth.

"She's healthy and still a good producer," says Sue. "She's not due for culling unless she gets mastitis or develops some other problem."

Of the sixty-seven cows on the look-at list, Sue has marked twenty-eight as "dry," fifteen for "vet check," fourteen as "wait," four "in heat," one "aborted," and five for "beef."

The first cow on the beef list is 821. At thirty pounds of milk, she missed the thirty-two-pound cutoff by one quart of milk. "She's a big, black cow, a nice-looking animal," says Sue. "Generally, she's been in good health and an above-average milker. But she aborted in April. Then we put her with the bull, but she didn't get rebred. She's nearly eight years old, in her fifth lactation. That's old. She's paid her dues."

Adds Sue, "It'll be good for you to watch her because she's got some personality—kind of high-strung. She knows what's going on around her."

Next is 4927, who gave twenty-five pounds. "She's an absolute pig," says Sue. "I call her an 'alley rat' because she'll lie in the manure in the aisle rather than walk into a stall. She's lazy—like someone who falls asleep on the couch because it's easier than going up to bed." Now in her third lactation, this cow hasn't gotten pregnant, and her production has declined.

Cow 5657 gave just five pounds of milk, the lowest producer on the list. She's three and a half years old and in her second lactation. "I AI'd her five times, put her on BST, but she just never produced," says Sue. "I never understood why she didn't do more."

Next is 5772. She gave twenty-eight pounds. "This cow has always had a problem with her front feet," says Sue. "When she walks, they kind of cross each other." Sue thinks the cow could have a "hardware problem," meaning she might have eaten some metal that got into her stomach. "Sometimes that can cause crossed feet. I don't know why that is, but it is."

The last cow, 5983, is young, in her first lactation. With BST, she's been milking 402 days, but despite AI and going with the bull, she hasn't gotten pregnant. "Why an otherwise healthy animal just doesn't conceive," says Sue, "I don't know. Something's just not right there."

I ask Sue if any of the five she's put on the beef list were close calls.

"No. These are cut-and-dried," she says. "They're out of here."

Early Monday morning, Sue will move the five cull cows to a collection point in the main barn.

"When I go out there to collect cows," she says, "they know it's their time. I try to get them out of the group and sometimes they won't go, especially the older animals. They know when stuff happens. They're not stupid."

I have one more question—I'm afraid Sue might find it odd, but I'm curious.

"When you round up the cows for culling," I begin, "do you ever, out loud or silently, sort of thank them for producing milk for the farm and your family?"

"No, I don't pay tribute," she says firmly.

.   .   .

Two days later, on Sunday afternoon, I return to Lawnel to watch the five cows selected for culling go through their last day of milking. Kirsty Smith is working in the milking parlor today along with Elaine, a middle-aged woman who is a part-time employee.

Elaine says they're running about an hour late. I wander into a barn to see if I can find 4927, the cow Sue calls an "alley rat." Sure enough, she is lying in the aisle, front hooves folded under her chest, rump and flanks covered with mud.

In another barn, I easily spot 821. She's a big cow, all black except for a white mark on her forehead that looks like the Nike "swoosh."

And in another barn I find 5772, the cow with crossed front legs. She stands in the aisle with her left leg straight under her chest and the right one crossed over. The hoof on her right front foot is grotesquely elongated. Her hipbones stick out in front of her sunken rump; I can count seven ribs. Her udder is thin, and short. Sue said this cow probably gets in a stall and doesn't get out to eat.

Joe Krenzer, the farmhand who walks with a limp, herds the cows toward the parlor.

Elaine calls, "Walk out, girls!" to those in the holding area, and activates the crowd gate. With a loud buzz, it pushes the cows toward the parlor entrance.

Kirsty sings and whistles them into the stalls, just as I've heard her mother do. "C'mon," she calls. "Get in there!"

The alley rat enters the parlor.

"C'mon, piggy!" Kirsty calls.

This big cow takes a position in a stall on the right side of the parlor, her head hanging low. She holds her front left hoof off the ground as if it hurts to touch it to the concrete. All of her underside, including her udder, is caked with mud and manure.

From the pit, Elaine wipes the filth from the alley rat's teats.

I ask Kirsty if she likes working Sunday afternoons in the parlor.

"I'd rather be doing something else," she says, "but this gives me spending money, and I get a lot else from the farm. I think it's expected of me, too."

Kirsty works about eight hours a week, usually on the weekend. She's paid the same as the other help: seven dollars an hour.

Just before coming here, she was at home watching television and doing homework. A junior at York Central High School, she's made the honor roll nearly every year, and competes on the volleyball and swim teams.

Dressed in jeans and a black T-shirt, Kirsty chews gum while she milks and we talk.

She has Andrew's blue eyes, and cuts her dirty blond hair short, like Sue's. She's strong like her dad and handles cows with the ease and grace of her mother.

"I'm closer to my mother than my dad," she says. "They say 'Daddy's little girl,' but I'm not Daddy's girl at all. I tell Mom everything. My dad and I get along okay, but we don't really talk that much."

"This cow," I say to Kirsty, gesturing toward the alley rat in the milking stall above us, "is getting shipped tomorrow."

"Oh, is she?" Kirsty replies, as she walks down the aisle to bring the next group in.

"Get up! C'mon," she shouts, and then whistles.

Kirsty's just beginning to think about college. She'd like to become a large-animal veterinarian. She didn't do as well on the PSAT as she'd hoped, but says she often doesn't score high on standardized tests.

"I do my homework and have a lot of common sense, so that's how I get as far as I do in school," she says.

Kirsty urges the next group of cows into the milking stalls.

I'm curious what she eats. My own daughter, Sarah, who's close to Kirsty's age, is vegetarian, as are several of her high school friends.

"I eat hamburger," she tells me, "but I wouldn't eat one of these cows." She points toward the "alley rat" and the other cows being milked.

Why not?

"Because they're mine and I've seen 'em since they were little."

She says she also doesn't eat veal because "they're too little." Veal is made from bull calves slaughtered at four months of age or younger.

Elaine brings another group of cows into the left side of the parlor, including 821—the beefy, stocky black animal with the white "swoosh" on her forehead. This cow's legs are black except for a line of white around each front hoof, as if she were wearing spats. Yellow tags in both ears have "821" hand-lettered in black marker; her original printed tags must have pulled out.

I try to pet her nose, but she jerks her huge head up and away from me.

This big old cow, I remember Sue commenting, had "paid her dues." If she's been milked three times a day for an average of 305 days a year for five years, that would be more than 4,500 trips through the milk parlor. When the exit gate suddenly rises with a loud hydraulic gush, releasing cows from the stalls, the cow doesn't even blink.

"Kirsty," I say, "your mom knows all the animals by their three- or four-digit numbers. How does she do that in a herd of almost nine hundred cows?"

"Yeah, and if she doesn't know the cow right away, she'll think about it and then remember," agrees Kirsty. "Mom knows every cow here. It's an amazing ability."

"Where do you think that comes from?" I ask.

"From her being here seventeen hours a day," she says.

When the cows are done milking and on their way back to the barn, Kirsty grabs a squeegee on a long stick and begins scraping manure and urine from the holding area before the sick and lame cows come in.

Would she want to be a dairy cow, I ask her.

"No, it's a tough life," she says, pushing the squeegee. "They're on their feet all the time, they have to come into the parlor three times a day, spend about an hour here. I wouldn't mind being a pregnant cow, though—they're lazy and seem to like that part, just eating and drinking and laying around."

Kirsty says her friends at school, most of whom don't live on farms, don't appreciate what her family does. "They don't understand how much hard work it is. They think milk comes from the store."

The vacuum pumps that pull milk from the cows' udders pulse twice a second, like a clock running at double time. Except for their pulsing, the parlor is quiet. Kirsty doesn't play the radio; she says Elaine prefers not to have it on.

Some kids resent her family having a big farm, she confides. "They think I'm rich. But I pay for everything I buy. I work a lot."

She does. In the three hours I've been watching, she hasn't stopped moving.

Kirsty and Elaine have milked three hundred cows and cleaned the parlor. They still need to milk the sick and lame cows before finishing their shift.

"Milking is a lot harder than, say, baby-sitting," says Kirsty. "I'm ready to go home."

Two weeks from now, on Christmas morning, Kirsty will start working at 5:00 A.M., along with Sue, Andrew, and her brother, Amos. "We do it every year," she says. Nonfamily employees have the day off. "After work, we all get home around one P.M., shower, and then open presents. I don't mind it and I get paid."

• • •

At 7:00 P.M., several hours after Kirsty and Elaine have left Lawnel, it's time for another group of cows to be milked. Powerful halogen lights illuminate the barn and the alleys leading to the parlor. 5772, the cow with crossed legs, walks along the wall. She steps slowly with her left foot, then brings her right foot—the one that's elongated—up to meet it, then repeats the move, as if carefully walking down the aisle in a wedding procession.

"C'mon, ladies, c'mon, girls," a young man, one of the night milkers, calls. "C'mon, ladies, walk it up."

The cow enters the parlor and moves into the fifth stall on the left side.

Three of the teats on her small udder are pink and one is black. I touch them. They are warm and spongy, like a soft thumb.

The sight glass on the milking unit fills with a modest gush of milk, but after less than two minutes the unit automatically drops off.

The cow raises her head forcefully, as if to leave the milking stall.

"Not so fast, lady, you ain't done yet," says the night milker, whose name is Jack. He wears brown coveralls, and on the side of his thick neck is a generous display of hickeys. Jack sprays 5772's teats with iodine, but his aim is off and he leaves a brownish stain on part of the udder.

When the other cows finish, the exit gate rises and 5772 begins her slow processional out of the parlor, past the holding area, back to the barn, for her last night at Lawnel.

. . . .

On Monday morning I'm up at five-thirty, after maybe two hours' sleep. I'm anxious about following the Lawnel cows to auction, and then maybe to slaughter.

When cull dairy cows are auctioned at Pavilion, I've learned, four or five companies do most of the bidding. Two of them, Moyer Packing and Taylor Packing, are major businesses with plants in Pennsylvania, just across the New York border. Moyer makes patties for Wendy's, and Taylor makes hamburger for McDonald's.

Though I'm uneasy about seeing these animals slaughtered, if I have the opportunity I'll go to Taylor—after all, McDonald's is where this whole effort began, when I took my daughter in search of Beanie Babies.

But first I'll have to see if Taylor buys any of the Lawnel cows. If it does, then I'll need to arrange permission to get into the plant. I'm sure slaughterhouses are reluctant to have writers—or anybody else—come in and observe what they're doing.

Heavy rain and fog this morning make the drive to York harrowing. When I arrive at Lawnel at seven, I see Elaine is already back in the milking parlor for the morning shift.

Is Sue here yet?

Elaine says she was, but went home to rest—she'll be back soon. But why was Sue here during the night?

"Night milkers quit on her," says Elaine. "She had to come in the middle of the night and do the milking till five this morning."

So, while I was lying in bed anxious about going to the slaughterhouse, Sue Smith was in the milk parlor, working.

Elaine says one of the milkers called Sue at home at nine last evening and quit. "Sue said the guy was talkin' real funny, like he was on drugs or something."

. . .

Outside the parlor, the fourteen-wheel, stainless-steel milk truck that comes to Lawnel every morning is already backed up to the milk house.

"What are you up to today?" the driver asks me.

"Following cull cows to Pavilion," I say.

"McDonald's, huh? Burger King?"

"I guess so," I answer.

. . .

Andrew arrives at eight. He says Jack called at 9:45 last night and said he and Bob, the other milker, were leaving.

"Those two are brain-dead," says Andrew. Andrew and Sue got up to do the milking and stayed until 3:00 A.M.

"Them two must of been on drugs and in a real hurry to get some more. Either that or they had a couple of girls waiting for them," Andrew says.

I mention that I had noticed Jack's hickeys.

"Oh yeah. Jack's hickeys! His badge of honor."

Later, Sue told me that when the milker called, she was in bed reading *A Day No Pigs Would Die,* the book I'd discussed earlier with Andrew. "I'd just finished the book—like the very last sentence," she said, "and I was sitting back to kind of think about the ending—how the boy has to help his father slaughter his own pet pig—and that's when the phone rang."

Sue returns to the farm just after 8:30 A.M., and immediately begins rounding up the five cows on today's beef list.

In the barn, she looks for 5772, the cow with crossed legs.

"C'mon, 5772," she calls. "C'mon, sweetie, you ready to rock and roll?"

Sue nearly grabs the cow, but at the last moment it makes a tight turn in the aisle and heads the other way. I'm surprised how fast this lame cow can move.

"Heh, heh, don't try it," calls Sue, following after 5772. "Up an' at 'em, let's go!"

Cows are running and turning away from her.

"When you're sorting cows," says Sue, "they know something's up. Someone's going somewhere or something's gonna happen. It's a break in their routine, and they don't like it."

Sue keeps after 5772. Calmly she opens and closes swinging gates, narrowing choices until there's no place for the cow with crossed legs to go but where Sue wants her to go. Within five minutes the cow is secured.

All five cows are now isolated in a thickly bedded holding area in the main barn. They've had their last milking. The older black cow paces back and forth; the others stand quietly, except the "alley rat," who lies in the straw, her sides and udder still caked with mud. The cross-legged cow eats feed from a trough. The younger white cow seems most agitated: vapor comes from her nostrils and steam off the top of her back. She's hot, I suppose, from having tried to elude Sue in the barn. Briefly, she butts heads with the big black cow.

Rain drums on the barn's tin roof.

Sue borrows my pen to write on a sheet of white paper the numbers of the five cows on the beef list. She tapes the paper to the barn door:

5 Cows to Market

5 Cows

5772 4927

821 5657

5983

Also 9 Bull Calves

Joe Hopper, the cattle hauler, should be here within the hour to pick up the cows and also a group of newborn bull calves for the trip to Pavilion.

As Sue and I leave the barn, I ask if the cows will be fed at Pavilion.

"I don't know if they will," she says. "I just don't know what goes on there."

She concedes she's never been to Pavilion to see any of her cows auctioned.

Earlier, Sue had told me that as a girl she often went to an auction barn near her family's dairy. "I used to go because I liked the smell," she said. "It smelled so clean and sawdusty . . . and I loved to sit up there and watch all the animals come in and the people bid on them. It was kind of thrilling."

"How about coming to Pavilion with me today?" I suggest.

"I don't want to," says Sue. "I'd find it depressing. I have no desire to go there."

"Because you're not interested or because you wouldn't like to see it?" I ask.

"Because I know I would find it depressing and I just don't want to see it," she says.

. . .

Minutes later, Joe Hopper's stock trailer rattles up the Lawnel driveway. Joe backs the trailer up to the barn and gets out of the cab, carrying two frozen Butterball turkeys, Christmas gifts for the Smiths: one for Sue and Andrew and one for Andrew's parents. He takes them into the farm office.

Joe's been hauling cattle for Lawnel for about ten years.

"No one could ever say anything bad about this family," he says, "especially that Susie. I never once had a bad word with her—never once. Just too bad she has to work so darn hard. In the summer I see her sweatin'—she works so hard. I don't know how she does it. She's one in a million."

Joe, fifty, wears a black hooded sweatshirt over muddy brown coveralls, a dark blue farm cap, and brown gloves. He has a round, gentle face and a warm smile.

Inside the barn, Sue herds the five cull cows toward the metal ramp leading up into Joe's trailer.

"Heh, heh, heh. Up, c'mon, get up!" she calls.

5657, a mostly white cow, is the first to climb into the trailer. The one with crossed legs is next, but she stops at the bottom of the ramp.

"All right, ladies, let's go. Get in there," says Sue as she leaves to get the other three cows.

The cow with crossed legs gets in, but the first cow now turns around and starts walking back down the ramp.

Joe calls to Sue, "I got a white one here that's bein' kinda goofy!"

Joe needs help with the reluctant cow. Since a tree fell on him some years ago and crushed a disk, he walks with a slight stoop and is careful about not straining his back.

Sue returns and pushes the cow up the ramp, and then helps Joe load the others.

Joe closes the back of the trailer. The last visible part of the five Lawnel cows is the weirdly long hoof of the cow with crossed legs. The cow retracts her hoof at the last possible moment, just as Joe slams the door shut.

Joe drives over to the outdoor superhutch. Nine newborn bull calves are ready to go.

"They sure are shitty, aren't they?" says Joe. I'm not sure whether he means that the calves are covered with dirt and mud—because it is muddy today—or if he's referring to three of them near the back of the hutch who are, in fact, smeared with light-brown feces from lying in their own waste.

"C'mon, kids, let's go," he says.

None of the calves are old enough to walk on their own, so Joe, supporting them under their necks and rumps, walks them into the back of his trailer. "Can't lift 'em like I used to—my back," he says.

Sometimes Joe has trouble getting a calf on its feet, so he gives it a few light jabs with a three-foot-long electric prod called a "Hot Shot."

"I take this out 'cause it's savin' a lot of beatin' on 'em," he says. "It don't hurt 'em none."

With the five cull cows and nine bull calves loaded, we're ready for the ten-mile drive to Pavilion.

Joe's trailer, made of steel, has two compartments: one in front for cows and one in back for calves. The floor is lightly bedded with sawdust. Holes along the sides let air in, but if you passed Joe's trailer on the road you wouldn't be able to see inside to know what he was hauling.

The odometer on Joe's twelve-year-old Chevy truck says 146,000 miles, but that's just when it stopped working. "After two years, it just quit," says Joe. "It's been eight years since then. I guess it's over four hundred thousand now, but that might be low."

Joe's eyeglasses hang on a cord from the cab's rearview mirror; on the seat between us rests a thermos of coffee.

"Where's my dog today?" Joe asks as we pull out of the Lawnel driveway and head down Craig Road.

Dog?

"Dogs love me!" he says with a big smile, and then explains that on a farm across from Lawnel and down the road a hundred yards or so, there's a dog that a couple of years ago chased after his truck. Joe threw the dog a bone, and ever since, when he drives by, the dog runs after the truck and Joe throws it a biscuit.

"That's just how I am with animals, what can I say?" he says.

Sure enough, as we pass a neighboring farm on Craig Road at forty miles an hour, a large brown shepherd shoots out from behind the farmhouse and races toward us. Joe rolls down the window and tosses a biscuit, which falls to the road.

"He's a little slow today," says Joe. "He'll find it later."

Joe asks who I think will read my book. City people, I say, who are curious about where their food comes from and who the people are who make it.

"People don't know what's going on," says Joe. "I saw a TV show a few years ago and—I'll never forget it—this lady says, 'What do we need farmers for?

I buy my meat at the store.' I don't know, do people think their food comes out of the sky?"

Joe charges Lawnel ten dollars to haul a cow, and a few dollars for each calf.

"By the end of the day," he says, "your tires, gas, your time, you don't make much. You do it because you like it. I see people, talk to them—I talk a lot. It gets me out of the house."

Joe was born in nearby Perry, New York, where he still resides. "My brother and me both quit school to work on our farm with my dad. That was the fashion in those days—people didn't hire from the outside. But I see people who went to college and what are they doin'—there's no jobs for them. Always works out for the best in the end, is what I say."

We're about halfway to Pavilion, driving on a two-lane back road.

What does it feel like, I ask Joe, to take animals to auction, knowing most of them will soon be slaughtered?

"It bothers me the young calves got no life," he says. "You're born one week and dead the next.

"When I was growing up, we had a hundred cows on our farm. They became pets. Sometimes cows can get like a dog or a cat—you get attached. We'd have tears in our eyes when we took them to market.

"But these big farms, like Sue's, they've got so many animals they can't get attached to them.

"I don't hurt nothin'," he continues. "The reason I use the prod—you'll see at the auction when we come in, they'll hit 'em on the head. They'll get a bruise, but with the prod you just touch 'em. It don't hurt 'em."

A rifle with a powerful scope rests next to me on the front seat. Is it for deer hunting?

"I got one deer this season," he says, "but that was with a bow." He says he doesn't hunt much anymore. "Did more when I was younger," he says.

I ask Joe if he has any family. He says he has two grown children, but he is divorced. His marriage broke up when he was in his late twenties.

"I went to work one day, and when I came home, the house was empty," he begins. "Turns out my wife had gone to Alaska with her boyfriend and took the kids: our boy, who was six, and our daughter, three. I just loved my wife and kids, and they were gone—it's like losin' both your legs.

"Next morning I didn't come up for milking and my dad came down to the house. He said I looked like I was sleepin', but my eyes were wide open. When he got me up I was like a wild man—out of control. Doc came and gave me a shot—it took two guys to hold me down. They put me in the hospital—I had a nervous breakdown. Then one day I woke up and said to myself, 'What am I doing here?'"

After eleven days, Joe left the hospital. Six months later he met a woman who, some years later, became his second wife. Joe's two kids, when they were older, came back to live with him.

"I hold no grudges," he says. "You only got but one life. That's why I say if a marriage don't work out, get somebody else. Get happy. And if you don't love your wife, let her find someone she can have a happy life with."

Suddenly we're at the auction barn in Pavilion. The four unloading docks are filled by other trucks, so Joe idles his in the driveway. As the cows and calves in the back move about, I feel the trailer rock slightly. I was so taken with Joe's story, I'd forgotten there were animals back there.

• • •

Pavilion, though larger than York, is still a small community. Government offices are open only on Mondays and Tuesdays. In the center of town, in a little triangle of grass just off the only intersection with a traffic light, a memorial plaque lists local residents killed in military service: one in Korea, one in Vietnam.

But to the farm animals of this region, Pavilion is a hub. It's where each year more than fifty thousand cattle change owners and stock trailers. The action happens every Monday and Wednesday at the livestock auction with the matter-of-fact name Empire Livestock Marketing.

The auction barn, a two-story building that slopes to one story on either side, appears to have endured many additions. Some sections are built of cinder block, others of wood and steel.

An unloading dock opens, and Joe backs up his truck. We walk around to the back of the trailer, and Joe swings open the gate. The five Lawnel cows, encouraged by a few touches from Joe's electric prod, walk across a metal ramp into the auction barn.

"C'mon, you fuckin' cunt!" yells a man in a red farm cap. Nearly all the cows coming in get hit with canes, often on the forehead.

Another man stands astride a wooden chute and gives each cow a quick once-over as it enters. He reads the numbers on the cows' ear tags and then assigns them new numbers for the auction. The Lawnel cows will be numbers 615 through 619.

"615 has a barn tag of 5657!" he calls, and slaps a white, round tag with large black numerals on the cow's left side. The tag sticks with a compound called "back-tag cement."

A woman named Paula records the old and new numbers on a clipboard.

"617 got a barn tag of 821!" the man calls to her as the big black cow with the Nike swoosh on her forehead comes through.

Paula is a short woman with wavy blond hair. In the way she carries a heavy stock cane, and banters and wisecracks with the men here, she reminds me of Ma Joad in *The Grapes of Wrath*. Yet her smile is open and warm, and I see that generally she has a gentle touch with the animals, especially calves.

"We got a lot of shit going on today," Paula says to me, by which she means there's an unusually large number of cull cows coming through. "Must be everyone's cleaning house before Christmas."

Paula and the men on the unloading ramp sort incoming cows by physical condition into three categories. Healthy cows are "good" or "straight." When the first two Lawnel cows come in, for example, the man straddling the wooden chute calls to Paula, "Both good cows!" Weaker cows, such as those who are lame, are called "slow cows" or sometimes "exes," and go into a separate area. The weakest animals are "double-exes" or, as one young man working on the ramp candidly puts it, "about-to-die" cows. These are also referred to as "wall" cows because as soon as they come in they are moved to an area next to a wall just past the unloading ramp.

The auction barn is sensitive about sick and weak cows. A sign displayed near the unloading ramp says DISABLED ANIMALS WILL NOT BE ACCEPTED FOR SALE.

All five Lawnel cows—even the one with crossed legs—are classified "good," and herded into a pen not far from the unloading ramp.

Joe Hopper gets a receipt for his load, and leaves. I'm staying; earlier I brought my car to Pavilion and parked at the auction.

· · ·

This wooden barn is cavernous and cold. All the loading bays are open. Even though you're inside, it feels as if you're outside, and outside it's only 20 degrees.

I climb wooden stairs to a catwalk overlooking more than seventy holding pens. In one narrow pen, a huge brown steer bellows loudly, emitting with the noise a jet of vapor that hangs for a moment beside his head like an empty dialogue balloon.

Cattle vocalize for a variety of reasons, but constant or intense vocalizing is generally a sign of distress, hunger, or fear. On a well-run dairy farm like Lawnel, where there is little break in daily routine and all the sights and people are familiar, cows normally are quiet. It is only in transit, or in an unfamiliar setting like an auction barn or slaughterhouse, that there is plenty of noise.

A large wooden pen over which I pass is crowded with Holstein cows. They are packed tightly together, like billiard balls in a rack. I realize it would be easy to count them because none of them can move. I count the black-and-white leather backs pressed against one fence and then the number pressed against the adjacent fence, and multiply. There are fifty cows in the pen.

From the catwalk, I gaze down at the five Lawnel cows. They've all been put in pen number 30, an enclosure about fifteen feet long on each side. Viewed from up here, you don't see the cows' faces, just the contours of their bodies: the length of the back, the heaviness of the flanks and rump. I note how thick or thin the covering of fat is over their hips and tailbones.

821, the old black cow, raises her head and bellows loudly, twice.

The bellowing from these pens is constant; occasionally a sheep bleats. 821 bellows again. 5983, the young Lawnel cow in her first lactation, bellows too.

Men with hardwood canes and high-brimmed caps continue unloading cattle and herding them to pens inside.

Sales of cows and other large animals won't begin until later this afternoon. Until then, the only business being done is at the calf auction.

· · · ·

Up a half-flight of wooden stairs, and down another, I enter a dim little room lit by one bare bulb and two short fluorescent lights suspended from the ceiling. A haze of cigarette smoke hangs in the air. There are just three rows of seats. The front row has six or seven battered wooden armchairs; rips in the plastic upholstery have been patched with duct tape. The second row is made of two wooden benches set end to end. The back row is a collection of wooden stools and a few molded plastic chairs of the kind you see in bus stations.

The auction is already in progress. There are maybe a dozen people here. The back two rows are mostly occupied by old-timers. They sit without bidding. My guess is they come mostly to watch, because on a cold December afternoon in western New York, there aren't a lot of other places to go for live entertainment and to see your friends. They seem to me like the farm equivalent of retired business executives hanging out at a Merrill Lynch office watching the stock prices and looking to pick up a lunch date.

The calf ring, a cement floor covered in sawdust, is just twenty feet long. This tiny ring, the handful of seats, the one lightbulb—the whole room is to miniature scale. What's being sold here, after all, are newborn calves. Some have umbilical cords still hanging from their undersides. Most, like those brought from Lawnel, are just a day or two old. They are unsteady, jerky on their feet.

Two "ring men" work the calf auction today. Their job is to control each animal as it moves through the ring.

I know the right-side ring man, Don Yahn, and nod hello. Don is the auction manager as well as head auctioneer. At forty-seven, he has short brown hair just beginning to go gray, brown eyes, and a round, open face. His voice is a clear, strong bass.

I'd called Don nearly two years ago to introduce myself and explain my plans to write about the life cycle of one dairy animal. One afternoon we spent a quiet couple of hours together, most of it after closing time in Don's private office. The other employees had left, the livestock pens were empty, the building was silent. Maybe it was the darkness of a late afternoon or the stillness of this empty, sprawling building, but our conversation that day assumed a familiarity that I think surprised us both.

Don told me he had long aspired to be an auctioneer, and as a boy practiced by selling household goods at firehouse auctions. After some training, he auctioned whatever he could, often for charity benefits: antiques, the contents of a dress shop, farm machinery. The first time he was allowed to work a cattle auction was when the regular auctioneer got laryngitis, just like in the opera.

We talked of our families. He had two grown daughters. One of them, Torre, twenty years old, had been struggling for four years with a potentially fatal disease. They were hoping to find a donor so Torre could have a bone marrow transplant.

At one point, Don turned around a picture frame on his desk and handed it to me.

"This is my other daughter," he said.

The picture showed a woman, probably in her late twenties, holding a mixed-race child about one year old.

"Your daughter adopted a child?" I asked.

"No," he said. "She had a boyfriend who left her before the child was born.

She's working as a hairdresser now and living at home with my wife and me. We're helping her raise the child."

I was moved by the photograph, but unsure how to respond.

The room was silent.

I said, "Don, you and your wife are helping raise this child for your older daughter, and your younger daughter is ill. How do you do it?"

"We take what comes," he said. "You do the best you can. Life is okay, if you don't weaken."

A few months later, Don's daughter, Torre Lynn Yahn, died at Strong Memorial Hospital in Rochester.

Today, Don fills in as ring man while another employee, a young man in a black cowboy hat, conducts the calf auction. The auctioneer sits at a folding table a few feet above the ring.

I take a seat in the second row to watch.

Behind where the auctioneer sits, off to the left, stands a man well over six feet tall. The embroidery on the pocket of his fringed shirt says "Everett." Everett brings calves in, one at a time, from group pens outside, where they have been confined since being unloaded. He grabs one of the calves—a Holstein—around the shoulders, pulls it up a short ramp, and shoves it forward toward the ring.

Everett's push sends the calf onto an electric floor scale. In red numerals on a sign above the auctioneer's head, the calf's weight in pounds is displayed: 68. Everett steps forward and shoves the calf out into the ring, but for half a second, while the calf is off the scale and Everett is on it, his own weight is displayed: 264.

Once in the ring, the calf plants his front feet against further motion, and looks around. He sniffs and takes an awkward half step toward a Styrofoam coffee cup resting on the half wall that separates the front row of seats from the ring. But just as the calf is about to touch its black nose to the cup, the left-side ring man pokes the calf with a hardwood cane—once in the shoulder, then near the rectum—prodding it into the center of the ring.

The auctioneer, microphone in one hand and gavel in the other, calls out the calf's sex and weight. This one is a "bob," or male calf. He tries to start the bidding at forty cents a pound, but there are no bids, so he drops the price a half cent.

"Bob calf, sixty-eight pounds. Am I bid forty, forty, forty, am I bid forty, forty, forty, thirty-nine and a half, thirty-nine and a half, thirty-nine and a half . . ."

Don and the other ring man poke the calf on either side with their canes. Their aim is to get the calf "spinning"—turning in circles—so that bidders can examine it from both sides. The calf resists, but more pokes near the rectum from the left ring man, and a hit on the side of the face from Don, gets the calf circling.

"I'm bid thirty-nine and a half, am I bid forty, forty, I'm bid forty, I'm bid forty-one, am I bid forty-one and a half, forty-one and a half, forty-one and a half, sold, Foss."

The sale—from floor scale to gavel—takes just fifteen seconds. Already the next calf is in the center of the ring, being spun.

The bidding on every second or third calf, I notice, ends with the auctioneer declaring, "Sold, Foss." "Foss," it turns out, is Jim Foss, a buyer who sits in what strikes me as the best seat in the room—the one in the front row all the way to the left. This seat offers the first look at the calves as Everett pushes them into the ring.

From behind, I watch as Foss makes slash marks with a pencil on a white buyer's card, keeping track of how many calves he's bought. He keeps three columns: one for the smallest and weakest calves that will go immediately to slaughter, one for "grower" calves to be raised for veal, and one for the largest calves, which will be raised for beef.

Foss strikes me as a big man in a small room. He's not a man of height, but of heft; like a beef animal himself, he's built low to the ground and heavy in front. His large head and face remind me of the actor Ed Asner, although he is jowly in a way Asner is not. He combs his silver-gray hair, which is thinning just a bit, straight back. His mouth holds the butt of an unlit cigar.

Farmers' high-brimmed caps, like the rest of their clothing, typically are dark: navy, olive green, gray, or black. But Foss wears a cap that is orange; bright, Day-Glo orange, bright like the orange of a freshly washed traffic cone. On the brim, in solid black letters, the cap says JAMES N. FOSS, INC. DEALERS IN LIVESTOCK.

I watch as Foss buys dozens of calves, yet I'm puzzled: How does he bid? He doesn't speak, and other than chewing on his cigar, he sits nearly motionless.

Then I notice: a calf comes through the ring and Foss lifts the second and third knuckles on his left hand. That's it; he flexes two knuckles. I've seen people move their fingers in this way before: violinists' fingers move that way when they finger the strings on their instrument. As a boy I played trumpet; raising those two fingers would change the note from E to G.

The arbitrary power this burly man wields with the motion of his fingers makes me uneasy. Curious to know him better, a few weeks later I went to visit him at his cattle-buying station.

• • •

Foss's office is a shack, really, set up next to a barn where farmers unload live-stock. The morning I visited, Foss sat on a swivel chair at his desk. He wore high boots that were so caked with dried mud I could not even guess what color they were, or of what material they were made. Near the desk, a rifle leaned against a wall. On a shelf nearby, a bright red bumper sticker insisted DON'T COMPLAIN ABOUT FARMERS WITH YOUR MOUTH FULL.

Foss had a light stubble of beard on his chin and jowls, and looked tired. His left eye was tearing. He said he had a cold in his eye. He dabbed witch hazel on it with a cotton ball held in one hand; in the other hand he held an unlit cigar.

"Why would I read anything you write about the cattle business?" Foss asked me. I was surprised by the immediacy of his challenge; I'd barely sat down. He said it loudly enough, too, for the two other people in the office to hear: a young man with long black hair doing paperwork at a desk in a little alcove, and a middle-aged woman, whom I took to be the office manager, at a desk next to us. Foss hadn't introduced me to either of them.

"Even if you talk to dozens of people and read a lot of books and visit a lot of farms, you're not going to know anything about the cattle business that I don't already know after being in it forty-five years."

I leaned forward and said to Foss that even though he might not learn much, other people—many of whom know little about where their food comes from—would learn a lot. This seemed to satisfy him. He bit off a piece of his cigar.

Then he told me about his business, how his dad had started it and how his three sons now worked with him.

I asked Foss what he looked for in buying calves.

"You're looking at their weight, first," he explained. "If they're eighty-five pounds or less, generally speaking, they're going to slaughter, you understand what I'm saying?" Foss slurred his words a little, and often used the phrase "you under-stand what I'm saying?" at the end of sentences when he was trying to explain something. "If they're more than ninety pounds and solid, if they've got good legs, they can go for veal."

"Also," he continued, "you don't want runny eyes or scours under the tail, you understand what I'm saying?" Scours is what farmers call diarrhea in animals.

"And you want a soft navel. A hard navel indicates an infection, maybe they've picked up something from lying in manure on a barn floor." Several times during the auction I saw Foss or other bidders reach over the half wall into the ring to feel a calf's navel.

"What you want is an animal that looks healthy and vigorous, not sick or weak. The general appearance will dictate the price."

Finally, I confessed to Foss my puzzlement at his method of bidding, and my surprise at discovering the movement of his knuckles.

"Oh," he said with a grin, "I have lots of ways to bid. Sometimes I move my fingers, sometimes I just look. If I'm looking down like this"—he dropped his eyes—"the auctioneer knows I'm not interested. If I'm staring him right in the eye, I'm bidding."

The phone rang and Foss took the call. Someone was placing an order for heifers. I used the break to get up and introduce myself to the other two people in the office.

The office manager, Myrna, has worked for Foss for fourteen years.

The young man at the desk in the alcove appeared to be in his early twenties. His dark hair hung to his shoulders, unusually long for a young man working around a farm, in my experience. He was also thin, not robust at all. And there was something about the way he sat in the wooden office chair on wheels that seemed not quite right. When he swiveled around to shake my hand, he grasped one arm of the chair with his other hand and moved the chair and himself all in one motion.

He introduced himself as Burt, and said he processes all the paperwork on cattle sales required by New York State and the federal government. I asked Burt how long he'd been with Foss.

"My parents dropped me off here when I was thirteen, and Jim's raised me ever since like his own son," he said.

Foss was still talking to the heifer buyer on the phone; cattle bellowed outside as they were herded off trucks.

"So you decided to stay and work here at the buying station?" I asked.

"Well, after the accident, Jim gave me a job here in the office," he said.

Now I understood; he had a back injury. I wasn't sure whether he could walk or not.

"Was your accident with some kind of farm equipment?" I asked.

"No," he said. "It was in the car, when I was nineteen."

Foss hung up the phone. I retook my seat and noticed photographs of two little girls on the desk in front of him. They are his grandchildren, he later explained.

I saw Jim Foss then as a grandfather with a cold in his eye who once took in a child in need of a home. He now keeps him on the payroll doing paperwork because after breaking his back the young man can't do much else. And I was reminded of a Talmudic commentary: "Do not judge a person until you have seen him in his own town."

·   ·   ·

The last few animals to come through the calf auction can barely stand or walk. A few have what appear to be broken or damaged legs; one walks on its right foreleg.

I watch through an interior window as Everett, working in the holding pens, pokes one calf who won't get up twenty-two times by my count with an electric prod on the back, rump, behind the shoulder, and then the underbelly and around the genitals. A boy about twelve years old tries to help by lifting the calf by the ears. When the animal finally stands, Everett pulls it up the ramp and pushes it into the ring, where the ring men get it to spin a time or two. Foss buys the calf for five cents a pound, about three dollars. A man drags it from the ring by one hind leg.

Neither the auctioneer nor Don Yahn nor the eight or ten people still in the seats say anything about these last few animals being so sick and lame. They must have seen this so often that they're no longer moved by it.

The auction ends at 2:00 P.M. I calculate that, at fifteen seconds per calf for two hours, about four hundred calves were sold. The red light connected to the floor scale is shut off. The old men, the young boys, and Jim Foss file out of the dark little room; some head for the cafeteria to get a drink or a bite to eat before the sale of large animals begins later this afternoon in the main ring upstairs.

·   ·   ·

Pen number 30 is empty. The Lawnel cows, I find, have been moved to a much larger pen where some seventy-five other cows mill about. Hay bales are stacked above the rafters, but a feed bunk in the middle of the pen is empty. Nor do I see any water. A sign near the auction office says HELD-OVER LIVESTOCK WILL HAVE ACCESS TO FEED AND WATER WITHIN 24 HOURS, but for the cows arriving today, it hasn't been twenty-four hours yet. Most have missed at least one meal, though, and for those accustomed to three milkings a day, they've missed a milking, too.

The big black Lawnel cow, 821, stands in the pen directly below me. She bellows, but there are no farmhands here to respond.

All social structures among these cows, which come from dozens of different herds, have been disrupted. Two cows lower their heads to push and butt each other. I suppose they're trying to establish dominance.

The sale of cull cows won't begin until 4:00 P.M. at the earliest. I could use a rest. I drive into Pavilion and park in front of the tiny public library. After telling the librarian not to be alarmed if someone reports a man lying in the back of a car in the parking lot, I climb into mine, set the alarm on my watch for an hour and a half, cover myself with a comforter, and fall asleep.

· · ·

At 4:00 P.M., back at the auction barn, the large pen that earlier held seventy-five cows is now jammed with at least twice that number. There's hardly room for any to move; many stand motionless. From all over the building and from every pen on either side of me, cows bellow. It's wrap-around sound, and doesn't let up.

I see "wall cows" now—the weakest of the group. Some lean against the wall; others limp nearby, rising and falling with big, halting steps; one lies in a heap.

In the main ring, manager Don Yahn is auctioning "feeder" calves—beef animals from three to six hundred pounds that need more feeding before they are ready for slaughter. If I had brought my calves here today from Peter Vonglis's farm, they'd be sold as feeders.

Outside, just off the parking lot, the large cow pen opens onto a barn door enclosed by a swinging gate. I go down to take a closer look at the 150 or so cows inside.

Not yet five o'clock, already it's dark outside, nearly black.

In the parking lot are twenty-three stock trailers, and a dozen cars and pickups, many with rifles mounted in the windows of the cabs. Some have bumper stickers: I'M A FARMER: I CARE FOR MY ANIMALS; BEEF. IT'S WHAT'S FOR DINNER; and MY OTHER CAR IS A TRACTOR.

The halogen light inside the barn shines on the cows nearest the gate. Among them is one of the Lawnel cows: big black 821. I try to remain a detached observer, but pull up a little grass from around the gate and offer it to her. She won't take it.

Cows from dozens of different herds are here, as evidenced by the variety of ear tags: yellow tags, red tags, lavender tags, green tags, brown tags, tags with two digits, tags with three and four digits; tags with printed numerals, tags written by hand.

I offer grass to the big black cow again, but she still won't take it.

Among the cows at the gate stands a bull with a brass ring in his nose. A huge animal, he is as powerless now as all the cows he mounted over the years at whatever dairy he served—the piece of jewelry in his nose that once proclaimed his status now just seems an obvious irony. Before the evening's over, he'll be sold along with the females.

A few of these cows have no voice left; they're sick, or they've bellowed too much already. But from the others, the bellowing is unceasing, a *basso continuo* over which, from the main ring inside, I can hear the steady drone of Don Yahn auctioning feeder calves.

Sheep begin coming through the main auction ring just after 6:00 P.M. The young man in a black shirt and cowboy hat, who earlier conducted the calf auction, takes over for Don.

After the sheep come pigs.

The main ring is set up like an amphitheater with about 150 seats covered in red leather-type material overlooking the twenty-five-foot-long, sawdust-covered concrete ring. Perched in front directly over the ring, like a press box at a sports stadium, is the auctioneer's box.

This evening only seventeen seats are filled. Way over on the left, a heavyset woman with graying hair sits alone, sipping soda from a can and doing needlepoint. Everyone else here is male, most in coveralls and farm caps. The average age looks to be about seventy. "Last night I was dreamin' 'bout Rita Hayworth," a man in front of me tells two others seated nearby. They rib him good-naturedly, questioning what interest Rita Hayworth would have in him.

Seated directly in front of me, still wearing his trademark bright orange cap, is cattle dealer Jim Foss.

At six-thirty the steers come through. The ring man on the right, an old man in black coveralls, pulls open a door for the animals to enter one at a time. If necessary, he can protect himself by jumping behind a swinging gate. Don Yahn, in jeans and hooded gray sweatshirt, acts as left ring man. If Don needs protection, he can jump behind two metal posts nearby. But most of the steers seem calm.

At 7:00 P.M., two bulls, each with a nose ring, enter the ring, one at a time.

The auctioneer announces their weight: 1,500 pounds for one, 1,730 pounds for the other. Both are bought by slaughterhouses.

Jim Foss turns around to a man seated next to me.

"Bill, you got any cigars? I'll never make it through the sale unless I have one."

"You ever smoke one, Jim?" the man asks.

"Nah, I don't smoke 'em," says Foss. "I just chew 'em."

By seven-thirty, when the first cull cows come through, there are just nine people, including me, watching the auction.

"Number 615, boys, seventeen fifty pounds," begins the auctioneer.

I know this animal. She's one of the five Lawnel cows. She was 5657, a mostly white cow, the first to climb into Joe Hopper's trailer before she turned around and tried to get out. Three and a half years old, she gave just five pounds of milk, the lowest producer on Sue's "look-at" list.

It's startling to me actually to recognize an animal entering the auction ring—like looking at a stranger's home movies and catching a glimpse of someone you know.

I see now why at the unloading ramp they stick the auction tags on the cows' left sides. It's so that when the animals enter the ring through the right door, the tag numbers are instantly visible to the spectators.

Don Yahn and the other ring man poke the Lawnel cow a few times on either side to start her spinning.

She's been without food or water for nearly twelve hours.

After twenty seconds, Don opens the left door and the first of the Lawnel cows is gone. The bidding on her, however, continues for another ten seconds.

"Taylor, forty and a half," declares the auctioneer. The cow has been bought by Taylor Packing for forty and one-half cents per pound, just over seven hundred dollars.

Well, that's it. If I want to watch a Lawnel cow come one step closer to becoming a Big Mac, I'll now have the opportunity.

Of the next ten cows to be sold, their average time in the ring is twenty-one seconds. Their demeanors range from placid and dull to jittery and jumpy. The ring men spin each one two or three times. Cane hits are soft thuds if against flesh, loud cracks if against bone.

After another fifteen minutes, Don Yahn takes over the auctioning. I like Don as an auctioneer. I like his voice and style, and how, even though he's younger than most of his audience, he gently refers to the old men bidding as "boys." Up in the auctioneer's box, with a bottle of spring water by his side, Don leans his elbows on the table, holds the microphone in both hands up close to his mouth, and croons.

He usually begins with the cow's weight, repeats it a few times, then seamlessly rolls it into the price, in cents per pound, at which he'd like the bidding to start: "This one here weighs twelve ninety-five, boys . . . twelve ninety-five pounds . . . twelve ninety-five, twelve ninety-five, twelve ninety-five . . . forty-one, forty-one, forty-one, forty-one . . . what'ya give on her . . . forty-one and a half, forty-one and a half," and so on, ending abruptly with the name of the buyer and the price: "Taylor, forty-one and a half."

None of the bidders calls out. They mouth silently, nod, or move a finger.

The next Lawnel cow comes through so fast I miss the weight and price. It was 5983. Schreiber, another slaughterhouse, is the buyer.

Many of these cows are thin, with ribs and hipbones showing; others are well filled out and look healthy—they're probably here because of reproductive problems. Some of their udders are tremendous; a few seem almost to drag in the sawdust on the floor.

The "alley rat" is next. She weighs in at 1,395 pounds. In fifteen seconds, Taylor buys her for thirty-four cents a pound.

An hour passes. It's late. Everyone seems tired.

"Keep 'em comin', boys," Don calls to the men behind the gates who push the cows one at a time into the ring.

I go downstairs to check on the large pen that earlier held about 150 animals. It's not as crowded as it was before; about seventy-five cows remain to be sold. There's a lot of bellowing; most of these animals have now missed two milkings and two meals.

Back in the ring, a cow defecates a stream of diarrhea as the ring men spin her. I don't know what it smells like, but given the audible force with which the stream is expelled, it sounds like it smells bad.

At eight-thirty there's a short break in the action. I head for the coffee shop, which is on the second floor above the large cow pen. Two waitresses in pink aprons are still on duty. I take a seat at the counter.

The only other customer here is one of the active bidders, a man I've met before, John Weidman. We order sixty-five-cent bowls of chicken noodle soup.

At thirty-six, John is the youngest man here, and probably the tallest, standing well over six feet. He has golden brown hair, which he parts in the middle, blue-green eyes, and a strong, Jay Leno–type jaw.

I rode with John one day about two years ago when he was working as a cattle buyer for a slaughterhouse. I marveled at how he could wade into a barnyard with dozens of cattle—many kicking up mud and manure as they raced away from him—and quickly pick out the five or six he wanted to buy.

"That one'll grade. She's ready," he'd say. "Them steers'll grade."

By "grade," John means that when the animal is slaughtered, a government inspector will give it one of the high-quality grades, such as Prime or Choice. The other grades, in descending order, are Select, Standard, Commercial, Utility, Cutter, and Canner. Marbling (the amount and distribution of fat within the muscle) and maturity—the age of the animal and the size and hardness of the bone—are the main factors that determine the quality grade.

Cows receive the same quality grades as steers, except they are not eligible for Prime. Young cows that have been culled not for illness but for reproductive problems may grade Select or Standard, but older ones that are sick or lame are likely to receive the lowest grades: Canner and Cutter. Their meat has little or no marbling. "This grade of beef is not presented to the buying public in retail markets," note the authors of *The Meat We Eat* (Interstate Publishers, 1994), a standard work on the meat industry, "instead, it is processed into frankfurters, bologna, and hamburger."

To predict what quality grade a carcass might receive, John imagines how a live animal will look "opened up." That's a phrase he uses a lot: "when she's opened up" or "how them cattle will open up."

In one barn he pointed to several steers and explained how he looked at the thickness of fat over the pin bones (at the rump), the fatness on the flank and brisket (chest), and the fatness over the loin (back).

"I look at the outside of cattle and I can see their inside," he told me. "I see that rump and I can picture the marbling in the meat. I've done it with thousands and thousands of head."

As animals are spun in the ring, buyers have only seconds to estimate the quality and grade the carcasses might receive, calculate the current market price for that type of meat, and bid.

"I love the competition," John told me. "I've got three seconds to think quick and outsmart the other guy."

Since our first meeting, John has changed jobs and now works for the livestock auction. He also buys cattle for a few Midwestern slaughterhouses, which is what he's doing here tonight.

As we finish our soup, John repeats an offer he made to me earlier: If I want to follow any of the Lawnel cows to Taylor Packing, he'll be glad to call the president, Tom Taylor, and try to arrange for me to get in. He knows Tom Taylor—and confirms the company sells ground beef to McDonald's—because earlier in his career he worked for Taylor Packing.

John's offer is important to me. With a capacity to kill more than 1,900 animals a day, more than $500 million in annual sales, and one thousand employees, Taylor Packing ranks among the ten largest slaughterhouses in the country. A slaughterhouse that big surely will be wary of a writer coming to visit.

A menu on the cafeteria wall offers desserts—"candy, gum, Rolaids"—but John and I finish our soup and head back to the auction.

The next Lawnel cow through the ring is 821, the big black animal with the white Nike swoosh on her forehead. She's the one who missed the milk-weight cutoff by two pounds—a single quart of milk. Taylor Packing buys her for thirty-six and a half cents a pound.

That's three out of four Lawnel cows going to Taylor.

The right ring man opens the door for the next cow to enter, but none does. I can see through the opening that the cow has got herself turned around. She tries to back into the ring, but can't manage. A man in the holding area smacks her half a dozen times on the face before she turns around and enters the ring.

It's after 8:30 P.M. Don Yahn is pumping. He's sold hundreds of cows without a break. A second or two is all he rests between sales. His auction patter is rapid and hypnotic, like someone chanting in prayer. There's something oddly comforting in it.

Just eight of us are left in the bidders' seats.

The cows coming through seem increasingly thin and weak: skin and bones hauling around huge, swollen udders.

"Twenty more good cows and about forty slow ones," says a man behind me who has just checked the holding pens.

By 9:00 P.M., just seven of us remain.

At 9:02, a thin cow with crossed front legs enters the ring. She's the last of the five Lawnel cows. "Eight hundred ninety-five pounds, that's what she weighs, boys," sings Don. Her turn in the spotlight is brief. Two spins and she's out. Fifteen seconds.

"Sold, Taylor-X, twenty-eight cents," says Don.

The "X" after a buyer's name means the animal is a slow cow. Slow cows are the first to be hauled away from the livestock auction so they can arrive at the slaughterhouse first.

The auctions I've watched today—the stumbling, matted little calves, the cull cows—are among hundreds held across the country each week. From these come the beef on which we feed. And what is so sad here will later be transformed into something joyful for so many: Happy Meals, Whoppers, and jolly Ronald McDonald and smiling, red-haired Wendy. The dirty beige of sawdust floors, the browns of the farmers' coveralls and winter jackets, the black and white of the animals themselves—all will be lost in the brilliance of bright primary colors: reds and yellows, neon lights and Golden Arches.

Only Jim Foss's bright orange farm cap foreshadows the transformation.

The auction should end in another fifteen minutes or so, but I'm ready to go home. It's been a long and tiring day, and I'm too drained to watch the rest of the lame, the injured, and the ill—the "slow" cows—go through the ring.

Even if John Weidman could reach his former boss, Tom Taylor, at home at this late hour and arrange for me to visit the plant tomorrow morning, I just don't have it in me to drive the three or four hours overnight to Pennsylvania; it's been too long a day. I would do it if at least one of the Lawnel cows going tonight was an animal I knew better, one I had observed for more than just the past few days. If Sue Smith had culled 4923, for example, the mother of my twin calves, and that cow was going to Taylor, then I'd go.

The parking lot behind the auction barn is unlighted and black. All that's visible are the red taillights and yellow running lights of two long, double-level stock trailers backed up to the loading ramps, their engines idling.

"How many you got in that pen, Jim?" a driver yells to someone inside the building.

I can't hear the reply.

With a loud clang, the man closes the gate on the back of the truck and drives off.

8

Beefed

"PETER, THIS IS SUE SMITH. I'm sorry, but I have some bad news on your cow, 4923. Call me."

The message is on the answering machine when I arrive at my office on a Friday morning just two days after my visit to the livestock auction at Pavilion. When I call Sue back at the Lawnel herd office, there's no answer.

I reach Andrew Smith in the machine shop.

"Do you know anything about 4923? Sue left a message on my machine."

"Yeah," he says. "She's open." That means the cow isn't pregnant as Sue had thought.

"So what's she going to do with her?" I ask.

"Beef her," he says.

"When?"

"Monday."

I leave the office, stop at home to pick up my coveralls, and drive immediately to Lawnel. There I find Sue in the milk parlor, spraying teats.

"4923 is the mother of the calves you bought, isn't she?" she asks. "Andrew pulled those twins last year, right?"

She says she was going to move 4923 on Wednesday to Valley View Farm, where dry cows stay until ready to give birth, but Dave Hale, the vet, checked her again this morning and found she wasn't pregnant after all.

"Dave thinks she was pregnant but absorbed the calf—miscarried but retained the fetus," says Sue. "That would explain why she was showing a lot of fluids, why she kept looking pregnant."

Will Sue try to breed 4923 again?

"No, her milk weight has dropped off," she says. "At three lactations, she's just too old to keep."

4923 has given birth to two heifers, each of which is now grown and in the milking herd, and my bull-heifer twins—7 and 8—but in the last measured milking, she gave just twelve pounds, well below the thirty-two-pound cutoff Sue uses to cull cows.

"Well, it's not so bad for her," says Sue. "She's in her third lactation and that's about typical to be beefed."

Sue says Joe Hopper, the cattle hauler, is off next Monday, so instead Andrew will take 4923 to Pavilion.

It's a cold Sunday morning in late December; bare, ice-covered tree limbs glisten in the sunlight. At Lawnel, the east and west sides of the cow barns have been covered with plastic sheeting to cut the wind. Steam rises off bagels rotting in the commodity shed. Outside the maternity barn, dead calves, their limbs stiff, lie in a heap, waiting to become compost.

In the cow barn, I spot 4923 by the white reverse question mark on her black forehead. She stands in the aisle ruminating, head low. Bulging on the right side, she still appears pregnant. Her back left hoof must be sore: she holds it off the concrete as she stands, touching it only lightly to the floor when she walks.

It is arresting to look at a living thing—particularly one so large as it exhales visible breath—and to know for a certainty it will soon be dead.

As I did with the five other cull cows, I've come to Lawnel to observe 4923 on her last day of milking. Then I'll go to auction with her, and if Taylor Packing buys her, I'll try to follow her to the slaughterhouse. Of course, the animal I should really watch slaughtered is my own bull calf, 8, but I'm still unsure what to do with him and his twin sister. At least by watching 4923, I'll see what it's like at Taylor, and if that's where I'll want to send my own calves if I do decide to slaughter them—kind of a trial run.

Once inside the parlor, 4923 moves into the fifth stall on the right side. From the pit, I can see her up close. Near her left thigh is a bare patch of skin. Pink flesh shows through the dark hair. There's also a spot that looks sore on her left hind leg where the hair has been rubbed away.

The afternoon milker says 4923 limps because she has hairy warts on her left front hoof. Now that he points it out, I can see the large brown patches of flesh growing around the hoof. These are common among dairy cows. If 4923 weren't on the beef list, the warts would be treated. The problem on the left knee, he says, is probably a rub burn "from lying on her side on concrete." The stalls in her barn, he says, don't have rubber mats under the straw bedding as most of the other barns do. The injury on her side is probably from hitting against a sharp object in the barn, or rubbing against a nail on a broken fence.

The milker connects the milking unit to 4923's teats. The milk comes in a trickle. In just three minutes the unit automatically disengages.

Outside, the Smiths—Andrew, Sue, Kirsty, and Amos—drive by in their sport utility vehicle. They're on their way to a mall near Rochester this Sunday morning to go to a wholesale shopping club.

With a whoosh of compressed air, the rapid-exit bar on the milking machine rises, releasing 4923.

·   ·   ·

"Hey, hey, hey!" calls Sue. "Move it up!"

It's Monday morning, and Sue is herding three cows out of the barn and up a ramp into the stock trailer. The last of the three, 4923, balks, her back right hoof hanging off the ramp, refusing to enter.

"C'mon, move up!" orders Sue.

"Move that rear axle!" shouts Andrew, working beside his wife.

Andrew kicks the hoof with his own booted foot until 4923 pulls it inside just before Sue pushes the truck gate closed.

At the superhutch, Andrew stops the trailer to load seven newborn bull calves. Then we turn right out of the farm and onto Craig Road. The same dog that chased Joe Hopper's truck last week dashes after us through a field of cut corn. I tell Andrew how Joe throws biscuits to the dog.

"I killed the last dog at this place," he says. "Ran it over."

·   ·   ·

As we approach Pavilion, I ask Andrew if he's ever been to the auction to see Lawnel cows sold.

"Never have been there," he says. "Just drop 'em off and Sayonara!"

At the unloading dock, Paula helps us unload the bull calves.

"C'mon, tiny tot," she says gently to one. "Oh, you got four legs and you don't know how to use any of 'em."

Andrew asks Paula if it would be okay if he carries the calf in. She says it would, and he does.

"That's the last time he'll be carried today, I can guarantee it," Paula says to Andrew.

Andrew carefully puts the calf down inside the loading ramp. Paula taps it gently with her cane to coax it toward a nearby pen.

"This way, Bubba," she says to the calf.

Now Andrew unloads the three cows.

"Good cow!" the man straddling the wooden chute calls as 4923 comes through. He cements a round auction tag—171—on her left side and moves her into a large holding pen.

Paula says there are a lot fewer cows coming in today than last Monday, when 943 animals were sold. She guesses all the cows today will be sold by late afternoon.

Unfortunately, I won't be here to see 4923 go through the ring. The Smiths have invited my wife and me to the annual Lawnel Christmas party, which begins late this afternoon. Instead, I arrange to call John Weidman, who works at the auction, to tell me who buys 4923. If Taylor buys her, I'll ask John to call Tom Taylor, his former boss, at Taylor Packing in Pennsylvania and see if he can get me permission to enter the plant and watch 4923 slaughtered. If he can, I'll follow 4923 to Pennsylvania.

I ride back to Lawnel with Andrew Smith. What feelings does he have, I ask, when he drops three of his farm's cows at auction?

"The white one, I think she knows it's the end of the line," he says, referring not to 4923 but to one of the other cows.

How would she know that?

"'Cause she turned around in the trailer and didn't want to get out. She knows," he says.

Could she just be reacting to the change of setting?

"No, I think she knows the end is near."

Then Andrew asks me, "They got any food or water in there for the animals?"

I say I haven't seen any on my previous visits, but there is a sign that says livestock are supposed to be given food and water within twenty-four hours.

There's a pause in our conversation.

"When I reach the end of the line," says Andrew, "I hope I know it's my time." Another pause.

"I like the way cows finish," he says. "They go right from productivity to death. One day they're productive animals and the next day they're hamburger.

"I wouldn't want to lie on my deathbed for two years. Grandpa Smith, he spends a lot of time on family genealogy, which I'm not particularly interested in," says Andrew, not quite completing the thought. Andrew's grandfather Nelson founded the family farm in 1945. He's ninety-two now, and lives in an assisted-living facility.

. . .

This is my second Lawnel Christmas party. It's at the same party house as last year, in a private dining room on the second floor. Andrew Smith, in a brown suit, and Sue Smith, in a long blue dress, stand at the top of the stairs, greeting their guests: farmhands, suppliers, relatives, and friends.

I'm talking to people at the party, but I'm really thinking about the call I have to make later this evening to John Weidman to find out what happened to 4923. If Taylor Packing bought her, I really need to watch her be slaughtered. I'm uneasy, though, both about being inside a place that kills 1,900 animals a day and about watching this particular cow—the mother of my calves—killed. I'm concerned, too, about whether Taylor will let me in—even with an introduction from Weidman— or whether I'll drive overnight to rural Pennsylvania only to be turned away in the morning because someone decides they don't want a writer nosing around.

My wife and I remain after dinner, talking with Sue and a few of the Lawnel employees, but then people start coming up the stairs for the second seating at 7:30 P.M., so it's time for us to leave. At a pay phone downstairs, I call John Weidman at his home.

"So, who bought 4923?" I ask.

"Taylor," he says, "just after five-thirty. Went for forty-one cents a pound."

My stomach sinks; now I'm really going to have to go there. I ask John to telephone Tom Taylor in the morning and see if he can arrange for me to visit.

"Can't do it," he says, surprising me. "Them cows have already left. They'll probably be slaughtered overnight. You'd never make it there. If you want to arrange a visit, you really need to call Tom ahead of time and arrange it on your own."

I'm greatly relieved, and suddenly hungry for the chicken, buttered rolls, and green beans I'd left on my plate at the party.

. . .

The next morning, my older daughter wakes me at six-thirty. She needs an early ride to school. I dress and drive her to school, but when I return home, I'm suddenly curious: Was John Weidman being honest with me when he said 4923 had already left for Pennsylvania? Somehow he sounded too certain, as though maybe he'd gone home, talked it over with his wife, and decided he just didn't want to get in the middle between Tom Taylor—his former boss and now an important customer of the livestock auction—and me, someone he really doesn't know well. If so, I can understand his reluctance.

I call Pavilion. A man named Jeff answers and confirms that the slow cows from yesterday's auction left for Taylor on an overnight truck, but the good cows—the healthier ones—are still there and probably won't leave until this afternoon.

I pack an overnight bag, pull on my coveralls, and drive the forty-five minutes to Pavilion. There, I find 4923 lying among thirty-five other cows in the large pen, her sale tag still glued to her left side.

Don Yahn, the auction manager, offers to call Taylor's truck dispatcher in Pennsylvania. The dispatcher confirms that the cows will leave this afternoon and are not scheduled to be killed until tomorrow morning.

Don says that if I want to call Tom Taylor, I can use a phone in the customer lounge.

For me to contact a large company like Taylor, without a personal introduction, carries some risk. If they ask around, they might find that twenty years ago, when I was just out of school, I did some work for the Humane Society. I've made a point of mentioning this to each of the principal people I'm writing about, and no one's seemed concerned. A big company, though, could make an issue of it— even tag me incorrectly as an animal-rights person—and damage the goodwill I've built up with so many people, even jeopardize my ability to finish the book.

In my notebook, I outline what I'll say to Tom Taylor if I'm able to reach him on the phone. I even practice the call once or twice to myself.

Then I place a long-distance call to Taylor Packing and ask for the president, Tom Taylor.

In a moment, I'm connected.

"This is Tom Taylor," says a strong, serious voice.

I introduce myself by mentioning a few people we know in common, John Weidman among them. I try to sound calm, as though this is no big deal. I say that for a book, I've been observing cattle for a year and a half at a nine-hundred-head dairy farm called Lawnel Farms in York, New York. I explain I've followed the progress of one cow and a couple of her calves, that the cow was just culled and bought at auction by his company, and will leave this afternoon for the plant. Would it be okay if I just came by and watched it go "through the line"?

"Yes, that would be fine," he says. "Come on down."

I need to exhale and breathe, but don't know how to do it without making a loud noise into the phone, so I move the phone away from my face for a moment. When I bring it back to my ear, Tom is saying something about tomorrow morning.

"Sorry," I say, "I couldn't hear you for a moment."

Tom repeats that he has a nine-thirty dentist's appointment tomorrow morning, but we can meet at his office when he gets back. Then he transfers me to his plant manager, Tony Noll, who he says will arrange for me to see the cow go through the line and also give me directions to the plant.

I'm put on hold for a moment. Then Tony comes on.

"Tom says you're coming to the plant tomorrow," he begins. "How can I help?"

I tell Tony about 4923.

The kill-chain will start at 6:45 A.M., he says. They'll do the slow cows first and then the lot from Pavilion at about nine. He suggests I arrive at the plant around eight o'clock, park in the visitors' lot, and have him paged. Tony then gives me directions to the plant in Wyalusing, Pennsylvania—he says the drive should take about three and a half hours—and recommends I stay overnight in Towanda, a town about twelve miles from the plant, at a Comfort Inn.

When I hang up with Tony, my dread of going to the slaughterhouse has vanished, at least temporarily. Instead, I'm elated. I handled the call well—I didn't need John Weidman to make it for me after all. Tom Taylor sounds like a nice person and a successful businessman, and he's given me the go-ahead. It's quite a coup. Most farmers I've met—Andrew and Sue Smith included—don't even go to the auction, let alone the slaughterhouse, but I'm going all the way. I'm going to the slaughterhouse.

·   ·   ·

At a strip mall about ten miles outside Pavilion, I buy a tuna sub sandwich to eat in the car on the way to Pennsylvania, and a copy of the *New York Times* to read later at the motel, and then head south on a divided highway.

The road is smooth for fifty miles, until just outside the town of Dansville, where I hit a patch of rough concrete. I wonder how 4923's front left hoof, the one with hairy warts, will feel on this bumpy stretch when the stock trailer she's on rides over it later today.

Just past the bumpy stretch, there's a McDonald's, its Golden Arches perched atop a tall pole, so as to be visible to motorists speeding along this road.

Traveling east on Route 17 through southern New York State, I pass Corning, Elmira, and then Ithaca. I think of Bonanza, the stud bull at Genex Cooperative in Ithaca, with whose semen 4923 was bred nearly two years ago. I haven't gotten back to Genex to see Bonanza again, but I've called and been told he's still an active and popular sire, still being "collected" twice each week.

I pass Binghamton and head south out of New York State. How ironic it will be for me, having grown up so sensitive about the way animals are treated, for me to be the guest of the president of one of the country's largest slaughterhouses. By choice, it's not a place I'd go, but professionally, it's important for me to make this visit. I push aside my ambivalence, and focus on preparing for my interview tomorrow.

Northeastern Pennsylvania is not rolling farmland like western New York, but steep hills with winding roads and straight drop-offs. The deeper I drive into it, the more vulnerable and unsafe I feel. Or maybe it's anxiety about witnessing the kill-chain tomorrow.

· · ·

I reach the Towanda Comfort Inn at just after 3:00 P.M. With no stops, the drive took three and a half hours, just as Tony Noll, the plant manager, had said it would. Instead of stopping, however, I drive on to Wyalusing. I want to prepare for the meeting tomorrow by seeing the town and the Taylor plant, at least from the outside.

The extra twelve miles are harrowing. A fog has descended and much of the road is narrow, with hairpin turns around steep cliffs that rise above the Susquehanna River.

Wyalusing is a small old town with a few streets of shops and public buildings at the center. About a half mile outside of town, the road bends to the right and down a steep hill. On the right, just before the entrance to Taylor Packing, is a small farm with a single Holstein cow lying in a pasture.

In front of a huge complex of off-white factory buildings is a large parking lot. Beyond, hard to see in the fog, are one or more smokestacks. In front of a section of the lot labeled VISITORS, there's a security guard. That's where I'll go tomorrow, but now I'm worn out and beginning to feel some pressure in my sinuses, maybe the start of a cold. I enter the parking area only to turn around, head back up the hill and through the town of Wyalusing, and drive twelve miles back to Towanda.

By the time I reach the Comfort Inn, at around 4:30 P.M., night has fallen. Today is the winter solstice, the shortest, darkest day of the year. The exact time of the solstice will be 2:14 A.M.; it will become winter overnight.

My room, on the first floor, faces the road. I lie on the bed and immediately feel the back of my neck cramp; I can't turn my head left or right. Fortunately, the motel has a small indoor heated pool. A half-hour swim helps a little, but when I get back to the room I feel a sharp pain in the back of my left lower leg, like a charley horse. I'm sure this is all just about the tension of going to the slaughter plant tomorrow, but it hurts nonetheless.

At 6:00 P.M., I leave the Comfort Inn to find something to eat. The cramp in my neck forces me to hold my head at an odd angle. Within walking distance, there are two choices: Bonanza, a family restaurant specializing in steak, chicken, and seafood; and McDonald's. Both present easy ironies: Bonanza because that's the name of the bull whose semen I saw collected and was later used to insemi-nate 4923, the mother of my calves and the cow who at this very moment is on her way to the slaughterhouse; and McDonald's because that's where 4923's meat may end up. I choose Bonanza when I see that on the hot buffet they have mac-aroni and cottage cheese, the comfort food my mom used to give me when I was a kid and not feeling well. Maybe it's even Friendship brand cottage cheese, which now I know is made, in part, from the milk of Lawnel cows. Maybe it's even made from 4923's milk.

As I eat, I imagine that the stock trailer carrying 4923 has by now gone over the bumps in the road outside Dansville and may have crossed into Pennsylvania. Sometime this evening it will pass in front of the Comfort Inn on its way to Wyalusing. I wonder, once they reach the plant, if the cows stay on the truck overnight or are off-loaded into a holding area before the kill-line starts up in the morning. I'll need to ask Tom Taylor that tomorrow. I also want to ask him other questions, and in my notebook I prepare a list under the head-ing "Qs for Taylor":

> —After 4923 was killed, how did her meat grade? Choice? Select? Or a lesser grade like Cutter or Canner?

—Where does her meat go? Can it be traced to a particular McDonald's?

—Where does her hide go?

—What happens to the cow magnets?

—How does Taylor coordinate the timing so well? Don Yahn called Taylor from Pavilion and was told exactly when his load of thirty-two cows would be picked up and what time they'd be slaughtered the next morning. Taylor must buy from scores of livestock auctions; how do they arrange the schedule so precisely?

—How long do cows generally stay in the plant before slaughter? Two hours? Half a day?

—Has he noticed any change over the years in the age and condition of cull cows? As higher production goals shorten the life of the average cow, is he seeing younger animals? Also, does use of BST as a growth hormone create more emaciated cows, as some farmers have said?

—How did he and his brother manage to build one of the largest slaughterhouses in the country?

—How did Taylor come to specialize in cull cows, as opposed to beef cattle, or pigs, or sheep?

—If he has teenagers or kids in college, any vegetarians in the family?

．　．　．

I return to my room around 7:00 P.M. and call home. I review the day's events with my wife, catch up with my kids, and then talk with my wife again.

"Oh, there was a message for you on the answering machine," she says. "It was kind of hard to hear—we need to change the tape—but I think a man named Tony from Taylor Packing is trying to reach you. He has some questions."

"Oh, shit!" I say. "That's not good."

I say a hurried good night and try to figure out what to do. The switchboard at Taylor Packing already has closed for the evening. I rifle through the slim, local phone directory and find Tony Noll's home number.

"Yeah, we were talking about this," Tony begins, "and we do let people come by to watch their own animals killed, but someone writing a book is a different thing. Anyway, people got discussing it."

"People? What people?" I interrupt. "Tom Taylor's the president, isn't he? When I spoke with him this morning, he said 'Fine, come on down.'"

"Well, the board of directors disagrees," says Tony. "We really can't have you see the kill floor. Which is your cow again? We don't even want to handle it. We'll take it out when the truck arrives and you can pick it up."

I tell Tony it's not *my* cow; it came from Lawnel Farms and was bought at auction by Taylor. I'm just watching it.

"Well, you can't come in. We have federal inspectors in there, and there are some sensitive public-health issues."

I explain to Tony that my book's not about public-health issues. I'm just trying to follow a cow from the farm to slaughter.

"We're a prosperous plant," he says. "We've made lots of improvements in the last ten or fifteen years, when maybe we did have some conditions that needed upgrading."

Sounds like Taylor might have had some problems in the past. I tell Tony I'm not interested in exposing conditions, good or otherwise. If it would help, I'll agree to almost any restrictions they might want. If they like, I won't even mention the name or location of the plant.

He still says no.

"But I've just driven one hundred seventy-five miles to get here, and I'm already checked into this Comfort Inn where you yourself told me to stay," I say, a little too desperately.

"Well, we've talked about it . . ." he says.

I calm down, and try again to explain to Tony what I'm doing. My interest is only in the cow and in the people caring for it, including the people working in the plant.

"Well, the Taylor family is very interesting," he says. "They're third-generation. Two of the boys came back from Vietnam in '66 and built this business from thirty-four employees to eleven hundred today—we're the largest plant on the East Coast."

I tell Tony I was raised in a family with a family-owned business, and I can appreciate the Taylor family's right to privacy. But isn't there any way we can work this out so the Taylors can be comfortable with my coming into the plant?

He says he can't think of any. The best I can get from him is that if I want, I can stop by the gate at nine-thirty in the morning. They'll have just had their morning management meeting, and if anything has changed in their position he'll let me know.

It doesn't sound promising. I'm not sure what to do.

If they don't let me in, I'll never know how I would have reacted to seeing the kill-line and watching 4923 slaughtered, and I won't get answers to the questions I prepared for Tom Taylor. And sending my own calves there to be slaughtered is out of the question if they won't let me in to watch.

The whole thing is frustrating.

But I'm also relieved. Of course I don't want to see the kill-line. My whole body's rebelled against it since I left Pavilion this morning.

I'm concerned, too, why Tom Taylor changed his mind after we spoke, and why he didn't call me himself. Maybe they think I'm writing an exposé. If so, I doubt I could stand at the plant gate and convince him otherwise.

I've done all I could do to get in, and they've said no. I could keep pushing—show up at the plant in the morning and try to talk my way in—but I don't have it in me.

I call Tony again. I've got my professional, controlled voice back.

"Tony, thanks for taking the time to consider my request, but it doesn't look like this will work out. I'm just going to go home in the morning. Hope you and your family have a nice holiday."

I'm achy and chilled, and begin sneezing. From the bathroom I remove a box of tissues from a metal holder under the sink, and bring it over to the bed. My neck is sore, and now I've got a cold.

• • •

I'm up and out of the hotel early and skip the breakfast I'd planned at McDonald's. Instead, I get on the road, and by nine I have crossed back into New York. By now, I think, 4923 probably has been slaughtered. I try to imagine what's become of her body and the white reverse question mark on her black forehead, but I can't quite get a picture.

Later in the morning, on the way home, I stop at Lawnel. The talk is mostly about how nice the Christmas party had been.

Andrew is in the equipment shed, fitting the chopper with a snow plow and loading the engine with antifreeze. He'll use the chopper to plow the farm's driveway this winter. Andrew thanks me for a framed photograph I gave him at the

Christmas party. It shows him in front of the silos at dawn, spray-cleaning a tractor, silhouetted by the rising sun.

Sue is in the parlor giving BST shots. She's wearing a brown stocking cap with
a long tail—kind of Christmassy. I tell her of my aborted 340-mile round-trip
adventure to Wyalusing. She says, "If I went to a slaughterhouse and they didn't
let me in, I'd be relieved."

I'm glad to hear her say that. If Sue, who selects the cows for culling, would
be relieved not to see them slaughtered, then who could fault me for having the
same feelings? Still, as I drive home, I think maybe I should have pushed harder
to get into the plant. I know I've lost an opportunity, and now the answer to my
dilemma about what to do with my calves seems even less clear.

9

Choices

IT IS AN OVERCAST AND RAINY afternoon in late January. The sky has not brightened all day; since morning, it has looked like evening.

In the intensive care unit of Rochester's Strong Memorial Hospital, Shelly Vonglis sits beside an elderly woman hooked up to a heart monitor. While her patient rests, Shelly studies a nursing school text. I've never seen Shelly at work outside her home, so I'm glad to be able to visit with her at the hospital today.

She looks terrific, the best I've ever seen her. Her shiny auburn hair has been nicely cut to frame her face, especially her intense blue eyes. She says she recently has been exercising and feels well.

Shelly found this part-time job by responding to a newspaper ad for a private-duty nurse. Her patient, it turns out, is the mother of a friend of mine. Even so, when I ask Shelly about the woman's condition, she politely declines to answer, properly citing confidentiality.

Nursing school is going well, she says, but she has some disturbing news about Peter: Scot Batzing, who had invited Peter to become an owner of the Batzing Farm because none of Scot's children was interested in farming, now says one of his daughters has quit college and is coming back to the farm.

"We don't know what this means yet," says Shelly. "But if Peter can't get shares in the farm, I doubt he'll stay there. For me, I'm just focused on my nursing degree so I can get a good job when I'm done."

Shelly checks her patient's monitors.

"So have you decided what you'll do with your calves?" she asks me.

It feels awkward—embarrassing even—to be asked about my calves while people in the same room cling to life.

I tell Shelly, honestly, that I haven't reached a decision.

"Well, I'm definitely buying one," she says. "Right now I'm buying hamburger at the supermarket and I don't like that, so I want to get the freezer filled. I'd buy both of them if I could, but I can only fit one in the freezer."

To hear Shelly say she's "definitely" buying the meat from one of my calves makes me uneasy, because I haven't even decided yet if I'm going to slaughter them.

I've got to do something, though. Peter has said he will ship his five steers to slaughter in April or May, and since I've committed to having him raise mine as he raises his, if I choose to slaughter mine, they should go when his go. There isn't a lot of time to explore what the other choices might be—and my suburban backyard isn't one of them. Keeping them indefinitely with Peter and Shelly is also out of the question. Even if I were willing to continue paying ninety dollars a month to board them there for life, which I'm not, the Vonglises have no interest in keeping them, especially a male such as 8, who could grow to weigh three thousand pounds.

At any rate, if I do send them to slaughter, I'll probably just make a gift of some of the meat to Peter and Shelly, rather than sell it to them.

I ask Shelly which calf she would want.

"Oh, no, I'm not picking." she says. "That's up to Peter."

"But would you prefer the boy or the girl?" I ask playfully.

"I'm not choosing!" she insists, her voice rising. "They'll all go at once—all seven of them—and all I'll know is that there's beef in the freezer. I don't want to know which calf it came from."

She continues, "That's why I don't go out there and spend time with them anymore. I just glance at the barnyard to see whether they're in the barn or the running shed or on that little wooden bridge over the creek—they like to play on the bridge—but I don't look any of them in the eyes."

Shelly and I talk more about her work in the ICU. I tell her my friend's mom is lucky to have her as her nurse.

"Actually," she says, "Peter seemed worried about my taking this job, like if I screwed up it could hurt his reputation in Avon."

Shelly's patient is the mother of a prominent family in Avon, a town just north of York where Peter grew up.

"Maybe a better way to think about it," I suggest, "is that if you do a good job—which I'm sure you will—you'll enhance both your own and Peter's reputations."

She says she's never thought of it that way.

On my way out of the hospital, I stop in the lobby. A middle-aged woman pushes an older woman—her mother, I imagine—in a wheelchair. The mother is obese and holds a potted poinsettia with leaves but no blossoms. Dozens of people are seated. Most, I suppose, are visiting friends or relatives who are ill. Some probably are ill themselves.

But I am focused on the fate of two Holstein calves lying in a barn thirty-five miles away.

• • •

Two weeks later, Shelly calls me at home in the evening. When I ask how my friend's mother is doing, she says she doesn't know. Her own son, Colin, two years old, has pneumonia and she doesn't feel she can care for him, keep up with nursing school, and work as a private-duty nurse all at the same time, so she's quit the part-time job.

What she is calling for, however, is to tell me that Peter is going to take my two animals and one of his own to his father's farm to weigh them. He wants to see how fast they're gaining on the corn finishing diet, so that he can decide when to slaughter them. Peter doesn't have his own livestock scale, so he uses his father's. She says if I want to see the weighing, Peter will call me the day before he goes, and I can arrange to ride with him.

• • •

I hadn't known there was a Hindu ashram near where I live until one day about two years ago I typed "cow" into an Internet search engine and came up with several listings for "sacred cows." Among these was Sri Puri Dhama Vaishnava Community in Lockport, New York, just fifty miles west of Rochester. I e-mailed the ashram, asking permission to visit. The reply, from someone named Jagannatha Dasa Puripadasat, was, "You are most welcome. We will entertain you until the sacred cows come home."

The ashram sits on ten acres overlooking the Erie Canal as it enters the old industrial town of Lockport, near Buffalo. The main building, constructed in the late 1800s, is a brick mansion with tall, narrow windows and white-painted wood trim. On that first visit, as I stepped from my car, a boy in his mid-teens, with a shaved head and a ponytail, showed me a young Holstein cow, horns and tail intact, tied to a long tether in the backyard.

"We worship cow," he said.

When I approached to rub the cow's neck, she didn't flinch—a marked difference from most dairy cows I've met. The boy showed me a barn where the cow sleeps. He then emptied half a dozen ten-pound bags of store-bought cut broccoli, cauliflower, and baby carrots into a large bowl for the cow to eat.

Inside, the mansion looked a little shabby. Paint peeled off a wall in the kitchen, and a stairway to the second floor was entirely without a handrail. Yet a temple room with a marble floor was filled with colorful murals and marble statues of Hindu gods and goddesses. Oddly, in a hallway, I noticed one bookshelf completely filled with biographies of rock-'n'-roll stars. I supposed it might reflect the musical tastes of the young man who showed me in.

"Jagannatha is at doctor's office with daughter," he told me, as he led me into a large sitting room. "You wait here."

The high-ceilinged room was dominated at one end by a large-screen TV. Shelves held religious objects, but the walls were mostly decorated with framed covers of books about the Beatles.

Just then the door burst open and a middle-aged man with a large belly strode in, barefoot. He wore a green sweatshirt and sweatpants. His hair, brown with some gray at the temples, was combed straight back in a short pony tail. His face was round and fleshy.

This was His Holiness Jagannatha Dasa Puripadasat. Immediately he sat on a blue floor mat in the center of the room, near the TV, and began lecturing me about cruelty to animals.

"All things the cow gives us—milk, ice cream, cheese, ghee—and what do we do? We slit her throat!"

He was almost shouting.

I tried to take notes, but he talked too fast, and then I thought I heard him say something about having been Ronald McDonald.

"Wait, please," I interrupted. "Say that again—the part about Ronald McDonald."

"I was Ronald McDonald!" he screamed. "Didn't you read my website?"

I only scanned it, I admitted.

"Shame on you, a journalist! Go to my website, click on 'Vegetarianism,' and follow the prompts."

Jagannatha calmed down a bit, and told me his story.

He was born Geoffrey Giuliano in Rochester, New York, in 1953. After receiving a master's degree in acting from the State University of New York, he took a job on Cape Cod playing a promotional character for Burger King. Twenty years later he could still recite the jingle in a clownish singsong: "I'm the Marvelous Magical Burger King. I can do most anything. I like magic and food that's fun. I've got fun, fun, fun for everyone. At Burger King!"

"It was like vaudeville," he recalled. "We had a stage on the back of this RV and we'd go around to shopping centers and restaurants and do a magic show. The message was that our food was wholesome and we were promoting good family values.

"I did that gig for a while, but heard the real money was with McDonald's, so I called up and asked, 'Is there any place in the world you need a Ronald?' Next thing I know, I'm hired and they give me a fancy corporate office in Toronto."

On a mantel over a fireplace near where I sat, I then noticed several black-and-white publicity photos of a younger and slimmer Jagannatha dressed as Ronald McDonald.

But Giuliano soured on the McDonald's job when he became concerned about the animals that were used to make Big Macs.

"I was told to tell children, if they ask where hamburger comes from, to say it comes from a hamburger patch," he recalled, "but of course the truth was they were murdering millions of animals for the Big Macs I was pushing."

He began to get excited again.

"McDonald's promotes a disconnect in people, especially children. The violence kids see on TV isn't real, but the violence behind McDonald's is real! They're child molesters in the sense that they are desensitizing generations of young people to the violence inherent in their food."

So Geoffrey Giuliano quit being Ronald McDonald and became a Hindu, in part "to atone for all the animal cruelty I helped promote," as he put it. He studied in India, became His Holiness Jagannatha Dasa Puripadasat, and founded SRI, the Spiritual Realization Institute, in Lockport. In addition to providing a spiritual setting for its followers, the temple cares for its sacred cow and funds vegetarian food pantries in India and western New York.

Jagannatha himself teaches and hosts spiritual retreats.

He also has become a successful author—under the name Giuliano—specializing in biographies of international rock celebrities.

"I went out one day to buy a good Beatles book and couldn't find one, so I wrote twenty," he said.

All the books on the shelf, all the framed covers, I then realized, were his:

Blackbird: The Life and Times of Paul McCartney; John Lennon: My Brother; Dark Horse: The Secret Life of George Harrison, among others.

•   •   •

Since that first visit, I had kept in occasional touch with Jagannatha. Now, in early March, I pay another visit to the ashram. He has something I may need: a small pasture.

There are two cows in the yard: a large white one with up-pointed horns—I think she's the same cow I saw here last visit—and also a bull calf about a year old. A young Indian-looking man, but not the same one I met earlier, shows me into the house.

In the TV room, Jagannatha sits barefoot and cross-legged on an old sofa. He wears cream-colored pants and a lime-green shirt.

Jagannatha is anxious today. The first reviews are appearing of his new book, *Lennon in America,* which he says is based partly on secret diaries of former Beatle John Lennon.

What will he do with the money, I ask, if the book is successful?

"I'll use it to make people aware of their responsibilities on this earth," he answers. "For myself, I don't need money. I wear rags. This kurta"—he fingers the sleeve of his shirt—"it's a four-dollar outfit."

The young man who greeted me enters the room and silently places a glass of cranberry juice on the floor in front of Jagannatha.

"Thank you, Vishnu," says Jagannatha.

The young man leaves. Vishnu, eighteen, arrived only a few months ago from Nepal, explains Jagannatha. He'd seen Vishnu waiting tables in a restaurant in Kathmandu and invited him to come to America to lead a religious life, help care for the ashram, and eventually study medicine to become a doctor.

"He's my disciple," says Jagannatha.

"Disciple?" I ask.

"You're in a religious cult here, dude!" he shouts, with a half smile. "He's my disciple!"

Now Jagannatha begins to lecture me.

"In America we have a two-hundred-year-old culture versus a five-thousand-year-old culture in India. We're a bunch of fuckin' lunkheads over here. We're so busy working and consuming we don't take time to consider the bigger questions. We're distracted and desensitized."

He's warmed up now, rocking forward and back on the sofa, sometimes to the sides. He gestures grandly, speaks rapidly and loudly.

"And who's the first to suffer by our lack of spirituality? The animals!

"If you ask Americans why they eat meat, they'll say, 'I don't know. I just do.' There is no philosophy of meat-eating except that people make money from it. It's just an idea unenlightened people have had for a long time and that lots of other people have bought into: 'Hey, let's eat this animal and let's not think about what we're doing!' I say make the world a better place: don't hurt these animals. Choose not to be a party to the violence."

Now Jagannatha addresses me.

"When I talk to you, you're always saying, 'Oh, I admire these farmers so much. They work so hard. They provide a service and feel unappreciated.'

"Well, breeding animals and cutting their tails off and slitting their throats is hard work!" he screams. "It's also evil!

"While you're around the farm," he continues, "the farmers can put a bell on the cow's neck, pat her on the head, and call her Betsy, but they're molesting her! The truth is they'll exploit these animals and when there's no longer money in it, they'll murder them!

"I say to the farmers, that's an unacceptable way to earn your living. Grow fuckin' tomatoes instead!"

I'm never quite sure what to make of Jagannatha. I can imagine a few people being convinced by him, and others being turned off. But I'm neither. I just like him, and for some of the same reasons I like many of the farmers I meet. He has an enormous capacity for work; he's churned out nearly twenty books in as many years. He's created his own place of business in a lovely rural setting, has a clear philosophy of life that guides him, and he's not afraid to tell you exactly what he thinks.

He also seems vulnerable.

"My mind and heart have been completely resculpted by my embracing Hindu philosophy," he confides. "My personality, on the other hand, is the same—often obnoxious."

Jagannatha lives alone in this big house except for his "disciple," Vishnu, and his three-year-old-grandson, Kashi. His teenage son has been jailed for a probation violation, and his teenage daughter has serious drug problems. His wife, Vrnda, has taken their two other daughters, both preteens, to a Hindu community school in North Carolina. "We got the girls out fast when the two older ones got into trouble," he explains.

Our conversation finally gets around to my calves.

I ask Jagannatha to explain the Hindu view of cows.

"Cows are thought to be our second mother," he says. "We believe that on every hair of a cow live ten thousand demigods, and if you kill the cow you have to be reincarnated—in very abject conditions—as many times as there are hairs on the cow."

"Are bulls also sacred?" I ask.

He says they are. "The bull is the symbol of the Vedic religion," he explains.

Not surprisingly, Jagannatha is appalled that I am even considering killing my calves.

"Hey, stupid," he says, "you're not going to live forever. You know not where you come from or where you go—in between, at least try to make the world a better place. Let the cows alone. You want to live unperturbed and unmolested, why not spread that to all creatures? It's the Golden Rule, man."

"But if I don't kill them," I ask, "what would I do with them?"

"Give them to me! I'll take them. They can live out their lives in peace here."

I try to explain the view that farmers have of cows as a renewable resource.

"Renewable resource?" he cries. "My daughter's a renewable resource. It's bullshit. Go kill a potato. Potatoes don't suckle their young!

"Give the cows to me!" he repeats. "I'll assume all feed and veterinary costs. That would be a beautiful ending to your book. Give the cows to Ronald McDonald to live out their lives in peace."

"I don't know," I say. "Even if I didn't eat the meat, I could give it to the farmers or to a food bank."

"They don't need meat to live, and you shouldn't have those cows' blood on your hands, man!" he says.

"But as a journalist," I say, "I made a commitment to see this thing through from conception to consumption. To do that, I need to slaughter the cow."

"Fuck journalism!" he shouts. "What's more important, journalism or life? God put this cow here, and you're going to kill it for journalism? That cow is innocent, powerless, has no voice, has no advocate. He didn't do anything wrong. He wants to live!"

Jagannatha is interrupted when his grandson, Kashi, enters the room and starts jumping on a nearby sofa. Kashi has a shaved head with a small ponytail. He's taken off his pants and is wearing only a red shirt. As he jumps, he throws the pants in the air and catches them.

"Kashi, stop that now!" cries Jagannatha.

The boy begins to whimper.

"Just imagine," says Jagannatha, returning his attention to me, "you die and you're up in front of Saint Peter or whoever the Jews have up there. The guy says, 'Welcome. Can I see some ID, please?' So you give him your credit card or library card. He says, 'Just one moment,' and types your name into the computer. Then there's this buzz and an electronic voice says, 'Entry denied.'

"You say, 'Why? What'd I do wrong? I tried to raise my children right. I tried to do well, et cetera.' But the guy looks at the computer and says, 'Hmmm, was there something about a cow or cows? You were writing a book, and after examining the situation FOR TWO YEARS, you decided in the end to kill them? You had your chance and you BLEW IT! Now get the fuck out of here, Junior!' And then the guy gives a nasty smile and says, 'Wait over there. The shuttle will be along in a minute.'

"I'd think twice, dude," Jagannatha warns. "Either that, or you can name your book *How I Fucked Myself Forever!*"

"Kashi! Stop the crap!" he shouts. His grandson is still jumping on the couch and throwing his pants in the air.

"Don't talk to me!" screams Kashi.

"I'll give you a count of three to stop crying," Jagannatha threatens. "Stop it! Stop it! Immediately stop it!"

When our meeting ends, Vishnu shows me to my car. On the way, we stop in the yard to see the sacred cow and calf again. Jagannatha called her "the luckiest cow on earth," but I'm not so sure. She and the calf just stand there on a small patch of snow-covered lawn, tethered to a tree by fifty-foot wires attached to nose rings. "The nose rings are necessary," Jagannatha had said. "We couldn't control them without it."

I'm not sure how I feel about bringing my calves here just to stand around on a wire tether. Still, it's nice to know the ashram is available if I need it.

·   ·   ·

Much of the next few weeks I spend driving around the rural areas outside Rochester, checking into possible places to put my calves. There's the Christian Heritage Farm, a working farm where developmentally disabled adults are brought each day to care for the animals. They've got a few Holstein steers housed in a well-kept barn. The director seems to like the idea of bringing in "celebrity" animals—those featured in a book—to help draw visitors and financial support, but the woman who's in charge of the livestock says they haven't got room for another large animal. They'd have to build a new barn, and they don't have the space or the money for that.

"So there's no room at the inn?" I ask.

"'Fraid not," she says, but she does refer me to Mary, down the road, who often takes in animals "who need a place to live," as she puts it.

I call Mary and arrange a visit. She and her husband, an accomplished taxidermist, have four young children and live on a sizable farm with plenty of space for more animals. She says she would be willing to take the calves, but would first want to meet them.

"I've got to see what their temperament is," she explains, "if they'd be safe to have around my kids. I can tell in a minute."

"Really? In a minute?" I ask.

"Sure, you know, just like when you meet people, you can tell what they're like."

I make a date to drive Mary to the Vonglis farm so she can meet 7 and 8, but when the day comes, just as I'm about to leave the house to pick her up—I have my coat on—she calls to cancel.

"I thought about it all night," she tells me, "and I'd just rather have a baby calf, one I can hand-raise with my kids. I'd be too nervous with steers I didn't raise."

Not long after, the woman who cuts my hair calls me at the office. Every couple of months when I see her I fill her in on the progress of my calves. She's thought it over, she says, and would be willing to adopt them. She grew up on a farm and now lives with her husband and thirteen-year-old daughter on five acres in the country. She keeps a couple of horses on pasture, but they eat too much grass and are getting fat. She's got room for my calves, and by sharing the pasture and eating much of the grass, they'd keep her horses from overeating. Her daughter has already picked out names for the calves: Gunther and Lucy. There's only one thing I need to know: they'll need a new, stronger fence for the pasture, and her husband wants me to pay for it.

A week later I drive out to their farm and meet with the husband. He grew up in Brooklyn, has a master's in set design from New York University, and is a professional designer of trade-show exhibits. He's picked out a white, vinyl-clad plastic fence: fifteen hundred linear feet at $7.25 a foot would run, with tax, just over $11,000.

. . .

Something a little more within my budget presents itself one day when I stop at York Town Hall. A display rack in a hallway holds pamphlets about local tourist attractions. One is from Farm Sanctuary, described as a "working farm that is home to hundreds of rescued pigs, turkeys, cattle, goats, and other animals." The Sanctuary is about an hour and a half from Rochester, near the town of Watkins Glen, in the southern Finger Lakes.

Farm Sanctuary sits on hilly terrain overlooking a valley between two lakes. When I arrive, Geoff, a college-age intern from Philadelphia, offers to show me around.

On a hundred-acre hillside pasture, several dozen cattle graze, many of them Holstein steers.

"This one is Snicker," says Geoff, but then corrects himself. "No, that might actually be Greta. Oh no, this is Garland, excuse me. Snicker's the one with a distended udder—chronic mastitis. Garland's got a bad leg."

The cattle don't have ear tags. Instead they wear blue cloth collars with red name tags, but if you're not facing the cow straight on, it's hard to see the tag.

"Robbins here is maybe ten or eleven years old," says Geoff, pointing to a steer that appears to be six feet tall at the shoulder. "He needs leg surgery."

Geoff points to another steer. "Lazarus just came from a stockyard. He was a downer."

Farm Sanctuary was started fifteen years ago by Lorri and Gene Bauston, a young couple concerned about injured or down cows abandoned at livestock auctions. Starting out with an annual budget of three thousand dollars, the two founded the shelter for neglected and abused farm animals.

The organization's growth has been impressive. Today it operates two shelters—this one and another in California—which together house more than one thousand animals. The Watkins Glen shelter alone employs some thirty people and receives more than five thousand visitors annually, some of whom stay at the Sanctuary's own bed-and-breakfast. Besides caring for the resident animals, the Sanctuary conducts educational programs, investigates cruelty, and lobbies for humane legislation. Today the group's combined annual budget—most of it from donations—is $1.8 million.

Geoff and I enter a large and airy barn housing a dozen or more pigs. A woman and her teenage daughter—they are visiting from Pennsylvania and say they have been Farm Sanctuary members for many years—watch the pigs. The mother says, "I can't believe how big they are! And they're all just lying around."

"Yeah, that's what they do most of the day," says Geoff. "They eat, they get done eating, and they sleep. This one might be Chris," he says, pointing to a huge pig about five feet long. The pig was rescued from medical research at the University of Rochester, says Geoff, where it was used in experiments involving laser surgery.

I'm not sure what he means by "rescued"—was the pig bought, donated, or filched?—but decide it might be impolite to ask.

"I think my daughter has fallen in love with that one over there," says the teenager's mom, pointing to the other side of the barn, where her daughter pets another large pig.

Geoff isn't sure which pig that is. The pigs don't wear name tags, he explains, although the newer ones are given microchips for identification.

Next, Geoff shows me the cattle barn, which houses the Sanctuary's current herd of forty-three cows, steers, and heifers. Many of the cows were brought here from an upstate dairy farm where the owner, apparently in financial trouble, had abandoned the cows, letting them starve. Some of the other cattle were downers found at livestock auctions. One cow, a large black one, was brought to the Sanctuary by a farmer who said the cow went blind and his wife didn't want to send it to slaughter.

This barn is so spacious, well-lit, and clean, it reminds me of the rec hall at my kids' summer camp. It even has an automatic watering system. In what would be the hayloft, I notice a window and a door.

"What's up there, behind that door?" I ask.

Geoff says it's the "caregiver's" apartment—it's where the woman in charge of the herd lives. There's a kitchen, a bedroom, and satellite TV up there, and a porch overlooking the barn. Later I learn that when Lorri and Gene Bauston started the Sanctuary, this same hayloft apartment was their first home.

I have to say that if I were a cow or steer, this is where I'd want to live out my days: large pasture overlooking the valley, comfortable barn with deep straw bedding, plenty of food and water, gentle treatment. For cows, this is the Four Seasons. There's no charge for boarding, either; if the Sanctuary agrees to take an animal, all expenses are covered.

Before I leave, I stop in the office and mention that I might have two Holsteins—

a steer and a heifer—in need of a place to live, and briefly explain the circumstances. A woman takes my name and says someone will be in touch. A few days later a letter arrives at my office. It begins, "Thank you for contacting Farm Sanctuary for information on farm animal placement. Unfortunately, our shelter facilities are currently full, and we do not anticipate any openings in the near future."

.   .   .

I stop at Lawnel Farms on my way back to Rochester; I need to discuss the fate of my animals.

It's a warm day for mid-March, but it's turned windy.

"Holy cow!" says Sue Smith. In a scene that reminds me of *The Wizard of Oz,* she and Andrew are hurriedly cranking down plastic curtains over the sides of the cow barns. "We're going to get some severe weather," she warns.

Sue has two tiny red scratches on her nose, which she says came from Mac, her new Scottish terrier puppy, when she and Mac were wrestling. The dog rides with Sue in the front seat of her pickup truck, and spends the day curled on a dog bed in the corner of the herd office.

I tell Sue I haven't decided what to do with my animals, and ask if it would make a difference to her what I decide. I'm concerned that if I don't send them to slaughter, it might be seen as insulting, as if I were rejecting her worldview.

"If you don't send your calves to slaughter, would I feel it was disrespectful of us?" she asks. "I don't think so. No, not at all. We've all faced situations like that, or can imagine it—when we get attached to an animal. It's just that economics force us to go ahead, but that may not apply to your situation. Like with Wart"— she refers to a cow she was once unable to cull—"I couldn't bear to send her to market."

I break in, "You've actually never been to market, though—to the Pavilion auction, right?"

"Yeah," says Sue. "You're ahead of me there."

As Andrew struggles to raise the plastic barn curtains, I tell him of my recent visits to the Hindu ashram, the Christian Heritage farm, and the Farm Sanctuary.

"You're researching more possibilities for those animals than most people have in their own lives," he says. I think he means this simply as a statement of fact, not a criticism.

What he says is true, of course, but I make no apologies. It's a confusing choice for me, and one I haven't faced before. I want to get it right.

I ask Andrew, too, if it would matter to him what I do with my calves. "No, it doesn't, I guess," he says. "We sold 'em to you. They're your babies. Do with 'em as you want."

.   .   .

At the Vonglis farm a couple of days later, on a cool, sunny afternoon, all seven calves lie in the running shed. Before I even open the car door, 8 lifts his head and switches his tail. If he were a dog, I'd say he was wagging his tail. He alone among the seven stands and faces me. He takes a few steps toward the center of the shed, alongside the feed wagon that holds the shell corn. Now 7 stands, too. Side by side, they walk toward me, picking their way through the deep mud of the barnyard.

Now the other steers rise and begin making their way toward me, too.

I pull on my black boots and enter the barnyard.

I sit on the wooden bridge over the tiny creek. Sit without moving. 7 and 8 both lick at my coverall legs and the sleeves of my winter parka. I try to stroke 8 under the neck, but he turns and walks away. 7, however, approaches again. This is unusual for her; usually she's the more timid of the two.

Slowly, 7 moves her huge head toward my face until my entire field of vision is nothing more than her black nostrils. She pulls away. I'm a little afraid of her being this close. A full minute passes. She approaches again. Whiskers, white and black, project from either side of her nostrils as she moves toward me. I try to sit as still as possible without flinching, like when a bee buzzes around your head. The sound of her exhaled breath not only fills my ears, I can feel it on my face. I think of possibly slaughtering her, and imagine her skinned carcass.

Again she pulls away, and I wait. A third time she approaches, her nostrils now inches from my own nose. Her mouth hangs open. I can see the bumps, the papillae, on her pink tongue. She lowers her head half an inch and quickly licks twice under my chin. Her rough tongue scrapes against the light stubble of hair on my neck. It hurts some, her coarseness against mine. I let the moisture dry on my skin.

.   .   .

Months ago I'd read Jane Goodall's account of observing chimpanzees in the wild and was intrigued by her description of watching them sleep at night, curled up in trees. I wonder if I could do the same: watch my calves sleep.

On an overcast but mild night in early spring, I arrive at Peter and Shelly's at 10:00 P.M. I park on the shoulder of Route 36 rather than in the Vonglises' driveway so I won't disturb their dog and start him barking. Their kids are probably already asleep. Only one room in the house has a light on; I think it's Peter and Shelly's bedroom.

I pull on my barn boots and cross the road to a section of old, slatted wooden fence that encloses the barnyard near the road.

All seven cattle lie in the running shed in a circle around the feed wagon; 8 is near the back. The light from one halogen bulb in the barn allows me to see. Immediately, 8 lifts his head, then stands. Did he hear me, or see me, or smell me? I don't know. He walks behind the feed wagon, and when he emerges on the other side, 7 is up and walking behind him, and together they walk across the barnyard toward me. So much for watching them sleep. In a minute the five other steers are up, too, and headed my way.

When 7 and 8 reach the fence, I pull up a little grass for them from next to the barn. At that moment the last light in Peter and Shelly's house goes off. I bend to pull more grass, but when I turn back to the fence, I see that 8 has reached his huge black head through the fence slats and is stuck! His head just hangs there like a moose head mounted on a wall.

"Oh shit!" I say out loud. "Get your head back!"

I try to push 8's head back, but it won't go. It's too big to fit through the wooden fence slats. I try to twist it to the left or right, but he holds it rigid.

7 and the other five steers stand quietly at the fence, watching.

I imagine Peter getting up in the morning, finding this steer stuck in his fence, and having to take apart the fence to free him—all because of my stupid idea of trying to watch my animals sleep.

I try again to twist his head and push it back inside the fence.

"You dumb ox!" I shout, in a whisper. "Move your goddamn head!"

Even as I say this, I realize it's the first time I've tried to get him to do something that he resists doing or can't figure out how to do, and I've responded by shouting and cursing—not unlike the men at the cattle auction whom I've always thought of as so much rougher than me. It didn't take much for me to join their ranks. If I had a stock cane or even an electric prod, I'd probably use it on 8 just to get him—and me—out of this jam.

I decide to put my notebook back in the car; maybe if I leave for a minute he'll get his head out by himself. I cross the dark road to the car and when I return—yes!—8 has freed his head.

On the drive back to Rochester, it occurs to me maybe 8's head wasn't really stuck at all; he probably just wanted more grass.

.   .   .

The phone rings in my office. It's Jagannatha from the ashram. He says he's been so upset since my visit that he's been unable to call until now.

"What upset you so much?" I ask.

"Because you said you're thinking of killing those two calves!

"Look," he says, "every time I talk to you, you go on and on about how much you admire these farmers 'cause they work so hard, but Jeffrey Dahmer worked hard, too, so do child pornographers. They're fucking devils! They should all be incarcerated for the rest of their lives for their careers built on animal slavery and massacre!"

I'm listening without comment.

"I know you've been with these farmers and developed some relationship with them," he continues, "but even the Devil can quote Scripture. God bless 'em, they should earn a living, but they can get jobs doing something else. Don't be fooled by these people!

"If you slaughter the cows, I condemn you. I condemn you! Don't ever call me. Don't ever see me!

"If you kill them, instant karma gonna get you and give you shit!"

.   .   .

The next day, Peter Vonglis calls. Tomorrow he'll take 7 and 8 and one of his own steers to his father's farm to weigh them. He wants to see, at sixteen months old, how close they are to being ready for slaughter.

I arrive at the Vonglis farm at four-thirty the next afternoon. Peter already has my animals and one of his own—13, a large black Angus with horns—in the livestock trailer. His other four steers are smaller; he won't bother weighing them.

The animals have definitely grown—mine stand nearly to my shoulder. But estimating their weight is difficult. When John Weidman, the buyer at the Pavilion livestock auction, visited in mid-December, he guessed they weighed around six hundred pounds. "Them cattle should be ready to ship in April, maybe May," he had said. "Get 'em up around one thousand or one thousand one hundred pounds."

Cattle are supposed to gain about three pounds a day on a finishing diet. It's now the end of March, so, since Weidman's visit, they may have gained as much as three hundred or even four hundred pounds, which would put them right up near slaughter weight.

Peter guesses my bull calf weighs nine hundred pounds, and I agree.

I get in the cab next to Peter, and in a minute we're on our way. Peter looks tired; he has at least a day's growth of beard. He's been busy repairing equipment at the Batzing Farm in preparation for spring planting. His hands are nearly black, his sweatshirt has dozens of tiny holes, and his brown winter coveralls are grimy with oil and mud; the cotton lining shows through at the knees.

"I can tell you in minutes exactly how long it takes to unload, weigh, and reload a steer at my dad's," says Peter as we drive east and then south toward his father's farm.

How long? I ask.

"About six minutes," he says.

That surprises me. I thought this was going to be a major operation. I had told my wife I wouldn't be home for dinner.

In just twenty minutes we arrive at John Vonglis's. His modest ranch house sits on a lovely, high plateau overlooking the Genesee Valley. The barn is far behind the house, and beyond the barn is a large field stretching nearly to the horizon.

Peter backs the trailer up the driveway, but needs to stop several times to correct his direction.

"I never backed in here in daylight," he says. "It's actually easier in the dark."

He explains that he hauls steers to auction for his father, but usually picks them up before work, around 4:00 A.M., when it's still dark.

Peter and his father look remarkably alike: short, dark hair; thin, angular face; slim but muscular. They both have the same strong, clipped speech, too. I can't imagine that between the two of them they ever waste a word.

Peter backs the truck up to a wooden stock chute that connects to a series of pens in which his father keeps nearly fifty steers that he raises for beef.

John shows me the scale. It's a metal platform five feet long, with a wooden chute built around it. The cattle walk in one at a time and stand on the scale.

John and Peter get right to business.

Peter opens the back of the trailer. Out first is my heifer, 7. She enters the chute and shifts nervously on the scale. John adjusts the weights like a nurse weighing a patient in a doctor's office. I can tell he guessed too high, because he has to remove some of the weights until he gets the scale to balance.

"Seven-fifty, Pete!" he calls to his son.

7 steps out of the chute and walks quickly into a large holding pen. Now my steer, 8, comes into the chute. He's quiet but edgy, moving back and forth within the small space.

"That's eight hundred right there!" calls John.

Eight hundred pounds? That's one hundred below what we thought—so 8's been gaining two pounds a day, not three. I am greatly relieved. This gives me at least another month, maybe two, to figure out what to do with him.

When Peter's black steer, 13, balks at entering the chute, Peter slaps him hard on the back.

"Seven hundred fifty-five pounds!" calls John.

So all three animals were lighter than we had guessed. It's back to the feeding trough.

Peter and his dad herd the three animals through a swinging gate back toward the open end of Peter's stock trailer.

7 enters the trailer first, but then, just as 8 is about to climb in, he makes a sharp and incredibly fast turn to the right through a narrow opening Peter has left between one of the gates and the back of the trailer.

In an instant, 8's out, free, running past me as I stand, holding my notebook, openmouthed. He heads around to the back of the barn, kicking up his hind legs, leaping like a deer.

Before any of us can react, Peter's black steer, 13, who was in line to board the truck just behind 8, escapes through the same opening.

My steer runs behind the barn, stops, then runs around the outside of a corral, where a dozen black steers turn their heads and watch. They rush to the fence as 8 comes near, then, as he rounds the other side of the yard, they follow. They run after him, back and forth, like movie fans mobbing a film star, or maybe just to be near greatness.

I hadn't noticed it before, but now that 8's running I can see how heavy he's gotten; on his sides, fat jiggles as he moves.

My steer runs like a horse, prancing on this high ground overlooking the valley—what a magnificent taste of freedom it must be. I'd forgotten that he can even run. If he wanted to, he could just take off behind the barn and keep running over that field as far as it goes.

He rounds the corner of the fenced corral and heads directly toward me, then stops to pull up some grass. Since last August he's eaten little but shell corn and pellets. I wonder how fresh spring grass tastes.

Against the green lawn, the brown, dormant field of cut corn behind, the bare trees in the valley below, and the overcast sky, 8 is the only thing black and white, the only thing moving and alive. He's a bull momentarily on top of the world, and I bet, at some level, he knows it.

"This has never happened before," says Peter. In all the times he's brought animals here to pick up, drop off, or weigh, none has ever escaped.

With arms outstretched, Peter and I position ourselves to herd the two steers back toward the truck. 13 we catch quickly—he never even made it behind the barn. "Ha! Ha! Heh!" Peter shouts at 8. Now his father joins the effort. It's only five minutes, maybe ten, before the three of us maneuver my steer to the far side of the barn and into a series of swinging gates that lead in only one direction: back to the truck. 8 slowly climbs in and Peter quickly closes the back.

As I come around the side of the trailer to get into the cab, I say good-bye and shake hands with John Vonglis.

"Did you let the steer get out?" he asks me, and by the way he says it I suspect he thinks I did.

"No, I didn't," I say, honestly, "but it was interesting to see."

· · ·

The next day I stop for lunch, as usual, at York Landing restaurant. Co-owner Joan Alexander is at the register, inviting a customer to choose a fresh brownie from the dessert case. She rings up the sale, then asks me, "So, have you decided what you're going to do with your calves?"

I tell Joan I haven't, but that I might send them to slaughter. It's what I signed on for, I say: conception to consumption.

"Oh, really?" she says, wincing. "I could never do that!"

I point to the chalkboard on the wall where the handwritten menu of today's specials includes a cheeseburger.

"You sell cheeseburgers. They're made from cows," I say.

"I know," says Joan. "But I don't have a relationship with them."

.   .   .

The following week, at our invitation, Peter and Shelly Vonglis come to Rochester on a Saturday evening to join my wife and me for dinner. We've chosen a trendy, Spanish-style restaurant downtown, partly because Shelly told us Peter likes to eat steak, and the menu there has a couple of fancy, sixteen-ounce steak entrees.

Peter and Shelly arrive more than half an hour after the scheduled time. "Sorry we're late," jokes Peter. "We found the restaurant okay, but I couldn't find a dirt lot to park the pickup on."

As we look over the menu, I point out the steaks to Peter, but he says he never eats steak in restaurants. "I've got plenty in my freezer," he explains. He decides instead to try the seafood paella, something new for him.

A minute after we've all ordered, Shelly leans across the table, wide-eyed, and asks me, "Are you *really* going to eat turtle?" It takes me a moment to realize she's thinking that what I ordered—red snapper, a dish she's never had before—is turtle rather than fish.

When the food comes, Shelly squirms to see the squid on Peter's plate. I ask why it upsets her.

"I don't eat anything with eyes," she says.

"But you want to eat my calves," I say. "They have eyes."

"But their eyes won't be on my plate," she says.

Peter has exciting news: Scot Batzing, the owner of the dairy farm where he works, has finally agreed to let Peter become a part owner. Even though Scot's own daughter is working now at the farm, he'll give Peter 10 percent of the stock in exchange for work already done, and additional stock in the coming years until he has at least 50 percent. Peter says he's waiting to see the papers from Scot's lawyers.

We drink a toast to congratulate Peter. This will be the realization of his dream to be the owner of a dairy farm.

Shelly also has good news. Her son, Colin, is fully recovered from pneumonia and she's gotten a new part-time job at a regional hospital. She says she was originally hired for five half-days a week but they like her work so much they've already increased her to six days. Shelly then tells a poignant story about one elderly patient who so appreciates how Shelly bathes and massages her and does her hair that she calls Shelly her "angel."

"Oh, by the way," says Peter, "I sold those four black steers at auction Monday at Pavilion."

This gets my attention. So the seven animals in the barnyard are now down to three: his last steer, 13, and my twins. The barnyard is emptying out and I'm still on the fence about what to do.

I ask Peter why he sold the steers so suddenly.

"We had a mortgage payment to make," he explains. He says he got sixty-nine cents a pound for the heaviest of the four, and seventy-two cents for the lighter ones. He made about $1,400 in total, or about $350 per steer.

"Anyway, I would have had to buy more corn to keep 'em much longer. As it is, the corn I've got left should be enough for your two and the one other I've still got in there."

Peter says he won't ship his last steer probably for another month, till mid-May. He'll take them to Kahn's, a small, local slaughterhouse just up the road from York, in Caledonia. He says he'll give me a couple of days' notice so I can call Kahn's and arrange to send mine at the same time, if that's what I decide to do. He'll haul them all together.

While Shelly and my wife, a nutritionist, discuss health care, I ask Peter the same question I'd put earlier to Sue and Andrew Smith at Lawnel: Would he feel I was devaluing his work in any way if I decided not to slaughter my calves?

"You mean you'd feel you were betraying me by not sending 'em to beef?" he asks.

"No," I say, a little defensively, "I wouldn't feel that way. I'm just wondering how you would feel."

"Personally, I really don't care what you do with 'em," he says. "They're your animals. I'm raising 'em for you the best I know how. You can take 'em into the city here and turn 'em loose for all I care. It's your decision. They're yours and it has no personal impact on me."

After the meal, my wife and I encourage Peter to try a cappuccino with dessert. He says he's never had one, but agrees to try it and later, I notice, drains the cup.

"How was the cappuccino?" I ask.

"Terrible," he says, making a face.

"But you drank it."

"Didn't want it to go to waste," he says.

We leave the restaurant and stroll a few blocks together. Shelly stares up at the ten- and fifteen-story office and apartment buildings as if we're in Manhattan. We cross a bridge over the Genesee River, which flows north through the middle of downtown Rochester.

"That's the same river that our little creek must feed into," she observes correctly, referring to the tiny stream that runs through their barnyard and from which my calves drink.

My wife and I mention that our daughter, Val, will soon celebrate her bat mitzvah. Shelly says she's never been to a synagogue and would like to come.

Peter says he was raised Catholic, but now is "no religion."

"Everyone dies," says Peter, "religion or no religion."

I ask him if farming provides a spiritual sense to his life that religion might offer to others.

"Well, if you plant a seed and watch it grow," he says, "that gives you tremendous satisfaction, doesn't it?"

I agree it does.

"Well, I plant thousands of seeds, millions of 'em."

·   ·   ·

A few days later, when I next visit Shelly at her home, I tell her how much my wife and I enjoyed having dinner with her and Peter.

"It was fun to be in Rochester," she says. "It's just fascinating to go someplace that's close to home but so completely different."

I tell her I know the feeling.

·   ·   ·

To celebrate my forty-seventh birthday, my wife and I stay overnight in York at a new bed-and-breakfast called the Silver Tendril. This two-story redbrick home, built in 1827, sits on Route 36 between Lawnel Farms and Peter and Shelly's house. I pass it often. In the warmer seasons, I've often seen a man seated on a stool in the side yard tending long rows of grapevines.

After settling in upstairs, my wife and I join Gary and Shirley Cox, the owners, in the parlor. Gary tells us he maintains 150 grapevines of forty-one European and domestic varieties. He crushes the grapes himself and makes about six hundred bottles a year.

As we enjoy cheese and crackers and a bottle of homemade wine, Gary says he hopes we're not bothered by the occasional odor from nearby fields where farmers spread manure this time of year.

"We're concerned about what Shirley and I refer to as the 'dairy-air,'" he says, obviously enjoying the pun.

Ironically, the field behind the B&B about which Gary is concerned is owned by Lawnel Farms. The one time I rode on a Lawnel manure spreader, it was on that very field.

I explain that of all possible guests, I'm the least likely—since I'm unable to smell—to be troubled by "dairy-air." Gary and Shirley are relieved, even more so when my wife says she also detects no odor.

The Coxes, we learn, are both retired educators. Shirley taught fourth grade in public school and Gary was until recently a professor of philosophy at nearby Geneseo College, part of the State University of New York. His area of specialty is moral philosophy.

I can't believe my good luck: the owner of the B&B turns out to be a professor of moral philosophy! Even if his knowledge of farming is academic, maybe he can help me figure out what to do with my calves.

In fact, Gary explains, he and his wife's social life has been more in the college town of Geneseo than in York and the immediate farming community. For example, they attend church in Geneseo rather than in York, and though they live only a half mile up the road from York Landing restaurant, they stop there only occasionally.

As we enjoy Gary's wine, I describe my efforts to follow the life of a cow from birth to slaughter, and the sense I have of how farmers are rooted and strengthened by their work.

Before responding, Gary pauses, and then offers a statement so polished it could only come from someone who has spent his entire career lecturing.

"Farmers may feel so grounded," he says in a rich, bass voice, "because on a scale of worthiness of one's work, with drug dealers and casino operators at one end, dairy farmers see themselves at the other."

He continues, "I suspect that when a dairy farmer meets his Maker, he may feel bitterness at how he was treated politically, and he may feel resentment that others did not always appreciate his work, but I believe he also feels the satisfaction of having spent his days engaged in labor that he believes greatly benefits his fellow man."

Gary says working in his vineyard—more than teaching—grounds him. He plants the vines, sees them go dormant in the fall and come back to life in the spring, harvests the crop, and finally sees a family member or friend enjoy the wine.

"I take a sip," he says, pausing to sip his own wine, "and I experience the process from beginning to end, like the life and death you witness at the farm."

I'm intrigued by Gary Cox's eyes. They're dark, with deep circles underneath. He shuts them while he thinks, and when he smiles, which is often, they nearly disappear in crinkles.

Our conversation gets around to the question with which I've been wrestling: what to do with my calves. It's mid-April; I expect Peter Vonglis will ship his last steer, 13, by mid-May. Our host takes a shot.

"I suspect if you had written this book fifty years ago," he begins, "you would not have faced this question because it would have been assumed that one needed the meat of these calves—and of other animals—to live.

"But we seem to have arrived at a time in history when it has become fairly clear that one can nourish oneself without meat—that you can get all the nutrients you need from other sources."

My wife, who teaches nutrition at a local college, nods in assent.

"One can't be sure," Gary continues, "but I would venture that perhaps in another fifty years the industry of raising animals for slaughter will have passed away. By that time, many people will have come to understand they can eat a vegetarian diet and be healthy, and others will have moved away from meat-eating because of moral concerns about the slaughter of animals. Sure, animals are going to die. We're all mortal. But the industry has tended to be insufficiently humane.

"So your dilemma, as I see it, may well be rooted in the particular time in which we live—when we are nearly exactly poised between these two radically different views of the human diet."

It's remarkable to hear someone right in the middle of York—a homeowner no less, whose property actually backs up to Lawnel Farms—openly predicting a vegetarian future. This would be heresy to the local Farm Bureau. Regrettably, though, I can't wait fifty years; I have two live animals and have to make a decision soon about what to do with them.

Gary suggests I could sell the calves to someone and "remove the issue" from my hands, but I quickly reject this as a cop-out.

"Unfortunately, then," he says, "there is no clear answer, no right answer except as it applies to you."

I try one of the arguments that seems most compelling to me in favor of slaughter.

"Someone, in this case a farmer named Peter Vonglis, has put substantial resources—his own labor and a lot of corn—into raising these animals for meat. Wouldn't it be a waste not to slaughter the animals and use the meat? Even if I don't want to eat the meat, I could give it to someone else who would, or donate it to the food pantry right here in York."

"Or you could make a cash donation to the food pantry equal to the value of the animals," Gary responds.

"Look," he says, "the danger here is that people would be pleased in different ways. You can't make your decision based on what would please other people or what other people would do. You've got to think carefully about what would be consistent in the long term with your own view, what you'll feel comfortable having done years from now."

.   .   .

Two weeks later, on a sunny afternoon in late April, I stop by Lawnel Farms to see what's going on. Sue Smith, I learn, is on vacation. She and Kirsty, who is on spring break from high school, are visiting Sue's sister in Arizona.

That Sue and her family can get away now and then is more the exception than the rule among farmers, many of whom find it nearly impossible to take vacations. The Smiths are able to do so, I think, because their farm is large and well established, with plenty of family and hired help to handle things while they're gone. For smaller farmers, like the Vonglises, it's extremely difficult to get away. In the two years I've known Peter Vonglis, he's taken just one weekend off each year, after harvest time. Another couple I met, who owned a sixty-head dairy farm, had taken four days off in twelve years. In the local farm newspaper, *Country Folk,* the same black-bordered advertisement appears in each issue: "DEAD FARMERS," it warns, "Can't Enjoy Vacations. Get Away Now While You Can Still Enjoy Life." The ad is placed by a "farm-sitting" service, but I've yet to meet anyone who has used it.

Outside the Lawnel maternity barn, in what I usually think of as the "dead pile" because that's where I often find newborn calves who have been born dead, a cow lies. Her head rests backward against her right side, her front left leg is stretched out forward, and her front right leg is tucked back under her chest. I assume she's dead, but then I'm startled when she lifts her head slightly, and bellows.

From various farmhands I piece together the story. At around 5:00 A.M. yesterday, while she was coming into the parlor to be milked, the cow "split out," that is, her back legs gave way and she fell. She'd had a calf five days before, which might have weakened her. The night milkers tried to get her up, but couldn't. Early today the vet checked her and found she was paralyzed below the neck. He prescribed some drugs, which didn't help, but the drugs are not allowed in meat, so the cow is now waiting to be picked up by a rendering company that takes only dead animals. When the truck comes, the driver will shoot the cow.

I've seen maybe a hundred dead calves lying in this spot, and several dead cows, but I've never seen a living cow shot to death.

From inside the barn, several cows stick their heads through openings in the wall and bellow toward the paralyzed cow. Others, at the feed trough, look around the corner of the barn at her and bellow, and then go back to eating.

Chris, the office manager, says she called the rendering company early this morning. They should be here sometime this afternoon, she says, although occasionally they don't show. She says there are two more cows, at Hanna and Valley View, that also need to be picked up today.

In the equipment shed where he's repairing a tractor, Andrew Smith agrees that the renderer tends to be unreliable about coming the day he's called. If he doesn't come by the time Andrew is ready to leave, Andrew says he'll shoot the cow himself. "I'm not gonna let her suffer overnight," he says, pointing to a rifle leaning against the wall.

"You want to shoot it?" he asks me, playfully.

As it turns out, neither of us has to shoot the cow.

At eleven minutes after five, a red container truck pulls into Lawnel and a slender man in his thirties with short, sandy brown hair and a neatly trimmed mustache gets out. He introduces himself—I'll call him Dan—and asks me where the down cows are.

I like when people come to Lawnel—contractors, suppliers, salespeople—and assume I work here. I'm certainly dressed as though I worked here: barn boots, blue coveralls, denim jacket, and farm cap.

I point to the cow lying next to the maternity barn, and say there are two more down cows at other locations. Dan gets back in the truck and backs it up to within a few feet of the paralyzed cow. This time when he gets out he carries a rifle.

After explaining to Dan that I don't work at Lawnel but am writing a book, I ask what kind of rifle he's got.

"A twenty-two," he says. "I don't know what make. It's the company's rifle. Probably a Kmart special."

He walks over to the cow and lifts the rifle to her head.

"Wait a minute!" I say. I didn't expect this to happen so quickly.

I back away three steps. Then five or six more—giant steps. I don't think I've ever been near a gun when it's been fired, let alone seen anything shot. Before I started coming to Lawnel, I don't think I'd ever even seen anything die. Since I've been here, though, I've seen lots of calves born dead, and I've seen others die minutes after they were born. I've seen cows die, too. Once Sue, Andrew, a niece of Sue's, and I stood around a cow while the vet sewed her up after a C-section. We were talking about our favorite restaurants when suddenly the vet got quiet and then chucked his needle into the open wound. In the silence that followed, the rest of us realized the cow had stopped breathing and died.

From twenty feet away, I ask Dan if there's any danger of ricochet. He says there's not. As he raises the gun to the cow's forehead, I kind of twist sideways and grimace, but keep my eyes open.

Pop!

It's a surprisingly small sound. I was expecting more.

Dan's shot the cow in the middle of her forehead. She lays her head down and bright red blood runs from her nose. But then she picks her head up again.

"Is she dead?" I ask, moving closer. She doesn't look dead, although now she lowers her head again.

"It takes eight to nine minutes for them to die," he says. "But the bullet paralyzes their central nervous system."

To check, Dan presses his thumb on the cow's open eye.

"No corneal reflex," he says.

I mention how quiet the gun sounded. Dan says he doesn't use anything bigger than a .22 because it would make a louder noise and startle the cows in the barn.

He lowers the back ramp of the container truck. The truck is nearly full, I suppose, because it's the end of the day. I can count five cows and four calves all piled on top of one another in a heap about ten feet high. Dan climbs over the carcasses toward a mechanical winch at the top.

Five minutes after she was shot, the cow lifts her head about three inches above the bloodstained ground. Her tail moves up and down a couple of times. Dan climbs down from the truck with a metal hook and loops it around the cow's front left leg, just above the knee.

He shoots her again, also in the forehead. I see no more movement.

Later I would ask Dan why he shot the cow a second time. "I just didn't think her eye reflexes looked like she was dead," he told me.

In another minute, Dan activates the winch and the cow is dragged up the metal ramp into the back of the truck. As her head reaches the top of the ramp it catches on the truck's side panel, twists all the way back, then snaps violently forward, spraying bits of blood onto the ground; a few drops land next to my boot. The winch pulls the cow up and over the other carcasses until she rests on top of the pile.

Dan invites me to ride with him to the two other Lawnel farms to pick up the other cows.

He tells me he's married and has a daughter ten years old. Today happens to be "take your daughter to work day," and I try not to ask, but can't resist, if he's ever taken his daughter to work.

"I wouldn't take my daughter, no," he answers. "I don't think she'd be too pleased with what I do. I tell her I pick up cows to make leather and dog food, but I don't mention that sometimes I have to shoot them."

I regret having asked the question.

We pull into the Hanna Farm, where Lawnel keeps cows in the later stages of pregnancy.

A large, but thin and bony, cow lies alone between two barns.

Andrew and his son, Amos, both in matching brown coveralls, are here checking on cows in Sue's absence. I ask Andrew what's wrong with the cow lying on the ground.

"She a Johne's animal," he says disgustedly, and points to a pool of light brown liquid manure behind the cow.

As Dan approaches the cow with his rifle, Andrew and Amos walk the other way. By the time Dan pulls the trigger, they are thirty feet away with their backs to us, and to their cow.

The cow rolls onto her side, but then holds all four legs up in the air. Her head shakes up and down slightly, her mouth hangs open, clear fluid drips from her nose.

Two minutes after shooting her, Dan bends to touch the cow's eye. No reflex, he says. I wonder, though, if she is insensitive or just unable to react.

Later I ask Dave Hale, the veterinarian, about this. He says a .22 is adequate to shoot a cow, and after being shot, if a cow has no "blink reflex," it is probably dead, although muscle spasms might continue for as long as fifteen to twenty minutes. He cautions, though, that cows have large sinuses in the front of the skull, and an inexperienced shooter could hit the frontal sinus rather than the brain.

At four minutes after the shooting, Dan begins to loop the metal chain around the cow's front leg. As he does so, however, the cow kicks out all four legs.

He shoots her twice more and, a minute later, shoots again.

On our way to Valley View, Dan says four shots are unusual, although when he started the job seven months ago, "sometimes I'd have to shoot 'em nine or ten times."

Before he took this job, Dan says, he sold insurance—accident and health, mostly. This is the first job he's had working with animals. "Funny thing is, I like animals," he says, noting that he doesn't hunt.

He says he drives three hundred miles five or six days a week, hauling mostly cows, horses, and pigs. On an average day he picks up ten or eleven cows, about one-fifth of which are alive and need to be "put down."

So how does it feel to haul dead animals and have to shoot cows?

"It's a paycheck," he says. "I'd rather be dealing with farmers anytime than selling insurance or 'driving truck' in the city. Really, the worst part of the job is the smell in the summer. Cows can deteriorate fast in the warm weather."

At Valley View, which is right next to Sue and Andrew's farmhouse, a large black cow with a white triangle on her forehead lies in front of the main gate on a lawn dotted with dandelions. This cow has Johne's disease, too. Twenty other cows, lined up behind the gate, watch as we approach.

Dan walks over to the cow. This time I don't flinch or back away. He shoots her twice in the head. Blood flows from the wounds and from her nose. She rolls onto her right side, her top leg held in the air. The mechanical winch drags her into the truck.

Dan drops me back at Lawnel, and I thank him for taking me along. I toss my barn boots into the trunk of my car and drive over to York Landing for dinner— a tuna sub with cheese, and a Danish pastry. I'm nearly done with the Danish when it occurs to me I just watched three cows shot in the head at close range and then immediately went to dinner, something I probably could not have done a couple of years ago.

. . .

After dinner, I drive the few miles down Route 36 to check on my calves at the Vonglises'. Peter is getting the kids ready for bed. He says Shelly is at a nearby

Presbyterian church, studying for her nursing exams. It's the one quiet place she's found where she can study, he explains.

I remind Peter that when we had dinner together, Shelly had said she would like to attend my daughter's bat mitzvah. I've brought a printed invitation for her, and ask Peter to be sure she gets it.

After saying good night to Peter and the kids, I go outside to the barnyard gate to watch my calves. It's a cool, clear evening. The sun is just beginning to set.

Now that Peter's four black steers are gone, there are just three animals left: my two, and the last one of Peter's, 13. The latter is nearly all black, about the same size as 8, but he has short horns that stick straight out to either side. Peter said he probably just forgot to take the horns off. 13 stands on the little wooden bridge just behind 8, and rubs his black neck over 8's rump; at the same time, 8 licks up grass I offer from my hand, and 7, next to him, scratches her neck on the gatepost.

It's a nice little trio out here at sunset.

8 takes my whole hand into his mouth. It's warm in there, the inside of a cow's mouth.

He's filled out a lot, and his hair has a nice shine to it on the back and sides. He's not nearly as muddy as he was, either, now that the spring rains have stopped and the barnyard has dried. I rub him on the neck and behind the ears.

I press my right hand against the white chalice on his forehead. In response, he presses with his head back against my arm. I feel my energy matched—much more than matched—by his.

If I don't kill you, I don't know what else to do with you. The system seems to overwhelm my efforts to find another path. Anyway, to fulfill my vow of watching from birth to death, I still need to observe a slaughter at the slaughterhouse; the three shootings at Lawnel today don't count.

My steer drops his head, holding it still and low, near my waist. I lay my right hand flat against his head, over the white hairs of the chalice. My fingers, pointing upward, grasp the occipital bone, the ridge that runs along the top of his skull. On my palm I can feel the stiff, short hairs of his forehead, and the slightly greasy feel of lanolin.

At my own bar mitzvah service, thirty-four years ago, the Torah portion I was assigned to read was *V'yikra,* the first chapters of the Book of Leviticus. The chapters concern animal sacrifices, a subject that then seemed remote, but now, eerily, is on point. As a thirteen-year-old, I had stood in the synagogue in front of the congregation and, in Hebrew, chanted these words: "And the Lord spoke unto Moses saying . . . tell the Children of Israel . . . when any man presents an offering of cattle . . . it shall be a male without blemish . . . and it will be accepted . . . and he shall lay his hand upon the head of the offering."

10

A Final Decision

WHEN I ARRIVE AT PETER VONGLIS'S at 6:15 A.M., the stock trailer is already loaded.

"Good morning, Peter!" he shouts cheerfully. "Today's the day! You ready for this?"

"I'm ready," I say. "It's what I signed on for."

I don't sound convincing, though, even to me.

Peter called two days ago to say it was time, that he'd be going to the slaughterhouse today. So here I am.

He closes the back of the trailer and we climb into the cab. He uses the wipers to clear the windshield of morning dew, waits for a couple of tractor-trailers to pass, and then pulls onto Route 36, heading north. The slaughterhouse, T.D. Kahn Country Meats, is outside Caledonia, about twelve miles up the road.

"Hey," Peter says, "your steer's a pretty friendly guy, did you know that?" He says last night he took Kalie, his thirteen-year-old daughter, with him into the barnyard and "she was pettin' him and everything."

"Yeah, I know he's pretty friendly," I say.

The forecast for today, May 11, is for clear skies, a relief after yesterday's thunderstorms. Already a brilliant sun is rising to our right over the Genesee River. Peter wears faded blue jeans, a blue sweatshirt, an oil-stained farm cap, and protective, wraparound sunglasses. I recall him explaining that his eyes hurt in bright sun because of a welding accident he had as a child.

Peter says he won't be staying to watch the slaughter. He has to get to the Batzing Farm to work. He's got a tractor to repair, and if it doesn't rain, he may be able to plant some corn.

"You've never actually seen an animal slaughtered, right?" I ask.

"That's right, never actually seen 'em slaughtered," he says. "I've been inside, seen the hooks and meat hanging, but there's nothing interesting in seeing 'em slaughtered."

Earlier, I'd asked Peter, "If I take these steers to slaughter and write about it, how do you think a reader would react?"

"Well," he had said, "it depends what you write. I mean, are you just going to say you stood there and watched them shoot the cow and it dropped? Or are you going to give gory details, like 'they hung it up on a hook and took its skin off and ripped its guts out'? 'Cause I don't know of too many people other than myself who could sit at McDonald's with a cheeseburger in their hand knowing that it used to be a cow and they shot it, cut its skin off, pulled its guts out, and cut it up into pieces of meat. How good would that hamburger taste to you?"

Route 36 runs north-south through the middle of York. So many of the people and places I've come to know these past two years are located along this two-lane country road.

Immediately to the right of Peter's driveway, we pass the barn and side yard where Peter kept my calves after they left the hay-bale hutches but before they were briefly on pasture. I'd sat in that little yard on a folding metal chair, waiting for my calf to let me touch him. One day, just after I'd gotten up to leave, I saw him go over to the chair and sniff it up and down.

At the first intersection, we pass Cook's, a combination gas station and restaurant. When I first started visiting Lawnel Farms, I asked Andrew Smith to lunch, thinking at the time that farmers, like office workers, actually went out to lunch. Andrew, accommodatingly, drove me here to pick up sub sandwiches, but we ate them back at the herd office.

A little farther on, on our left, Peter and I pass the Silver Tendril bed-and-breakfast. At this early hour, I envision owners Gary and Shirley Cox, comfortable in their retirement, still sleeping.

Now we pass Craig Road. To the left is Lawnel Farms, where my calves were born and where I marked their foreheads with orange chalk so that Joe Hopper, the cattle hauler, would know not to take them to the auction in Pavilion. I'm sure Sue and Andrew Smith are already up and working, she in the cow barns or milking parlor and he in the equipment shed.

To the right on Craig Road is the building shared by the local post of the Veterans of Foreign Wars and the York Sportsmen's Club. On a chilly day last fall, at Veterans Day services, a talented bugler from York High School played taps. I listened as the sound floated over the surrounding fields.

Peter slows the truck to thirty-five as we enter York. At the intersection, on the left, is York Landing, where I've spent so many hours at what owner Larry Alexander calls the Table of Knowledge, eating and reviewing my notes. The restaurant's been open for nearly an hour already. Through the front windows I can see Larry at the counter; Joan is probably out back, loading the Snack Shack.

A moment later we pass York Town Hall, where my wife and I square-danced last year. Partially hidden behind the building is the cemetery in which many of York's early Scottish settlers are interred.

I ask Peter how it feels when he takes animals he's fed and cared for to slaughter.

"Doesn't faze me," he says. "I look forward to the check. You can't look at it like 'Oh, you poor animals. I'm never going to see you again.' If you did, you wouldn't be in business long. Or you'd have a lot of sleepless nights. It's just part of making a living."

A couple of miles farther on, we pass Davis' Trailer World and Country Mall, where you can buy everything from barn boots to wedding dresses, and where, in the last two years, I've bought all my farm clothes: summer and winter coveralls, flannel shirts, thermal underwear, winter boots, flannel-lined jeans, hats, gloves, a denim jacket, and two pairs of barn boots.

There's a silence in the cab, which, after a minute or so, Peter breaks. This is unusual because typically, when we ride together, Peter's quiet until I ask a question.

"You asked once why I like farming," he says. "Well, last week I put seed in the ground and this week the plants are already this tall." He holds his thumb and index finger about an inch apart.

I don't recall the question, but his statement prompts me to ask if my being around and asking so many questions has caused him to think differently about his work.

He says it has. I ask for an example.

"Well, once when I was moving one group of animals into the barn with another group, you asked what I thought the animals might be thinking. I'd never even tried to imagine what a cow would think."

"So what did you think?" I ask.

"I thought you were goofy for asking the question," he says. "But I guess I did start to wonder about it. When you mix 'em up like that, they start sniffing. Like young kids, they sort of check each other out. Then they start playing together."

As we approach Caledonia, we pass the fairgrounds where last summer I watched my first rodeo and where Sue Smith and Shelly Vonglis almost came face to face.

We're only a minute away from Kahn's now. The folk song "Dona, Dona, Dona" comes to mind. We used to sing it at summer camp. It begins, "On a wagon bound for market, there's a calf with a mournful eye," and concludes: "Calves are easily bound and slaughtered, never knowing the reason why, but whoever treasures freedom, like the swallow will learn to fly."

The song, popularized by the folk singer Joan Baez, was written for the Yiddish theater in 1943, and may have been based on a story in the Talmud (Baba Metzia, 56b) about Judah the Prince, a revered rabbi.

One day, the story goes, Rabbi Judah was sitting at a café in a small town when a wagon came by carrying a calf to the slaughterhouse. The calf cried out to Rabbi Judah for mercy, but the rabbi replied, "Go, for this you were created." For his callousness, God punished Rabbi Judah with a painful illness lasting seventeen years. Then one day, seeing his housekeeper about to sweep a weasel from the house, Rabbi Judah told the woman to treat the animal gently, and his illness ended.

Talmudic scholars say the point of the story is not that Rabbi Judah should have saved the calf, only that he should not have been callous about its fate.

At a quiet traffic circle in the center of Caledonia, Peter turns right, drives through a short stretch of suburban housing, and then pulls into the gravel parking lot of T.D. Kahn Country Meats.

It's 6:45 A.M.; Kahn's doesn't open until seven. There's one other car in the lot.

"Looks like the inspector's the only one here," says Peter.

We park and wait. I can feel the trailer behind us rock slightly.

The slaughterhouse is a white-painted, one-story cinder-block structure with a corrugated tin roof.

A piece of pipe about four inches long sticks out from the side of the building directly in front of where Peter's parked the truck. On it sits a tiny brown bird. The dark color of its body contrasts sharply with the white cinder block.

"What kind of bird is that?" I ask Peter.

"I think he's a tweety bird," says Peter.

Peter must be joking.

"A tweety bird?" I ask.

"Chickadee is the real name, I think," he says. "I used to call 'em tweety birds. I used to shoot 'em all the time."

"Did you eat 'em?"

"Nah, just shot 'em."

"When you were a kid?"

"No, just whenever I see 'em. If I have a gun on me, I might shoot 'em, but Shelly doesn't like me having a gun around so I don't shoot much anymore, although I do have a few pigeons in the barn I've been meaning to get rid of."

Another car pulls into the lot. A man who appears to be in his thirties, with sandy-colored hair and a mustache, gets out, stretches, and comes over to us. This is Jim Taylor, the slaughterhouse manager.

"I thought this place opened at five!" Peter jokes.

"Nah, I get up at five," says Jim.

Peter and Jim seem friendly. Later, Peter tells me that for several years he's been bringing all his beef animals to Kahn's. He has gotten to know Jim and likes doing business with him.

Peter pulls the truck around to the rear of the plant and backs up to an unloading ramp.

Jim peers into the back of our trailer.

"Nice beef," he says.

When the trailer is emptied, Peter, pointing at me, says to Jim, "I'm leavin'— he's stayin'. If he gets out of line, you can hang him up, too!"

Peter's joking. In fact, he helped arrange for me to observe at Kahn's today. When I'd called Kahn's and asked permission to visit, Jim called Peter to check me out. Like Tom Taylor (same last name but no relation) at Taylor Packing in Pennsylvania, Jim Taylor was uneasy about letting a writer into the slaughterhouse, but Peter explained to Jim what I was doing, and so Jim agreed to let me in.

I get out of the cab and say good-bye to Peter. I've arranged for a friend to pick me up later in Caledonia.

"Hope you don't get too upset when they start shooting," says Peter.

•   •   •

Jim Taylor is a handsome six-footer with sandy brown hair, one green eye and one blue eye, and a well-trimmed mustache. He wears a tight black T-shirt over a long-sleeved, white thermal undershirt. He began working in slaughterhouses at seventeen, and started at Kahn's about eight years ago.

Jim shows me into the plant and introduces me to a man in a white lab coat. This is Dave Bulin, the federal inspector. Dave, about sixty years old, invites me to accompany him to the back of the building. I follow him down a dark passageway to several small holding pens. The one farthest in the back is for cattle.

Dave looks over both animals quickly, what he calls the "ante mortem inspection."

"I make sure the eyes are bright, look for abnormalities under the skin, lesions that might be visible. There are glands all over the body," he explains, "right behind the front legs and down the neck—just like on people. If there's a problem, you'd see them bulging."

Dave sees nothing abnormal. "Both very good looking," he says.

I follow Dave back to the kill-floor, passing on the way two other pens, one with two pigs, the other with eight.

The kill-floor is a room with a ceiling nearly twenty-five feet high. The walls are white-painted cinder block; the floor is cement, painted gray. Chains and hooks hang from metal rails attached to the ceiling; they glisten in the ample sunlight that streams in through large windows along three walls.

A red metal stanchion in which the animals are held—what the workers here call the "knocking pen"—stands in the far corner of the room in front of a white sliding door.

There are three workers on the kill-floor this morning. Two of them, whom we'll call Ed and George, both in their fifties, have worked at this facility for nearly thirty years—long before it was purchased by Kahn. Chris Schojan started here five months ago.

Ed wears a clear plastic smock over jeans and a green, flowered shirt. Knives of different shapes and sizes hang from a yellow chain around his waist. He sharpens a long knife by scraping it back and forth across a metal cylinder.

Suddenly, George slides open the door to the knocking pen.

I haven't been in the slaughterhouse ten minutes; this is all happening faster than I expected.

There's a shuffling of hooves against the concrete floor.

I hadn't noticed the rifle. It was resting on a ledge above the sliding door. George takes it and walks to the front of the knocking pen.

A vat of boiling water used to de-hair pigs sits just in front of the pen, steaming.

A radio, set to a classic oldies station, gives tomorrow's weather forecast.

I am standing no more than twenty feet away. Having already witnessed the shooting at close range of the Lawnel cows, I don't back up or twist around this time. My eyes follow George as he lifts the rifle, aims, and shoots.

Blam!

I was expecting a quiet pop, like when the renderer shot the cows at Lawnel, but this is a loud blast. I suppose the sound reverberates off the cinder-block walls and cement floor.

Ed lifts the side of the knocking pen, and the steer rolls out the side.

I can see the hole in his forehead.

I'm glad this isn't my steer. This is Peter's, 13, the last one he had left to ship. He's a black Angus, with short horns that stick straight out to either side, and curly black hair on the top of his head, which flops forward to cover a tiny patch of white on his forehead.

When Peter called to say he was ready to ship 13 to Kahn's, it seemed a good opportunity to witness a slaughter in order to prepare myself for the killing of 7 and 8. At the moment, they remain in Peter's barnyard.

Ed wraps a chain around 13's left hind hoof. With a screeching sound, a mechanical lift pulls the body up until 13's head hangs about a foot off the floor. His tongue hangs loosely from his mouth; clear fluid drips from his nose. Ed pushes 13 about eight feet along the overhead rail until he's positioned over a white barrel. Then, in a quick movement, George sticks 13 in the throat with a knife; as if a pipe had suddenly burst, a torrent of blood gushes from the wound.

It has been less than two minutes since 13 entered the knocking pen. As his body hangs and bleeds, it shows no movement.

The sliding door opens again, and a second steer, a brown Jersey from another farm, enters. I find it hard to believe that as a prey species this steer could be oblivious of the sights, sounds, and smells of danger on the kill-floor. I assume these would include 13's fresh blood on the wall a foot or two behind the knocking pen, and his body hanging upside down and bleeding eight feet away. Yet the Jersey seems relatively calm.

I've learned that prey animals in danger will sometimes try to appear calm so as not to attract a predator's attention. Is the Jersey really calm or just appearing calm? I don't know.

George approaches the Jersey with the rifle. He shoots, the animal falls, and George rolls him out of the knocking pen.

George's shots seem to kill more quickly than the renderer's at Lawnel, although both use a .22. It may just be that, unlike the downer cows at Lawnel, these animals are shot while standing, so their abrupt fall gives the appearance of a quick death.

Later I ask George what it's like to shoot cattle.

"It's like nothing," he says. "I just shoot 'em. I aim right between the eyes. Most times that kills 'em."

He says one time out of ten he may need to shoot twice. "If they move their head and you miss, that won't kill 'em. You gotta shoot 'em again."

Ed wraps a hook around the Jersey's hind leg, raises him on the rail, and positions him over a white barrel. George sticks him. This animal bleeds more slowly than 13, more like an open garden hose than a burst water pipe.

13 is done bleeding. George begins cutting away the skin from the sides of his head, over his eyes, and around his horns. He's cutting 13's face off. I didn't know 13 as well as I know my own animals, but he was in Peter's barnyard all the time I've been visiting my own. He was distinctive because alone among the seven steers there, he had horns.

At first I didn't pay much attention to 13, but then, after Peter sent his four small black calves to auction and just my two animals and 13 remained, I started noticing 13 more. Sometimes I'd slip him a little hay or grass when I came to feed my own calves. So this face being removed is a face I know, one that I fed, one that occasionally would lick the leg of my coverall or chew on my shirt sleeve.

"This is called skinning out the head," explains Dave, the inspector, as George cuts away the hide from around 13's nose and mouth. George removes the ears with a straight knife. "We've gotten so we call anyone in the meat market a butcher," says Dave, "but this is real butchering."

Dave has a deep bass voice, so rich-sounding that I can't resist asking if he ever considered going into radio. He says people often ask him that, but no, he's worked only in the meat industry for nearly forty years.

George holds 13's jaw in one hand, bends the head back, and then cuts through the Adam's apple and the first cervical vertebra, called the atlas joint. He carries the head to the wall just behind me and hangs it on a metal hook. In the skull, just above the eyes—which stare upward—I can see the hole where the bullet went in. George washes the head with a hose.

Dave cuts out the mandibular gland, near the lower jaw, and examines it. Then he cuts open the cheeks to check for cysts and parasites. The cheek flesh throbs rhythmically. I point this out. "That's normal," Dave says. "Just the muscles contracting."

It's strange to see, nonetheless.

As the flesh is removed, 13's head begins to look like a skull.

Over where 13's body still hangs upside down, the ears and the yellow ear tag with "13" printed on it remain on the hide, but the place where the head goes is empty because the head is behind me.

Ed, George, Chris, and Dave all stop what they're doing every few minutes to take a hose and wash blood and bits of flesh from their knives, aprons, and hands. They all work without gloves.

Dave cuts out 13's tongue. Just two days ago, as I fed 13, this tongue licked me.

Ed and George lower 13's headless body from the rail and lay it in the middle of the kill-floor, an area they call the "skinning bed." Like a dog on its back, waiting to have its stomach rubbed, 13's feet stick up in the air. In the clefts of the upraised hooves, I can still see bits of dried mud and straw from Peter's barnyard.

Kahn Country Meats is a small, custom slaughterhouse that, even on a busy day, kills no more than ten cattle. Dave assures me, however, that the procedures followed here are similar to those used at the big commercial slaughterhouses. I mention Taylor Packing in Pennsylvania, and he says he's familiar with it. The major difference, he says, is that here things go slower and are done by hand rather than by machine.

"At a big, modern plant," says Dave, "once the animal is up on the rail, it never comes off. It's all assembly-line. The hide is taken off by machine, and you have people who do nothing all day long but take legs off. Here we do it all by hand from start to finish. This is the old way."

Ed and George cut off 13's legs at the knees and toss them into a blue barrel labeled INEDIBLE.

Ed and George now spread 13's hoofless back legs wide apart and place between them a metal bar, called a "spreader." Later a hook attached to an overhead rail will hoist up the carcass and position it for further cutting.

Meanwhile, Chris, the new employee, begins to skin 13's carcass, cutting the hide off the legs. With 13's head gone, it takes me a moment to figure out which leg Chris is working on. Then he cuts open the anus and the chest, and slices through the hide down the middle.

Ed begins cutting the hide off under the belly, and I move closer to watch. I'm leaning right over his shoulder.

"How long you been working here?" I ask.

"Since '65," he says.

"You could probably do this in your sleep," I say.

"I try not to," he says, grinning, but I'm not sure whether he means that he tries to stay alert while he works, or whether, when he sleeps, he tries not to dream about butchering.

With 13's carcass still on the skinning bed, George opens the chest with an electric saw. He cuts out the top half of the esophagus, called the weasand, and ties off what's left. He also ties off the anus. When they rehang 13's carcass, having the esophagus and anus tied off will keep the contents of 13's guts from spilling out and contaminating the rest of the meat.

They now mechanically hoist and move 13's carcass a few feet to the "rumping station," where Ed and George remove the rest of the hide and the guts. The four-chambered stomach, a huge, bloated organ that resembles a large beach ball, is cut loose and falls into a vat. They remove the kidney, heart, and lungs separately.

Dave puts the liver, which is dark brown and about the size of a baseball mitt, on a metal tray and cuts it open to check for parasites. Then he cuts the lungs, looking for abnormalities such as tuberculosis. Both are fine.

George climbs a step stool. Using a four-foot-long electric saw, which is so loud I need to cover my ears, he splits 13's hanging carcass down the middle. As the two sides swing separately on the rail, a shift occurs in my perception: this body, which until moments ago still looked like steer 13 from Peter Vonglis's barnyard, now looks like meat. Ribs, muscle, and fat are what I see; traces of the animal I knew—head, ears, feet, hide—are gone.

Chris and Ed push the two carcass halves, still hanging from the rail, into the chilling room.

Remarkably, nearly an hour after 13's death, his carcass still moves: muscles quiver and twitch. Muscle fibers contract with the change in temperature from the kill-floor to the chilling room, explains Dave. "These are the normal processes of death."

I'm curious how 13's meat would grade, but Dave tells me Kahn's doesn't grade its meat. "It just isn't necessary at a small place like this," he says. "No one's that interested."

Still, I'd like to know.

"Well," he says, looking over the hanging meat, "a guesstimate would be Choice or Select." These are the two grades just below Prime. "This carcass," he continues, pointing to either the left or right half of 13—I can't tell anymore—"doesn't have a lot of fat on it, but the inside of the spinal column indicates a youthfulness."

The carcasses will chill overnight. Tomorrow they'll be cut into quarters and hung in the cooler.

* * *

Jim Taylor invites me into his office. He and his secretary, Della, are both seated at their desks, facing me and smoking.

I ask if there's much odor in the plant, explaining that I can't smell.

"Odor?" says Jim. "Well, right now they're scalding pigs on the kill-floor, so there is a little smell now of singed hair."

Della, about thirty years old, wears a sweatshirt from a local community college where she studied accounting, office management, and customer service. Her blond hair falls in waves to her shoulders.

Jim hired Della just a few months ago.

"When I started," she says, "I wouldn't walk out to the bathroom if any animals were on the kill-floor, 'cause I didn't want to see them. But then one day by accident I saw one killed—it was cattle—and after that it was okay."

Her friends are often impressed to learn where she works, says Della. "For a woman to be working in a slaughterhouse, it's cool. They think I'm tough."

Della herself has learned a lot about meat. "I know now that a cut of meat is better with the bone than without, because the bone gives you more flavor. So why pay for boned beef? Like Delmonico steak is basically rib steak without the bone, so you're paying to have the bone taken out and you're losing half the flavor. You're just paying for a fancy name."

This morning Della has been making flyers to distribute around Caledonia to promote Kahn's retail meat market, a part of the business they hope to expand. Kahn's is typical of custom slaughterhouses in the area except that one day a week it offers ritual Muslim slaughter, called Halal.

Spring is a slow season, says Jim, explaining why there were only two cattle and ten pigs slaughtered this morning. "Farmers are out in their fields now, they don't want to mess with beef." In the fall and winter, he says, they may handle ten cattle a day, plus up to forty pigs, sheep, lamb, and goats. During the fall hunting season, they also butcher deer.

Jim says they slaughter only a few cull cows, but those that do come through are often in bad shape. "We hang 'em in the freezer and they start breaking down after three to four days, rather than two weeks or more for a good beef animal. Truth is, they're composting on the hoof even before they get in here."

I excuse myself to go to the restroom, and quickly see what Della meant about having been afraid to go there: to get to the bathroom you have to cross directly in front of the kill-floor. No animals are being killed just now, but I do pass pig carcasses hanging in the chiller.

Just outside the bathroom, a telephone hangs on a wall. It's an old rotary phone, but the outer case has been removed so that the phone's innards—bell, screws, and wires—are exposed.

Back in the office, I remind Jim that when we'd spoken earlier he'd told me that when he first starting working at slaughterhouses, he had nightmares. He said he'd gotten over them, but I wonder if it's still sometimes difficult to work at a slaughterhouse.

It's not difficult, he says, he likes the work, but occasionally it is hard to see animals on the kill-floor.

"Which ones are the hardest?" I ask.

"The goats and lambs," he says, "because they go 'maa-maaa.'"

One of the most upsetting experiences he's had, however, involved people, not animals. About five years ago, he says, animal-rights activists attacked the building after hours.

"They let three lambs go, busted locks, set the building on fire, called in a bomb threat, and wrote things on the outside walls," he says.

"What did they write?"

"'Murdering Scum—We Have Declared War!'" he says with a grimace.

Jim isn't wearing it today, but when I first met him he had a cap that said WORLD'S BEST DAD. He says it was a Father's Day gift from his two daughters, ages seven and eleven.

The seven-year-old, especially, loves animals, he says. She came to the plant once and he let a pig out so she could ride it out back.

I ask if his girls have ever seen the kill-floor.

"No, but they understand the process," he says. "They know that what's on their plate comes from here."

· · ·

About a week later I return to Kahn's. Peter Vonglis has decided to sell the meat from 13 to his sister and three of her friends, and Jim Taylor has said it would be fine if I came and watched them cut the meat into pieces for retail packaging.

The killing floor is quiet this morning, and spotless: no blood anywhere. No animals have been brought in to be killed today.

Jim gives me a blue cloth coat to wear over my street clothes for protection. The coat is one of his; it says JIM over the breast pocket, and hangs below my knees.

The carcass halves from 13 have already been cut into quarters. This morning Ed and Chris will cut up one front quarter and one hind quarter, splitting the meat between two friends of Peter's sister: a family named Horn and a family named Zimmer.

In the cutting room, Ed works at a tabletop band saw. He's holding 13's front right quarter, with a leg attached. From it he cuts rib steaks—sixteen of them— each about three-quarters of an inch thick, with a quarter-inch of fat all around. Then he cuts off the brisket, or lower chest, and then the front leg. "That's where the soup bones come from," he says.

Ed, fifty-three, has three grown children, two girls and a boy, all of whom are employed as county sheriffs. An African-American, he has short black hair graying at the temples, and a mustache and beard. He wears a red cloth apron over the same type of blue cotton coat that I wear. He works bare-handed.

As he makes each cut, Ed lays the steaks in two white plastic bins—each about the size of a home recycling bin—that sit on a shelf directly in front of me. One bin is for the Horns, the other is for the Zimmers.

From the forequarter, the area along 13's neck and upper chest, Ed cuts chuck roasts. Each roast is about two inches thick and weighs about three pounds. The meat is deeply red and lightly marbled.

"Nice piece of beef," he comments.

On the table behind him, Ed makes a "hamburger" pile with pieces of meat he trims from the various cuts.

He now cuts arm roasts from the area just above 13's left shoulder.

A radio plays classic oldies. Ed cuts to the Rolling Stones' "Street Fighting Man." The white bins are beginning to fill.

At the table behind Ed, Chris trims the cuts Ed gives him, tossing the fat into a "fat barrel"; later it will go to a renderer.

Chris, thirty-one, worked for a supermarket chain for eighteen years. He met Jim Taylor through deer hunting. He recalls, "Jim asked me one day if I'd like to come out here and cut meat, and I said sure."

I ask Chris if he had any trouble adjusting to the slaughterhouse. "Lambs were tough," he says, echoing Jim, "'cause they make a noise, like 'baa, baa, baa,' and the pigs—they squeal. But you get used to it."

I watch Ed and Chris busy with their knives. "I suppose you've got to be careful not to cut yourselves," I say. "But you've both got all your fingers."

"I got 'em, but a lot of 'em ain't straight," says Ed. He holds up his left hand, the two smallest fingers are crooked and bent at the first joint. He says he cut them many years ago.

Ed's ready to work on another quarter. In the cooler, he selects one of 13's hindquarters. I press my bare hand against it as it hangs; it feels like cool, hard rubber, or maybe even plastic.

Back in the cutting room, Ed explains there are three major cuts from the hindquarters: the round, the loin, and the flank. The flank is located on the underside, behind where 13's penis was, or where the udder would be on a heifer. Ed trims off an outer layer of meat. It's usable only for hamburger, he explains, tossing it on the trim pile for Chris.

Each family has ordered four sirloin steaks. From an area on 13's back, just in front of the rump, Ed makes three-quarter-inch cuts and lays the steaks inside the two bins.

Each bin now holds a pile of steaks and roasts nearly a foot high.

With a handsaw, Ed saws the hindquarter in half. To separate the flank, he uses a knife to cut away a strip of muscle. Then, with his bare hands, he grabs the flank meat and—almost like pulling up a carpet—yanks it from the membrane that connects it to the bone.

I ask if I can try.

"It's tougher than you probably think," he cautions.

I put down my notebook, grasp the red flesh with both my hands, and pull as hard as I can. The meat moves only a few inches.

Ed finishes ripping the flank and puts it in the hamburger pile. It's just nine o'clock in the morning, but I'm beginning to feel hungry. In fact, my mouth is watering. I haven't eaten steak in years, except on a few occasions, but I'm salivating over this flank steak.

This isn't the reaction I expected.

Ed cuts three T-bone and five porterhouse steaks, and lays them on the ever-rising pile in the white bins. Behind us, meanwhile, Chris trims fat off chunks of stew meat.

Next, Ed cuts the round, a section of meat from the rump. As he does, he exposes the ball joint in 13's hip. He puts the top round on the band saw and cuts seven thick steaks.

"This is a lot of meat here without any bone," he says.

He cuts the eye of the round, a boneless cylinder of meat three inches in diameter and nearly a foot long, and puts the slabs through a cubing machine. This creates a waffle pattern on the meat and softens it.

"That's better cube steak than you'd buy in a store," says Chris. "It's fresher and doesn't sit in a bag for three weeks."

My mouth is watering. It's not that I have any desire actually to eat this meat, I don't—but seeing it causes me to salivate, anyway. I wonder if salivating for meat is something innate in the human species, or if I'm just reacting to a remembered taste from my youth, when I ate plenty of meat at my parents' home, particularly sirloin steaks, rib roasts, and brisket.

The white bins overflow with steak.

13's back leg—I've no idea if it used to be the left or right side—hangs from the rail now with no meat left on it. The bare white bone glistens.

Now Chris dumps all the meat he's trimmed into an electric grinding machine in a corner of the cutting room. Ed pushes in more meat—I toss a few pieces in, too—and turns on the motor. Out the other end come spaghetti-like strands of ground beef.

I'm reminded of something I haven't thought of since I was a child: an old Mutoscope flip-card machine at a photography museum in Rochester, on which you cranked a handle and cartoon drawings rapidly flipped over, giving the illusion of motion. In one, a man puts a live dog into a meat grinder and out the other end comes ground beef. I always found that disturbing, and wondered why anyone would enjoy watching it.

13's ground beef is pinkish orange.

"That's good," says Chris, explaining that the color shows the meat is not too fatty. He says Kahn's aims for ground beef to be 80 to 90 percent lean and 10 to 20 percent fat, which is standard in the industry. Too little fat and the meat will lose its flavor, too much and it will get mushy. Chris can adjust the levels of fat and lean by how closely he trims the meat. McDonald's and other fast-food companies do essentially the same thing: they control the taste and texture of their ground beef by mixing relatively fatty meat from corn-fed animals with the leaner meat of cull dairy cows.

Soon a tub the size of a laundry basket is filled with ground beef from 13. One family has requested hamburger in one-pound packages; the other wants two-pound packages. Chris molds the beef into softball shapes. "That's about one pound," he says, studying his handiwork. "You just guess as best you can."

Della comes in to help with the wrapping. She wears a white T-shirt tied at the navel; her wavy blond hair hangs across her shoulders. The three of them—Chris, Della, and Ed—stand at a counter in front of a window facing the parking lot. I watch from behind. On the right, Chris molds the ground beef into one- and two-pound balls; in the middle, Della wraps them in white freezer paper; on the left, Ed tapes the packages shut and puts them into cardboard cartons, one for each customer. The three of them—the young white man, the woman, the older black man—all in a row, wrap meat.

A moment later, Jim Taylor comes into the cutting room. I ask if he could wrap me up a little hamburger from 13 to take home. He says sure, and a short time later I leave Kahn's with two packages of ground beef, and also a slice of neck-bone that Jim offered for my dog.

. . .

From Caledonia, a friend drives me south on Route 36 back to the Vonglis farm to pick up my car and check on my animals. They're alone now. First Peter shipped the four black Angus calves to auction, then he and I took 13 to Kahn's. Only 7 and 8 are left in the barnyard.

As I get out of the car, the two of them come over to the fence. I pull up a little grass to feed them. Mud covers their hooves and to a point about six inches up their legs—just about where the hooves would be cut off after slaughter. I imagine the ball joint inside 8's hip—that's the naked bone I saw hanging on the rail at Kahn's as Ed cut steaks on the band saw. I imagine dotted lines on 8's hide showing the different cuts of meat. I see 8, as the cattle buyer John Weidman would say, "opened up." I see him as meat.

I open the gate to the barnyard and walk to the running shed at the far end to see how much shell corn remains in the feed wagon. 8 comes up behind me, but as I turn to rub his forehead and neck, he quickly lowers and then raises his head—it's a movement I haven't seen before, and it strikes me as aggressive. Suddenly I'm scared. I'm alone in this barnyard with two one-thousand-pound animals, and for the first time I'm frightened.

I walk back to the center of the barnyard, where I can't be crushed against a wall or fence. These animals could easily knock me down. They move toward me. I need to get out of here. I stand up tall, squaring my shoulders to appear larger and unafraid, and walk backward toward the gate, keeping my eyes on them. At the gate, my heart pounds.

I open a folding chair next to Peter and Shelly's house and sit in the shade, watching the animals.

Maybe 8's hungry, or it's the heat, or he's just bored now that 13 is gone. Maybe he smells the slaughterhouse on me, although when I came here last week after having been at Kahn's, he was gentle as usual. Or maybe he actually is gentle and I'm misinterpreting his behavior.

He turns his side to me. As I have done so often before, I see in the black-and-white pattern of his hair a man in a white hat. But this time I imagine Ed, at Kahn's, pulling back that hide and tying off 8's upper esophagus so his guts don't spill out when he's hung upside down. And I see a rump roast on his hind leg. This must be how Peter Vonglis and other farmers see cattle.

What changed at the slaughterhouse? That I saw a living thing, 13, transformed into meat? Death came quickly, and then my mouth watered. I saw good people working hard, and saw the value of their labor. 13 is gone, wrapped and boxed, and I can't say I care. Sentiments I've had about animals since childhood strike me as naive.

Maybe I should call Peter this evening and tell him to ship 7 and 8 to Kahn's tomorrow. I could make a blanket from 8's hide. I could ask Ed or George to skin out the chalice on his face, and then have it framed and hang it in my office.

Without reentering the barnyard, I leave the Vonglises' and head back to Rochester. I have dinner to make.

•   •   •

The two packages—both marked GROUND BEEF   T.D. KAHN MEAT PACKERS KEEP FROZEN—have warmed only a little during the forty-minute ride home. I put one in the freezer and the other I lay on the kitchen counter.

On the patio in back of the house, I load the black Weber grill with charcoal briquettes, douse the inside with lighter fluid, and put a match to it.

I throw an inch-long bone on the grass for our little dog, Champ. He begins to eat 13.

While I'm waiting for the grill to heat up, I relax on a patio chair.

Was 8 really aggressive with me today, or did I somehow convey an aggressive attitude to which he responded? Maybe if you watch a steer so degraded as to be cut into meat—and with your bare hands tear flesh from its bones—you can't help but seem threatening to the next steer you see.

A sliding door from the house opens. It's my older daughter, Sarah, who is vegetarian. She's just come from high school track practice.

"What are you doing?" she asks, indicating the grill.

"I'm firing up the grill to cook hamburger. It's from a steer I saw raised and then watched slaughtered."

"That's disgusting!" she says, in the way only teenagers can say it. "Why can't you just give it to Champ?"

"I want to see how it feels to eat it," I say. "It's for my book."

"It's still disgusting!" she says.

When the grill is hot, I go into the kitchen, wash my hands, and open the thawed, two-pound package of ground beef. I remember Sue Smith telling me her teenage daughter, Kirsty, eats meat but won't touch it, and Shelly Vonglis telling me her sister, a dairy farmer, uses a watermelon scoop to prepare ground beef because she also won't touch it.

I grab the softball-sized chunk of raw meat. It's cold and clammy. I squeeze and mold it into five thick patties. Back outside, I put the patties on the grill, plus two veggie burgers for Sarah. Champ's finished the bone. He sucked the marrow clean out; I can see right through what was 13's spine.

Seated behind the grill, I watch my six-year-old son, Ben, and two friends play soccer in the yard, their images distorted by the waves of heat rising off the grill.

I flip the burgers. Bits of fat cause the fire to flare up.

My other daughter, Val, thirteen, comes onto the patio. It was Val, my meat-eating daughter, whom I took to McDonald's more than two years ago in search of Beanie Babies.

"What are those?" she asks, pointing to the grill.

"Hamburgers," I say, "from steer number 13 on the farm."

"Oh my God! Oh, that's really gross!" she cries, and runs inside.

A moment later she comes back, apparently having talked with her mother.

"I thought it was your cow," she says. "You'd have been a real sicko for killing your cow and bringing it home to eat."

I remind her that my steer is number 8; this meat is from another animal in the same herd.

"It smells really good," she says.

. . .

At the table, Sarah takes a veggie burger, my wife, Val, and I each take a hamburger, and Ben, who doesn't like any burgers, eats pasta.

I wait for everyone else to begin eating, then bring the burger to my mouth, but I'm stopped by an image of 13's black head, short horns sticking straight out to either side, and the long, curly dark hair on top of his head that fell forward and covered a spot of white on his forehead. I put the burger down.

I pick it up again, but I'm stopped once more, this time by an image of myself standing at the gate of Peter Vonglis's barnyard feeding grass to my own calf, and 13 coming over and trying to push 8 out of the way to get some grass for himself.

I pick the burger up a third time. This time I force myself to think of Peter's labor: growing the corn to feed all the calves in the barnyard, filling the feed troughs late at night after a long day of planting or plowing, filling them all winter, and every week putting clean straw bedding in the barn. Peter opened his work and his life to me, and I want to honor his labor.

My family is watching. Conception to consumption. I take a bite.

. . .

It's been just over eighteen months since Peter Vonglis picked up my two calves at Lawnel Farms. I'd paid Lawnel twenty-five dollars for each, plus twenty-five dollars for the other bull calf I took as a backup in case one of the first two died. As it turned out, it was the backup who died. Peter was never sure why.

Sometimes I think it was a mistake to take ownership of the calves. I could have just arranged for Peter to buy them directly from Lawnel. Then I could have watched dispassionately as he raised them for beef and, at the proper time, took them to slaughter. That would have been easier for me, and probably for Peter, too. He wouldn't have had to put up with my questioning when he took the calves off pasture and later put them on the corn finishing diet.

On the other hand, owning them forced the question I had asked myself more than two years ago: What would happen if I were to follow from birth to slaughter one animal raised for meat? What would it mean to make a connection with one animal out of "billions and billions served"? If I hadn't bought the animals, my answer to that question would have been academic; instead, it became real.

I struggled with the decision, asked the advice of many people, wondered how farmers would react if I chose one way or the other.

In the end, though, I never had to make the decision. Instead, it came by itself, unforced, the day I watched Peter's last steer, 13, go to slaughter.

.   .   .

I had been in the slaughterhouse all that morning—observing, interviewing, taking notes. When it was over, I'd felt a great sense of accomplishment for having witnessed the process. But the real surprise was that I hadn't felt repulsed at all. I hadn't even been squeamish.

There had been, in fact, almost an intimacy to the place. The kill-floor was clean and well lit, the people were friendly. They were not anonymous workers. They had names: Ed, George, Jim, Dave, Della. The older two, Ed and George, had worked there nearly thirty years. Together they handled an animal from beginning to end.

Of course, only a handful of animals end their lives at a place like Kahn's; all the rest—all the Lawnel cows, for example—are killed at modern, mechanized plants like Taylor Packing in Pennsylvania. If they had let me into Taylor, I probably would have been repelled to see an assembly-line operation where 1,900 cows are slaughtered daily—on a ten-hour shift, that's three cows a minute—with machines ripping off hides and people with pneumatic saws cutting off thousands of hooves.

But Kahn's was no factory. There was no death-camp imagery to color my impression. There were just people trying to make a living, getting through the day.

Finally I understood the process of turning a living animal into food. It's what Peter Vonglis does.

Peter raises a steer, feeds and cares for it, feeds it no matter how tired he is, makes sure there is water available all winter, brings it grain and corn to eat—the fruit of his own labor of planting and reaping—and though he doesn't make a pet of it or indulge it, he doesn't knowingly mistreat it, either. When the time comes, he drives it a few miles up the road, and there, people who have worked together every day for years kill it quickly, and skillfully turn the carcass into meat. In this way Peter makes food for his family; the steer is the vehicle for that. If Peter works hard and does the right things, he can stock his freezer with beef.

That must be what making meat was all about before it became an industry, and how Peter and other farmers still view it. It's an image I'd somehow been missing, and it felt deeply calming finally to realize it, because it let me reconcile my respect for Peter and other farmers with an understanding of an essential part of their lives.

That revelation came two weeks ago. Since then, I've been busy making arrangements for my animals. Peter Vonglis is working at the Batzing Farm this week and can't take time off, so in order to move 7 and 8, I've had to hire a private livestock hauler.

On this warm but overcast August morning, I help herd 7 and 8 out of Peter's barnyard and into a livestock trailer. They enter without resistance. On recent visits they've been as gentle as ever. I still don't know if they were aggressive on that one occasion because I'd come from the slaughterhouse, or if I was just projecting onto them the violence I'd seen there.

8 probably weighs one thousand pounds, and 7 maybe a hundred pounds less. As the truck pulls onto Route 36, I can feel their weight, nearly a combined ton, shift in the back.

A few miles down the road, the driver stops at a combination restaurant and gas station. It's hot; we both could use a cold drink. There's some mooing from the trailer, but not much; my animals mostly are quiet. I wonder if through the trailer's air holes they can smell cooked meat from inside the restaurant.

While we drink, I glance at the front page of the weekly Livingston County newspaper: new regulations mean farmers will need extra permits to spread manure on their fields; a Caledonia woman was hurt in a car crash Saturday night; York Central High beat Avon High, 5 to 4, in ten innings.

I'll miss this community. I've felt a part of it, and it hurts to think that when I dispose of these animals and my work is done, I'll have no role here. In the past two years I've made well over one hundred trips to York, yet every time I come, it feels as if I've entered sacred ground. I've square-danced at the town hall, applauded at the cattle-judging, cheered at the rodeo. I've ridden with the inseminator, followed heifers in heat, rushed in the night to watch calves born, dipped their navels in iodine. I've worn coveralls and barn boots, thermal underwear, denim jackets, and my own collection of farm caps. I've milked cows, trimmed hooves, and been kissed by a steer. I've spent hours at the window table at York Landing, warming myself with coffee; I've bought pastry from the Snack Shack. I've ridden on tractors and combines, choppers and manure spreaders. I've planted and I've reaped. I've called 911 in a farm emergency, consoled people when their pets died, fawned over newborn puppies, celebrated engagements, attended holiday parties, signed get-well cards and farewell cards, learned to enjoy country music, and paid tribute to area veterans. I've given and received gifts, shared meals, and proudly brought family and friends to visit the farms, giving tours as if I lived here.

Finished with our drinks, we pull back onto the road. Again, I can feel the weight of 7 and 8 move in the back.

· · ·

Fifty miles from York, we turn left off a main road, proceed another half mile down an unpaved country lane, and turn right through an unlocked gate. The driver and I lower the back panel of the stock trailer, and 7 and 8 step out backward. Farm Sanctuary's co-director, Lorri Bauston, walks the animals into a small holding pen off the side of the main cattle barn. They'll stay here for a couple of weeks until the sanctuary's vet tests them for contagious diseases, then they'll join the herd— about forty steers, heifers, and cows—on one hundred acres of green pasture.

When I called Farm Sanctuary about a week ago, I made sure I spoke directly with Lorri Bauston. She was sufficiently intrigued by the story of my calves to make room at the sanctuary for both of them.

But 7 and 8 had been on the corn finishing diet for nearly ten months, and Lorri and I were both concerned about their health. At my request, Dave Hale, the veterinarian, stopped by the Vonglis farm one afternoon to check them out. He was surprised they hadn't gained more weight than they had, and concluded— given their age and size—that the corn diet hadn't stressed them physically as much as he had expected. "My earlier comments about liver abscesses don't apply," he said. "They both look well. You probably never had to worry."

I also asked Dr. Hale how long the animals might live once they went back to eating roughage. He said he couldn't be sure, since he seldom sees bulls more than four or five years old. "They get to that age, up around 2,500 pounds, and their feet and legs give out on them because they can't carry all that weight," he said.

Laurie Bauston also couldn't predict how long 7 and 8 might live. "I'm not sure what a natural life span is for cattle," she said, "but we've had some at the sanctuary since we started fifteen years ago, and so far none has died. We haven't lost a single one to old age; they're all still living."

Before we leave, I stop in the sanctuary office and sign a release form. It says, "I hereby release custody of one Holstein steer (#8) and one Holstein heifer (#7) to Farm Sanctuary, Inc. In doing so, I waive any and all future claims on said animals and am absolved of any and all responsibility."

.   .   .

On the drive back to York, I feel relieved, my responsibility for these animals finally is lifted. At the Vonglis farm, the livestock hauler lets me off so I can pick up my car.

The barnyard is empty, but hoofprints remain visible in the dried mud. I remember the seven cattle who made these prints: the four black Angus steers, Peter's steer 13, and my calves, 7 and 8.

Shelly's not home; she's probably out somewhere with the kids. She completed her first year of nursing school in good standing, and next year at this time she should have her degree and be a registered nurse. My only regret about Shelly is that in the two years I spent visiting with her and Sue Smith, I wasn't able to help the two of them make peace.

Peter's at work at the Batzing Farm. Scot Batzing, the owner, had offered him a share of the business, but so far nothing has happened, so Peter's dream of owning a dairy farm remains unresolved.

I drive the four miles up Route 36 to Lawnel Farms. The new cow barn that Sue and Andrew Smith and Andrew's father, Larry, had planned last winter is nearly complete. The wood frame is up and the cement floor has been poured. Soon the Smiths will add one hundred more cows to the herd, bringing the total closer to one thousand. Cow 6717, sired like my own calves from the stud bull Bonanza, is now nearly two years old. She was bred for the first time last winter, and this fall she should give birth and join the milking herd.

Sue Smith is in the parlor, helping milk cows. Back from her vacation in the Southwest, she seems re-energized. When she returned, she wrote on the parlor chalk board, "Thank you ALL for a wonderful vacation." One of the new Mexican milkers wrote below, *"De nada, señora,"* you're welcome.

Andrew Smith is out in the fields, planting. Jessica, the calf manager, rolls a cart through the greenhouse, pouring warm milk replacer into buckets that hang in front of the young heifer calves. Outside, six newborn bull calves lie in the super-hutch. Tomorrow Joe Hopper will come with his pickup and stock trailer to take them to the calf auction in Pavilion.

I pull off my barn boots and toss them in the trunk of my car.

. . .

On my way out of York, I stop one last time at the Landing restaurant. From the bakery case I select a brownie, and, from the cooler in the back, a cold drink. The Table of Knowledge is open. I take my usual seat facing the front door and the window onto Main Street.

It was at Kahn's slaughterhouse that I came to understand meat-eating, but it was also at Kahn's that I decided not to kill my calves. I remember the moment because I checked my watch: it was exactly ten minutes after Ed shot 13 in the forehead. 13's carcass had been lowered to the floor and Ed had taken off the head.

The head to which I'd fed hay the previous Tuesday was skinned and stuck on a post behind me. I had turned and looked at the bulging eyes, through the cheek-less jaw at the row of exposed teeth, and tried to imagine my own calf, 8, there: shot, hung, headless, hoofless, and skinned. Suddenly the decision I'd had so much difficulty making seemed easy. I didn't want to see either of my calves there. It was not an intellectual decision; I felt it in my gut. I simply didn't want them to disappear and become meat.

It's true, 7's and 8's meat could be used to feed people, and if I had to eat it to live or to feed my family, I would. Fortunately, though, that's not my situation; any of us can nourish ourselves, as my sixteen-year-old daughter does, without meat.

As a child I had seen herds of grazing cattle and been filled with wonder, and some fear, about how such creatures became food. Forty years later—through the appearance at McDonald's of a stuffed toy in the shape of a cow—I resolved to go to the heart of the matter, to connect if I could with just one live animal out of "billions and billions served."

One winter day in Peter Vonglis's barnyard, I'd made myself small so my calf wouldn't fear me. Slowly I got to know him. He is, as Peter himself observed, "a pretty friendly guy." He seems to me to have, as Albert Schweitzer said, a "will to live." I saw that the day he escaped behind John Vonglis's barn. I think he enjoys some of his life, the parts when the weather is good and the grass is fresh and moist.

In one sense, we all have calves in our lives: things that are small, voiceless, or vulnerable, and over which we have power. It might be a child, an older parent, a stream or a stretch of woods, or a Holstein calf. We have to decide what to do with them.

More than two years ago, I set out to connect all the dots from conception to consumption. To the Smiths and the Vonglises, and everyone else in York who helped me make these connections, I'm grateful. It seems to me now, however, that it was pure chance that a calf called 8 and his twin sister, 7, were the ones I saw born—an occurrence as random as the single sperm I happened to glimpse while viewing Bonanza's ejaculate under a microscope. In truth, it could have been any of millions of calves born on any farm in any state that I ended up watching. And if I had, in the end I probably would have chosen not to kill them, either. My hunch is, once you connect all the dots, you see that all the calves are number 8.

·   ·   ·

I'm finished; it's time to leave. I get up from the table, pay for my food at the counter, and push open the Landing's front door. Behind me, the cowbell hanging from the screen clangs gently. I get in my car, pull onto Route 36, and head home.

Epilogue

I WRITE THIS MORE THAN A year after I took 7 and 8 to the Farm Sanctuary. Since then, I try to get to York every couple of months just to enjoy lunch at York Landing restaurant and to see what's new with everyone.

Ken Schaeffer, the artificial inseminator, undertook a major career change. One day, he told me, he was browsing through a camping magazine and saw an ad for the sale of a small company in Sitka, Alaska, that sells kayaks and runs wilderness trips. Ken flew there to check it out, fell in love with the community, and after twenty-five years at Genex, quit his job, sold his home, and drove with Buster, his dog, to Alaska. Ken called and wrote me a few times, reporting that the business was doing well and that he loved the people and beauty of his new Alaskan home. Then he had a terrible accident. On November 8, 2001, while demonstrating kayaking techniques, Ken died. He would have turned fifty the following week. Ken Schaeffer is survived by his two grown sons, Daniel and Michael, his parents, siblings, cousins, and many friends in western New York.

Kirsty Smith, Andrew and Sue's daughter, graduated from York Central High School last spring. She was accepted to Cornell University's School of Agriculture and has already begun classes there, on her way to becoming a veterinarian.

For their part, Andrew and Sue report it's been a good year at Lawnel Farms. The price of milk has stabilized, and they've completed construction of not one but two new barns, bringing the milking herd to nearly one thousand cows. I notice when I visit there now that the cows seem almost invisible to me, as if I have to make an effort to see them as individual animals. Without a particular cow to which I can attach a story, they seem just a mass of animals, much as they did on my first visit years ago.

The Vonglises have had a good year, too. Peter finally made his deal with Scot Batzing and is now a 50 percent owner of the crop and harvesting portion of Batzing Farms. He oversees a half-dozen employees. In May, Shelly graduated— with honors—from nursing school. She and Peter had a graduation party at their home; a white tent was set up on the side of the house opposite the barnyard. Shelly now works at a hospital in Rochester and recently passed her exam to become a registered nurse.

I miss York. As I go through my day, I think often of what might be happening there at any given moment. Which group of cows is coming through the milk parlor at Lawnel? Is Andrew repairing a tractor in the machine shop or out planting corn? Will Shelly be home to fix Colin and Bridgette an after-school snack or is she working the night shift at the hospital? What's today's special at York Landing?

And what has become of 7 and 8? I visited them at the Farm Sanctuary just once, last winter. They were grazing on pasture in a herd of about fifty other Holsteins. I wasn't sure if I'd recognize them, or they me. By the white chalice on his forehead, however, I quickly spotted 8, and 7 was close by. Both appeared heavier and taller than I remembered. Their hair was longer, too; they'd grown their winter coats. Did they know me? I couldn't tell if 7 did, but 8 definitely seemed to; he let me walk right up to him and touch his face.

Captions for Photographs

Half title pages: Author and 8 at Vonglis farm.

Title spread: 7 and 8 in barnyard of Peter and Shelly Vonglis's farm.

Page xvi: 8 at Vonglis farm.

Page 32: York Landing restaurant on Route 36 (Main Street), in York, New York.

Page 54: Shelly Vonglis holding son Colin outside their home in Leicester, New York.

Page 80: Susan Smith walks in front of trench silos filled with feed at Lawnel Farms in York, New York.

Page 102: Peter Vonglis stands on his harvesting machine, or "chopper."

Page 134: Author and 8 in Vonglis barnyard.

Page 156: Andrew Smith enters the cab of his "chopper" at Lawnel Farms.

Page 186: Author and 8, Vonglis farm.

Page 200: Author and 8 go head-to-head, Vonglis farm.

Page 232: Andrew Smith power-washes a tractor at dawn on Lawnel Farms.

Selected Bibliography

Books

Adams, Carol J. *The Sexual Politics of Meat: A Feminist-Vegetarian Critical Theory.* New York: Continuum, 1995.

Beale, Irene A. *Genesee Valley Events: 1668–1986.* Geneseo, N.Y.: Chestnut Hill Press, 1986.

———. *Genesee Valley People: 1743–1962.* Geneseo, N.Y.: Chestnut Hill Press, 1983.

Eisnitz, Gail A. *Slaughterhouse.* Buffalo: Prometheus Books, 1997.

Ensminger, M. E. *Dairy Cattle Science.* 3d ed. Danville, Ill.: Interstate Publishers, 1993.

Ensminger, M. E. and R. C. Perry. *Beef Cattle Science.* 7th ed. Danville, Ill.: Interstate Publishers, 1997.

Fossey, Dian. *Gorillas in the Mist.* Boston: Houghton Mifflin, 1983.

Fraser, A. F., and D. M. Broom. *Farm Animal Behaviour and Welfare.* 3d ed. New York: CAB International, 1997.

Goodall, Jane Van Lawick. *In the Shadow of Man.* Boston: Houghton Mifflin, 1971.

Grandin, Temple. *Thinking in Pictures: And Other Reports from My Life with Autism.* New York: Vintage Books, 1996.

Hanson, Victor Davis. *Field Without Dreams: Defending the Agrarian Idea.* New York: Free Press Paperbacks, 1996.

Houpt, Katherine A. *Domestic Animal Behavior for Veterinarians and Animal Scientists.* 3d ed. Ames, Iowa: Iowa State University Press, 1998.

Kramer, Mark. *Three Farms: Making Milk, Meat and Money from the American Soil.* Boston: Little, Brown, 1977.

Kroc, Ray. *Grinding It Out: The Making of McDonald's.* Chicago: H. Regnery, 1977.

Mohin, Ann. *The Farm She Was.* Bridgehampton, N.Y.: Bridge Works Pub. Co. 1998.

Peck, Robert Newton. *A Day No Pigs Would Die.* New York: Random House, 1972.

Petersen, Ray. *Cowkind.* New York: St. Martin's Press, 1996.

Pukite, John. *A Field Guide to Cows.* New York: Penguin Books, 1998.

Rath, Sarah. *The Complete Cow.* Stillwater, Minn.: Voyageur Press, 1998.

Rhodes, Richard. *Farm: A Year in the Life of an American Farmer.* New York: Simon and Schuster, 1989.

Rifkin, Jeremy. *Beyond Beef: The Rise and Fall of the Cattle Culture.* New York: Penguin Books, 1992.

Rollin, Bernard E. *Farm Animal Welfare: Social, Bioethical, and Research Issues.* Ames, Iowa: Iowa State University Press, 1995.

Tennyson, Jeffrey. *Hamburger Heaven: The Illustrated History of the Hamburger.* New York: Hyperion, 1993.

Wall, Charles, J. *The Devil.* Detroit: Singing Tree Press, 1968.

Webster, John. *Calf Husbandry, Health and Welfare.* Boulder, Colo.: Westview Press, 1984.

———. *Understanding the Dairy Cow.* 2nd ed. Oxford: Blackwell Science, 1993.

Zeuner, Frederick E. *A History of Domesticated Animals.* London: Hutchinson & Co., Ltd., 1963.

Journal Articles

Egbert, W. Russell, Dale L. Huffman, et al. "Development of Low-Fat Ground Beef." *Food Technology* (June 1991): 64.

Nicol, C. J. "Farm Animal Cognition." *Animal Science* 62 (1996): 375.